WHERE THE OX DOES NOT PLOW ≡—

Where the Ox Does Not Plow

A MEXICAN AMERICAN BALLAD

Manuel Peña

UNIVERSITY OF NEW MEXICO PRESS ◈ ALBUQUERQUE

13 12 11 10 09 08   1 2 3 4 5 6

LIBRARY OF CONGRESS CATALOGING-IN-PUBLICATION DATA

Peña, Manuel H., 1942–

Where the ox does not plow :

a Mexican American ballad / Manuel Peña.

p. cm.

ISBN 978-0-8263-4421-2 (CLOTH : ALK. PAPER)

1. Peña, Manuel H., 1942–   2. Mexican Americans—Southwest, New—Biography.

3. Mexican Americans—Southwest, New—Cultural assimilation.

4. Mexican Americans—Southwest, New—Social conditions.

5. Southwest, New—Ethnic relations   6. Southwest, New—Social conditions.

7. Ethnicity—Southwest, New. I. Title.

E184.M5P396 2008

979.046872073—dc22

[B]

2008001035

Book design and type composition by Kathleen Sparkes.

The book type is set in Warnock Pro OT 10.5/14, 26P3,

the display type is also Warnock Pro.

Américo Paredes was right. The corrido *is an American ballad, invented right here in the Southwest. In its most epic form it speaks to the Chicano people's loftiest ideals and deepest sorrows.*

—Tomás Rivera, Address to the Chicano Student
Leadership Conference, Fresno, California (1984)

CONTENTS

The Light of
Consciousness

1
THE LIGHT OF CONSCIOUSNESS

"Papa, what is 'luz de conocimiento'?"

"'Luz de conocimiento,' son, is the light of awareness. It is the moment in our life when we become conscious of ourselves and of the world around us."

Eyes shut. Can't open. Hurt. Help me. Waaahhhhh . . .

"Imelda, look after Memito. He woke up with snot on his eyelids again, and he's been crying. See if you can wash his eyes out."

Water on my eyes. Water on my face. Cold. Ough!! Hurt, hurt. Waaahh . . .

"Mama, I can't take out the snot, and Memito just keeps crying. It's glued to his eyelids."

"Get them real wet first. It'll loosen up."

The hurt—going away now. I open my eyes. I see the light! I see the bowl with water. I see Imelda—Mama Imelda. No, that's Mama over there, that other woman. I see the brown walls. I smell the brown floor. The bright box on the wall—it's a little house. The little boy and the little girl. They are standing outside. I want to touch the house—pretty colors. Too high, too high, I can't reach . . .

The shoes on the floor next to me—they are so black, and so smooth and shiny and slippery. They shine and look so pretty, and they have such long— what do they call them? Tacones—heels. I smell them—oh, they smell so good, they smell new. Imelda, they belong to sister Imelda. She wears them to work every day. They smell like sister Imelda. The touch and the smell give me a strange feeling, a good feeling. It's all over my body. What is it? Why does it feel so good?

"Tiene pulmonía. What's his name, and how old is he?"

"Four. Manuel is four years old. He be five next month."

I hear the voices of the doctor and Papa; they seem to come from far away; they sound like an echo in my head. They drift in and out of my ears and the words sound like metal clicks. The doctor speaks to Papa in Spanish. He sounds strange. It is Spanish, but it sounds like that other language I have heard—English. I can't breathe, and my body is on fire. I want to stay awake, but I can't. Where am I? It's very cold—no, it's very hot. My hands, my arms, my lips, my tongue—they all feel swollen; they feel gigantic. I hear my heart beating in my ears; it beats very fast and sounds like the train engine when it pumps steam—chang, chang, chang, chang!

"He's a lucky young man. You brought him just in time. I'll give him a strong penicillin shot. He should feel better very soon."

The light is very bright. It hurts my eyes. Papa's holding me in his arms. They are strong and I feel safe so close to him. Close my eyes—sleep. Chang! Chang! Chang!

"Amorcito, corazón, yo tengo tentación de un beso. . . ."

"Oh, Francisco, listen to Memito sing. He carries that Trío Los Panchos tune so well. What's it called, Alessio?"

"'Amorcito corazón,' Mama."

"Yes, and the other day he was singing that *corrido* about Gregorio

Cortez. I think *m'hijo* has real talent. And he's only six. Why, already he's learning to play the guitar, just by watching his brother Alessio."

"Well, *vieja*, maybe he'll be a musician, like those uncles of yours, the Jassos in Monterrey. That talent comes from your family, you know, 'cause my family—what can I say? We're all tone deaf."

≡

"Francisco, I heard my Memito speaking English today, to that little gringo *garra*—that "rags" kid who lives across the road. I think that's remarkable; he's never been to an American school, and of course we never speak English at home. He must be learning it from that little *garrita*. He learns everything so fast. We should encourage him, *viejo*. God willing, he may make something of himself someday."

"Well, we don't want to spoil the little whelp. He's gonna have to pull his weight, just like his older bothers and Imelda did. But you're right, he does show some intelligence. Perhaps he will make something of himself, someday."

2

HOW WILL WE GET BACK HOME?

"*Yo creo que fue el cuarenta-y-siete*—I think it was in forty-seven, *comadre*, when we had to leave Weslaco for the first time to go *al norte*. Things were very bad, and Francisco just couldn't find enough work. So we left on the first *campaña. Ay, Dios*, there would be so many campañas. It was very sad to leave our little hovel. No matter how rundown, it was still ours, and at least it provided an anchor for us. We weren't vagrants then, rolling here and there like stones."

Our years as itinerant workers safely behind us, now that Papa was on Social Security, Mama was reminiscing about the day we left our ancestral home in the Rio Grande Valley, deep in South Texas. We were joining the migrant-labor stream for one of the campañas that would become for us yearly treks following the cotton harvest across Texas. As I heard her speak in her low, gentle voice, the scene passed through my mind's eye, and I began to remember some of the details of that eventful trip, fourteen years in the past. . . .

"Vieja," I heard Papa saying to Mama one night, after we were all in bed. "*No hay otro remedio.* We are out of money, and we must leave town and search for work. They say the cotton harvest is good up north, in Ribera. Maybe we can go there and see how things turn out for us."

Riviera—or "Ribera," as my parents called it. The name had a strange ring to it, and I wondered where the place could be. Until that moment, I had never been away from the little matchbox we called home, except for frequent trips to visit my spiritualist Tía Virginia, who lived fifteen miles up the Valley in the town of Edinburg, or "Limburgo," as the local folk called it.

My father would often visit his clairvoyant younger sister to consult about weighty family matters, such as where we should relocate our little shanty when the time came to move it to another part of town. *"Al oriente, Francisco, al lado oriente del pueblo,"* I heard my tía tell Papa in her domineering voice, *"Allí está tu destino*—On the east side, Francisco, on the east side of town. That's where your destiny lies." On another occasion, I overheard them secretively discussing what Papa had convinced himself was some kind of portent—a large black bird he had seen perched on his window sill one morning at the break of dawn. Recalling the flocks of black birds that periodically invaded the Valley, and unable to hold my tongue, I stuck my head into Tía Virginia's *consultorio* and blurted out, "Maybe it was a magpie, Tía!" My Aunt Virginia would laugh heartily every time she remembered my droll interpretation of Papa's omen.

At age five, I was thus already aware of the concept "pueblo," as in Weslaco and Limburgo, but Ribera seemed so far away. I began to feel a bit uneasy. The next day I asked Papa where this place, Ribera, was. "It's some distance away, m'hijo," he answered, "maybe about eighty miles to the north." "Yeah," added Alessio, my mischievous thirteen-year-old brother, "It's like from here to the moon, and they say little boys are often mysteriously lost along the way, so we might have to chain you to the truck."

As always, I took Alessio's words to heart, and over the next few days, every time Mama and Papa mentioned Riviera, I worried about my brother's warning. On the day before we left, when we started loading up our 1934 International Harvester, I stayed close to Mama, fearful something might happen if she strayed too far from my sight. I do not think I slept well that night, but in any case, I was awakened at dawn by the sound of my parents' voices. Normally, I would be sound asleep at this early hour, but on this momentous occasion I woke up easily enough. Unlike the previous days, however, on the morning of our departure, I found myself more excited than fearful at the prospect of traveling so far from home. I got up brimming with nervous energy, as seemed to be the case with my older brothers Alessio and José, or Plon, as we called him.

After a breakfast of egg-and-potato tacos and coffee (except for Elia, the toddler, who was too young to be served coffee), we set about loading up the *candongo* (old mule), as we affectionately called the Harvester.

Papa had taken the truck in for maintenance the day before, and it was now ready for travel. We had loaded many household items onto the flatbed, but only a few stood out in my memory—the portable kerosene stove Mama used for cooking, blankets to be used for bedding, the wash tub and buckets, and the indispensable *tallador*. I shall never forget the tallador, perhaps the ultimate tool that the men of Papa's generation used to impose their rule over domestic woman's labor. Mama spent endless hours hunched over hers, beads of sweat condensing on her forehead as she scrubbed back and forth, until she had laundered every stain out of our ultimately spotless clothes.

The candongo finally loaded with the necessary housewares, the Peñas were ready to face their first campaña. For the first time in my life, we were joining the thousands of fellow tejanos and their *norteño* kin from across the border as they swarmed like locusts over the harvest-ready cotton fields of Texas.

It was hot, but cloudy and windy, on that July day when we pulled out of the large lot on which our shanty stood. Papa, Mama, and little sister Elia rode in the candongo's cabin, while Alessio, middle brother Plon and I huddled in a corner of the makeshift camper Papa had fashioned on the truck's wooden flatbed. We left the old homestead shortly after sunrise, traveling at the rusty Harvester's maximum cruising speed—about thirty-five miles per hour.

Gradually, the skyline of Weslaco began to recede in the distance. The last we saw of our town was the cylindrical water tower perched on its five giant pillars, its concrete glistening white as it rose high above the housetops, dwarfing even the slender palm trees that swayed like hula dancers in the gusty breeze blowing in from the Gulf of Mexico. Emblems of the Valley's subtropical climate, the palms would always remain for me a token of Weslaco, the place Mama and Papa continued to call home even after they were long settled, many years later, in the state of California. Indeed, the words "palms" and "Weslaco" would in later years evoke a nostalgic yearning for my primordial roots, perhaps because those first few years seemed in retrospect the most blissful of my life. For a very long time, memories of that period conjured images of simple pleasures, like playing marbles with my friends Quique and Güero, or romping on cotton-filled trailers with la Minnie, my next-door neighbor. During those years, Papa often worked as foreman for local farmers, overseeing

Peña family, 1948

laborers from across the border, and sometimes he would park the cotton trailers in front of the house overnight.

As the candongo lumbered northward toward Elsa, the next town up State Highway 88, Alessio, Plon, and I watched the majestic water tower gradually shrink to a dot on the horizon. As it disappeared from view, Plon bet his two brothers that he would be the first to spot the white-washed concrete landmark when we made our return trip home.

We had traveled perhaps five or six miles when the old Harvester began to sputter, and then, suddenly, the engine died. As was his habit, Papa got out and blessed the truck with one of his *chingados*—an all-purpose expletive he used when things went wrong. *"¿Qué pasó, Francisco?"* Mama asked, with a trace of worry in her voice. *"Este troque chingado*—this damned truck," he muttered. Meanwhile, I suddenly remembered Alessio's warning, and a wave of panic swept over me. We were stranded in the middle of an unfamiliar place, far from home it seemed to me, and I was petrified at the prospect of being snatched from my family and never seeing them again. I began to cry.

"*Pobrecito*, my poor little Memito. I can still remember how tears filled his eyes when he realized the truck had broken down and we were stuck between Weslaco and Elsa. We had only driven about five or six miles. But he was always a very sensitive child, you know. And I think he became frightened at the idea of being stranded so far from home—or at least it seemed far to him. And the first thing he asked was, 'How will we get back home?' while the tears rolled down his cheeks. I felt very sorry for my little one, and I told him, 'Don't worry, *m'hijito*, Papa will get the truck fixed, and then we'll be on our way. Everything will be all right.'

"But it was sad, comadre, because what Memito didn't realize—none of us did, really—was that it would be many years before we would settle down in our home again. For ten long years we wandered. Sometimes we would come back and spend a month, maybe two or three, in Weslaco, but every time we tried to settle down, things would go bad for us, and we had to pull up stakes and go back on campaña. As I told you, it was very hard, the way we lived during those years, constantly on the move and never setting roots anywhere. So many times I was ashamed to let people see the poverty in which we lived—the rundown shacks, with no running water or electricity, and no tables or chairs to sit on, no beds to sleep in. I never want to do that again, to live like a drifter, on campaña."

3
THE TACO AND
THE SANDWICH
(An American Encounter)

Bigfoot Wallace, who was captured by Mexican troops after the Mier
Expedition, used his alleged sufferings in captivity as an excuse for the
barbarities he committed against Texas-Mexican civilians when he
was a member of Hays's Rangers during the Mexican War[. . . .] Wallace
complained that after being captured, and during the time he spent
along the Rio Grande, all he ever was given to eat were beans, tortillas
and goat meat. Nowadays, many of Wallace's fellow countrymen
journey all the way from Central Texas to "in" eating spots on the Rio
Grande, to satisfy their craving for beans, tortillas and goat meat.
> —Américo Paredes, "The Problem of Identity in a
> Changing Culture: Popular Expressions of Culture
> Conflict along the Lower Rio Grande Border"

I may look Mexican to you, but, believe me,
I'm as American as Taco Bell.
> —Professor Peña,
> addressing his folklore class

It was the second day of January, 1949, and it was my very first day of school. We had been picking cotton in Colorado City during the fall, and we returned to our winter sojourn in Edroy, Texas, not far from Corpus Christi, in December—too late for me to start school before the Christmas holidays. Early in the morning, Mama dressed me in the new jeans, plaid shirt, and woolen jacket Papa had bought for me in Colorado City. Feeling like a freshly minted coin (though a bit apprehensive), I was ready to begin my life as a grade-school student. My brother Plon, who was starting his third year, was also dressed, and together we walked the mile or so across the barren winter fields, making our way to the spot where the school bus would pick us up. It was still dark and cheek-numbingly cold when we left the tiny shack we called home.

Edroy Elementary was the imaginary story-book school on the American frontier—an old three-room, wood frame building painted rust-red with white trim. There couldn't have been more than a hundred students enrolled, almost all of them Mexicans, supervised by three teachers, each of whom was responsible for two grades. My teacher, Mrs. Mayfield, taught first grade and kindergarten (or "beginners," as we called it), the two classes totaling about thirty children. The school had no cafeteria, so we had to bring our own lunches.

For my first day of school, Mama had packed some tacos in a brand new metal lunch box Papa had bought for me, with a picture of Hopalong Cassidy and his horse stamped on the lid. In those days, anything wedged or wrapped in a tortilla was called a taco, and these were made of refried beans and potatoes mixed into a hash, which Mama had rolled into a home-made flour tortilla—what in later years came to be known as a burrito. During midmorning recess, I had met and befriended a couple of children, and when it came time to eat I joined them and two or three more in a little circle, where we all set about opening our lunch boxes and unwrapping our noon meals.

When the other children saw what I had brought for lunch, they all burst into simultaneous laughter. "Lookie, lookie," one of them jeered in his Mexicanized accent, "he's eating tortillas!" By this time I had learned a little English by listening to my older brothers and playing with a poor gringo neighbor's kid—what we called a *garra*—and when the other classmates joined in the taunting, I quickly found myself in a state of crushing embarrassment. I was unable to understand why my new friends were so disdainful of my food! But I knew what ridicule was in any language, and, feeling ashamed and near tears, I finally put my tortillas back in the pail and ran for comfort to my brother Plon, who was eating his tacos on the other side of the building. He was sharing the noon repast with a student from our neighborhood. Too upset to eat, I did not have lunch that day, and I felt miserable for the rest of the afternoon, the pangs of hunger gnawing at me while I tried to explain to myself what had happened during the noon hour.

As I rode the bus home that afternoon, the events of the day began to fall into place. Yes, I then realized, all the other students were eating white-bread sandwiches of bologna and lettuce. And they looked so clean and neatly put together, the gleaming white slices joined in perfect symmetry around the brown edges, in contrast to my lumpy bean tacos with the ugly burn spots that looked like warts on the flour tortillas Mama had cooked on the *comal*. Maybe that was why my classmates had made fun of me, because my tacos looked so, well, trashy. Trashy Mexican—that was it! I thought of the tacos, still lying in my lunch box waiting to be eaten. I wanted to rip them out of the pail and toss them through the bus window, but I was afraid the driver might see me and walk back to my seat and give me a good paddling for littering the road. I did nothing until I got home.

"Tomorrow I am not taking tortillas to school," I wailed to Mama as soon as I walked into our shack. Taken aback, Mama tried to find out what was wrong. "They made fun of me and made me feel ashamed," I complained. "They laughed and made fun of my tacos, and I'm never gonna eat them again!" "But m'hijito," Mama protested, "That's what we eat; that's what all Mexicans eat. I'll bet those kids who laughed at your tacos—were they Mexicans? I'll bet that's what they eat when they get home from school."

"I don't care. All I know is I'm never gonna take tacos to school again. I'd rather not eat. I'd rather not even go to school."

"Well, m'hijo, what do you expect us to do?"

"I want to eat *comida americana*, like the other kids do. I want a white-bread-and-bologna sandwich. With lettuce and mayonnaise."

"Francisco," I heard my mother say to Papa when he got home. "Memito was completely humiliated at school today. The other children all had white-bread sandwiches except him, and they taunted him because he brought tacos to school. Can you believe that? And they're all Mexican kids. Anyway, he's very upset, and he says he's not going to eat in school unless he takes sandwiches to eat. You know how sensitive he is. You must drive into Odem and get him the things he wants."

Papa was not particularly sympathetic to my plight—after all, Odem was seven miles from Edroy, and, tired as he was from a full day behind the steering wheel of a tractor, a trip into town was the last thing his aching body needed. Besides, the old candongo was not running very well, and Papa was afraid it might break down along the way. He was planning to fix it the next weekend. But in the end, after Mama reminded him how awful it must be for me to feel so left out and so ridiculed at school, he relented, and he finally turned to me. "Come with me, *cabrón*, so you can tell me what you want."

The next day at noon, I proudly pulled out my white-bread-and-bologna sandwich, complete with lettuce and mayonnaise trimmings. No one laughed or jeered this time. I was now one of them. But I had learned a lesson in this little encounter between American and Mexican culinary habits. For the first time in my young life, I had a vague notion of the difference between things American and the exclusively Mexican world I had known until yesterday. And, as I had quickly learned, in the social space defined by the school, anything Mexican was subject to shame and contempt. The irony lay in the facts of the lesson: it had been taught to me not by the americanos, but by Mexicans like me—tortilla-nourished children whose lives, too, were being reshaped by simple but powerfully symbolic things like the difference between a taco and a sandwich.

And here a further irony: none of us in 1949 could have dreamed that the taco, now hyper-commercialized and its ethnic symbolism properly sanitized, would someday be appropriated by the americanos and transformed into a national icon—*"Yo quiero Taco Bell"*—eclipsing the sandwich in popularity.

4
THE CHICKEN AND THE EGG

It was a special pleasure to get up every morning, open the creaking screen door, then jump from the porch and rush to the rear corner of the old house built on three-foot redwood piers, where I knew my farm-fresh breakfast was waiting for me. There, astride the pier on the corner, I would find the single egg the Leghorn pullet had recently laid. It was always in the nest the young hen had fashioned, deep within the tall grass and weeds, and I would gently scoop it out of its shelter, the small oval delicacy still warm and reeking of its mother's barnyard aroma. The gastric juices were flowing by the time I ran into the kitchen, handed the egg to Mama, and waited for her to cook it for me—usually with *nopalitos* (tender cacti), if they were in season, or at least with chorizo.

We raised flocks of chickens in those days, when we sharecropped with Mr. Elvin B. Gruene in Calvert, Texas, and they provided us ready food while we waited for the cotton crop and its hoped-for profit to come in. Early in March, Papa would go to the feed store in town and bring home three or four dozen newly hatched chicks, all chirping away in a cacophonous symphony of "peeiu-peeiu-peeius," their tiny bodies wrapped in soft, yellow down. They seemed so fragile to me as they huddled in the large cardboard boxes lit with electric bulbs to keep them warm. But they ate the grain feed Papa bought for them with a voracious appetite, and within a month had developed into gangly and awkward young birds—adolescent chickens, we might call them. At this stage in their development they began to take on the earmarks of their particular pedigrees—Plymouth Rocks (mostly the barred variety), black and white Leghorns, Rhode Island Reds, and a few Minorcas.

We raised the birds primarily for food, but Mama kept a handful of hens for eggs, and there were always a couple of roosters with particularly arresting plumage that we kept as pets. These were christened with the names of people my parents had known long ago, ghosts from the past with names such as "El Chacho" and "El Úrsulo." In those early Calvert years, Mama did most of the killing and preparation of the chickens. She would go out and spread feed grain, which the chickens flocked to eat, and, while they were all busy pecking and clucking at her feet, she would swoop down and grab the one chosen for the next meal. Her slaughtering method was simple: she squeezed the bird's head tightly with her hand and whirled it vigorously in a wide circle for a few seconds. By then, the neck had splintered like a wet twig, while the dead body bounced around wildly in post-mortem seizures. It was a gruesome but fascinating sight for me, and I enjoyed helping Mama pluck the feathers, which came off easily enough once the carcass had been dunked in hot water. Three years later, when we settled ten miles farther south, near Hearne, I learned from Mama the art of killing a bird, and I then became the assigned butcher.

When cooked, these freshly killed chickens tasted indescribably rich. The juices oozing out of the recently pulsating flesh seized the taste buds and reacted with our own salivary enzymes to deliver morsels of robust flavor and deeply satisfying bulk. As the main ingredient in the *guisados* Mama prepared, the fresh fryers blended with the strong aromas of cumin, garlic, onion, and other spices, offering a cuisine simple in its preparation but exuberant in its bouquet. Years later, resigned to the savorless rubber of the frozen birds sold in supermarkets, I would long nostalgically for the succulence of Mama's chicken, which, despite the passage of time, remained intact in the memory buds of my palate.

During the harvest season of 1950, Papa's younger brother, Benicio, or *Tío* Ben, as we called him, joined us in Calvert as our sharecropping partner. He was accompanied by his second wife, Lorenza, and their two small children, Chato and Alicia, as well as Israel, a grown son born of his late first wife. The arrival of my uncle meant sharing food and living accommodations with our kin, and so the four-room house we inhabited now became shelter to the combined families of Francisco and

Ben Peña—eleven people altogether. The extra bodies meant overcrowding, but Papa and Tío Ben enjoyed a close relationship, and the well-being of relatives was more important to my father than his children's personal convenience. In any case, sharing quarters with other families was no longer unusual for the Peñas; we had been doing it ever since we began our itinerant life in 1947, when the collapse of the Valley economy forced us to leave the three-room matchbox we called home. Indeed, as houses went, the one on Mr. Gruene's farm was superior to most other shacks we occupied during the ten years we spent as migrant farm workers on campaña.

Although it contained only four rooms, the house-on-stilts had a spacious feel to it, thanks to high ceilings and the two oversized front rooms, both of which had doors that opened onto the large porch spanning the length of the house. One of the rooms had an old butane stove in it and served as kitchen and dining area. The other contained a large wood-burning furnace for winter heating, and it functioned as a living room for us, although we had none of the requisite furniture, such as sofas, coffee tables, or recliners. The smaller rooms in the back served as sleeping quarters. With the arrival of our relatives, it became necessary to divide the sleeping accommodations between the two families. Uncle Ben, Lorenza, and their small children took one of the bedrooms in the back, while Mama, Papa, and little sister Elia took the other. The three Peña boys and our cousin Israel slept on army mattresses in the living room.

The presence of our relatives also meant tightening our belts during the winter and early spring months, when we depended heavily on the fifteen-dollar weekly advances from Mr. Gruene against future profits from the sale of the cotton harvest. Little or no wage work was available before spring planting began in March. The provisions Papa and Tío Ben purchased at Tom Mears's grocery-and-market thus consisted of the bare essentials—a small chuck steak, perhaps, and flour and lard for tortillas, as well as beans, potatoes, rice, *fideo* (vermicelli), and household necessities such as FAB detergent and Palmolive bar soap. Papa and Tío Ben always managed to scrape up enough money for my uncle's Bugler tobacco and beer for the Peña brothers' periodic *parranditas*, or mini-binges.

Despite the overcrowding, the tight finances, and the extra measures Papa took to demonstrate to Tío Ben that his children were well-behaved (mainly through tighter reins on our *travesuras*, or mischievous doings), the families got along reasonably well, and I was pretty much allowed the run of the area around the house and the nearby barnyard. Taking care of the chickens—providing them with water and feed—and looking after the vegetable garden was enough to keep me gainfully occupied. Especially satisfying to me was watching the tiny tomatoes emerge from the little yellow blossoms and then mature into sumptuous, juicy fruit, along with the *calabacitas* (zucchini) Mama planted. We also grew Serrano chiles, onions, and carrots, all of which found their way into Mama's delectable chicken guisados. But my favorite treat was what Mama called *bombón*, otherwise known as okra. While many people consider okra slimy and "yucky," like my mother, I developed a strong predilection for it early, and it was always a special occasion when Mama included it in a guisado.

In my spare moments, I would wander off to the nearby Brazos River bottom, where I engaged in many daydreams watching the river and its caramel-brown currents meander placidly toward the "Gulf of Dreams" (as a travel ad called the Gulf of Mexico), a hundred miles downstream. The luxuriant riverbank, with its cottonwoods, oaks, ivy, and other vegetation, provided an idyllic place to spin fantasies. Walking along its banks, I also found plenty of targets to practice marksmanship with what we called a *nigasura*—a transliteration of "nigger shooter," or slingshot.* A particularly exciting adventure was the walk to the usually dry arroyo not far from the farm, over which the Southern Pacific had built a curving bridge. The shape of the arroyo's channel was such that at its edge, the bridge dovetailed with the rising slope as the rails ran into the level ground above. I was able to squeeze into the crevice where the bridge ended and experience the roar of the railroad cars thundering by, no more than a couple of feet above me. The bridge shook with the ponderous weight of the speeding locomotive and its load, as did the earth beneath me. The sensation I felt was one of awe and a sort of controlled terror. It was as if I were in the bowels of a death machine, protected only by the sturdy redwood posts that held up its crushing weight. Flashes of this imagery would recur many times in future dreams.

---

*The term "*nigasura*" may be objectionable, but the Spanish term, "*tirador*," was unknown to us. Mexican American youngsters were unfamiliar with many other standard Spanish words, and we inevitably utilized English loan words, such as "mofle" ("muffler") and "mapeador" ("mop"). We were not aware of *nigasura*'s racist origins.

And, of course, there was the morning trip to the corner post behind the house-on-three-foot-stilts, where my special treat awaited.

One day, I got up and, as usual, went to my favorite corner—only to find an empty nest. I was sorely disappointed and frustrated, wondering what had happened to my egg-laying hen. I went in and shared my disappointment with Mama, but she said nothing. The next morning I got up a little earlier and, to my surprise, just as I was about to jump from the porch, I espied my Aunt Lorenza straightening up at the spot where the nest was located. She had my egg in her hand! I wanted to run up and grab the pearly ingot from her, and to give her a piece of my mind for stealing my breakfast, but respect for her and the fear of reprisal paralyzed me. Instead, I went in and complained to Mama in *sotto voce*, tears welling up when I recounted what I had seen. "Sht!" admonished Mama. "It's only an egg, Memito. I have others here that I can cook for you." Then, bending down, she whispered emphatically, "I don't want to hear any more," as my aunt walked in with my treasure.

Seething with rage, I ran outside and pulled out the tall grass and other weeds surrounding the corner post, and then I scattered the soft dirt all around, obliterating all traces of the nest. The hen never laid her egg there again, nor did I ever learn exactly where she had moved her nest. My Aunt Lorenza knew what I had done, but she recognized it as a child's selfish reaction and laughed it off. Indeed, the story of the chicken and the egg, and my willful destruction of the nest, became a family joke—a kind of morality tale about childish wrath. For my part, it took years to understand the motives that drove me to such a wanton act of destruction. Eventually, I came to the conclusion that I was angry not so much at the loss of an egg (after all, we had a *gallinero* nearby, where other hens laid their eggs), but at being deprived of a unique, almost talismanic object meant for me and no one else. Living in a world of hardship in which I seldom indulged in the thrill of material possessions, the idea of giving up this very personal treasure seemed grossly unfair, especially to someone like Tía Lorenza, an adult whose power over me was beyond challenge.

Thus, in its small way, the loss of the precious egg taught me a bitter lesson about the vagaries of life, the impermanence of worldly possessions, and, especially, about disempowerment. The moral of two old proverbs had been driven home: "*Nada en esta vida dura*—nothing in this life lasts forever," and "*El que tiene más saliva traga más pinole*—he with the most saliva swallows the most roasted corn powder," or, in more idiomatic terms, "the stronger get their way." Perhaps, after reflecting on her action, Tía Lorenza understood my anger, and that was why she, along with the other adults, sympathized with my predicament. And that is why, perhaps, the little episode with the chicken and the egg became a permanent addition to the Peña families' fund of oft-told stories.

5
DAY OF THE STORM

Every day for the previous few weeks, since late May, when the last substantial rain fell over the Calvert area, farmer Elvin B. Gruene and Papa had walked up the gravel path leading from Gruene's house to the neatly cultivated rows of cotton. They would go through what had now become a daily ritual—turning a few of the drooping leaves, inspecting the puny bolls, kicking at the sunbaked dirt, and expressing their hopes for a small deluge. Then, as if on cue, the two men—farmer and sharecropper—would turn their heads toward the blazing June glare and its bald sky. Except for a few scrawny cumulus drifting by, not a cloud was in sight. It had been dry and it had been hot, and ever-widening cracks were fissuring the red clay soil. The cotton crop was showing signs of real stress. "If it rains in the next two weeks," Mr. Gruene was telling Papa in his Southern drawl, "we might still get in a decent crop—maybe even a bale an acre." By the furrowed eyebrows and low voices, I could tell the two men were not especially hopeful.

We were introduced to sharecropping in 1950, when we first arrived on Mr. Gruene's farm. Ever since the big ice storm of '47 struck the Rio Grande Valley and wrecked the local agricultural economy, the Peñas had been forced to join the migrant labor stream that followed *la pizca*— the cotton harvest. Papa had heard about sharecropping opportunities in the Brazos Valley from acquaintances who had joined the exodus from the lower border to all points leading out—West Texas, North and East-Central Texas, the Midwest, California, and even Washington State and

Idaho. In the Calvert and Hearne vicinity of the Brazos Valley, Mexicans had been displacing urban-bound blacks since World War II. Many of these recent immigrants had been drawn into the tradition of sharecropping, long established in the region as in other areas of the deep South. Desperate for any economic arrangement that would carry us through the extended idle spell between the end of the West Texas harvest in December and the start of the new one in South Texas the following July, Papa had quickly come to terms with Mr. Gruene.

As Gruene and other growers had long practiced it, sharecropping was an informal agreement between a farmer and landless workers in which the latter were permitted to cultivate a certain number of acres of the farmer's land on a fifty-fifty basis. Fifty percent of the profits from the sale of the cotton harvest went to the landowner, fifty percent to the sharecropper. The workers were at a lopsided disadvantage, however, since they were held in virtual bondage by the debt they amassed while awaiting the sale of the harvest. Between the fallow months of winter and the summer harvest, they depended on the grower for cash credit, in order to buy supplies such as seed, fertilizer, and insecticides. Like other farmers, Elvin B. Gruene deducted the fifteen-dollars-per-week cash advances he made to his "halvers" at the time accounts were settled—although some of the advances were offset by wages Papa and the older boys earned while working on Gruene's portion of the land. That work included planting, plowing, hoeing, and picking, as well as other tasks, such as tending to the few hogs and cattle Mr. Gruene also raised.

One task I found fascinating was the tamping of the cottonseed once it was planted. Cottonseed needs compact soil to absorb moisture and to germinate, and so the soil around it must be compressed, or "tamped." By the 1950s, most farmers in the area had mechanized the process, using tractors with seed hoppers, cappers, press, and packing wheels to plant and tamp the seed simultaneously. But Mr. Gruene still clung to an ancient practice. He planted the seed mechanically, but lacking the implements to press the ground, he brought in two oxen he had owned for years, Nelly and Maine. Pulling an old-fashioned cart with steel rollers attached, the oxen trudged over the freshly planted rows, two at a time, until the whole field was done. Gruene saw no need to purchase the modern equipment other farmers used, citing the ready availability of his beasts, but Papa wondered whether our *patrón*'s reluctance had more to do with his desire to keep alive comfortable old habits. In any case, on a late-March day, one could see Mr. Gruene or Papa perched on the bare-metal seat of the two-wheel cart, harness in hand, calling out gently to Nelly and Maine as they came to the end of a row and nudging them on to the next one.

Despite the prodigious amount of labor we put into sharecropping, during the years we worked the land with Gruene and later with Joe Milano, we never received more than a couple of hundred dollars from the sale of a year's crop. During the drought year of 1950, there was even a deficit. That season, by the time la pizca was completed and the cotton from our twenty acres was sold, we owed our entire share to Gruene—and then a small bundle besides. But meager as the earnings from sharecropping may have been, we enjoyed at least a measure of economic security, especially during the long months of soil preparation, planting, thinning, chopping, and harvesting. Little earned income flowed in during this time, and the farmer's credit was all that kept us from going over the financial brink.*

E. B. Gruene's property was located about five miles south of Calvert, on the winding Farm-to-Market (F.M.) Road 1644, which follows the course of the Brazos River. Nestled in the fertile river bottom formed by the Brazos and its myriad tributaries (or "arms," the English for "brazos"), Gruene's eighty acres of cultivated land and livestock range stood amid a strand of rich, red clay capable of bountiful agricultural yields, especially when properly watered. In the early fifties, however, many growers such as Gruene had not yet introduced irrigation, and the dry farming they practiced could be risky, dependent as it was on the vagaries of climate—or, as my father would say, Providence. Once the cotton was planted, the farmer was at the mercy of the weather: an opportune gully-washer in late June could spell the difference between a bale-an-acre and a ruined crop. Not surprisingly, the word "rain" itself acquired a talismanic charm, its sound constantly playing like an incantation on the farmers' lips.

---

*In his book, *The White Scourge* (Berkeley: University of California Press, 1997), Neil Foley has trenchantly described the tradition of sharecropping in Texas and its relationship to race and class.

The years we sharecropped with Gruene—1950 and '51—were particularly difficult for dry farmers in the Brazos Valley. The first half of that decade was a period of drought in East-Central Texas, and rain was at a premium, especially during the critical months of June and July when the cotton was maturing. I shall always remember the nights my father roamed from window to window and in and out of the house, staying up late to watch the lightning from distant clouds and hoping they might drift our way. Meanwhile, by day he plotted the course of every promising cumulus that rolled overhead. But the rain never came, at least in 1950, and in the end farmer Gruene was forced to "forgive" some of the advances he had made to us earlier. That year, when we left Calvert after the harvest to go pick cotton on Mr. Billingsley's fields in Colorado City (which we had done since 1948), we were penniless. Only through the largess of "el viejo" Billingsley, who advanced us the cash we needed to buy our first provisions, were we kept from facing real hunger.

We thus returned to Gruene's farm reluctantly in the winter of 1951, but there seemed to be no other choice. Besides, my parents were still enthralled by stories of *medieros* ("halvers," or sharecroppers) who had cleared hefty profits from bumper crops. Perhaps the Peñas, too, might reap the windfall from a good harvest. Not that Papa and Mama were given to grand illusions about stumbling onto a fortune, but the stories we had heard sounded plausible enough, and at any rate Mama on occasion did allow her imagination a bit of room for the play of desire. Such was the case when I overheard them talking early one morning about the upcoming harvest.

"If we have a little money left over, Francisco," she was saying, "perhaps you can buy me a washing machine. Everybody has one now. I'm the only one still scrubbing away on the tallador."

"*Cállate*," he replied impatiently. "*Ya ves como nos fue el año pasado*—you know how badly we did last year."

Yet after gentle prodding on her part, he, too, began to speculate a bit. "*Quizás*," he finally allowed himself to say, "if things go well for us, I may even be able to buy a good truck to replace the candongo. *Pero, bueno, ahi veremos*—we shall see." And then, hedging his bets, he added, "But if we don't make it as medieros this year, we'll have to try something else. Maybe we can go back to Edroy or Robstown."

The Gruene homestead was perhaps typical of the smaller farms

Noe and Imelda Rodriguez at Gruene Farm, 1950

in the Brazos Valley. The farmer's house itself was unprepossessing. It couldn't have exceeded a thousand square feet in living area—just enough to accommodate the Gruenes and their two adolescent children, Ellie Mae and Elvin, "Bud," Jr. But it had traditional wood siding, always painted with fresh whitewash and green trim, and the small yard was kept in neat order by Mrs. Gruene, with roses lining the picket fence in front. The two-car garage was detached, and the driveway was lined with rows of perennials that blossomed every spring and summer. The house stood on the north side of the road and at a distance from the other buildings, which were located about three hundred feet further down the gravel path that ran like a spine through the middle of the farm. The path formed a circle around the Gruene home, passed between our place and the barn, then crossed the Southern Pacific rail on the south side, continuing all the way to the edge of the Brazos River.

Before F.M. 1644 was re-routed in 1951, the road separated the Gruene house from the other buildings on the farm—a barn, a tractor shed, a hen house, and the place on stilts that we called home. On the north side of the barn was a corral, and adjacent was the small pasture where the milk cows grazed. A larger pasture, extending to the edge of the river, lay on the south side of the railroad tracks. On the east side was a pig pen and a little further out, on a narrow dirt path, a silo. Just south of the farm and no more than ten yards from our place were the railroad tracks, where long freight trains often awakened us at night with their loud roaring and the "clackety-clack, clackety-clack" of steel wheels.

All in all, the Gruene farm had the rustic look and feel of rural America, its simple charm enhanced by the color of the outbuildings, which were painted a rusty red with white trim.

≡—

As the two men walked back from the field, Mr. Gruene kept reassuring Papa that there was still hope. "I've seen this happen before, Frank. You never know about the weather in East Texas this time of the year. Overnight, a storm out of the Gulf could send some good rains up in this direction." Papa, who was not altogether immune to optimism, did not seem terribly impressed, but he had lived in Texas all his life, and, like Mr. Gruene, he knew about the unpredictable Texas weather. "Maybe so, Mr. Gruene," he offered in his Mexicanized English (which nevertheless betrayed a slight Texas twang), "maybe we get a good rain one of these days."

Walking behind the two men, I was struck by our patrón's great size and noticeable limp. He had suffered a stroke a couple of years earlier and had lost some mobility in his right side. I remember him as a true redneck, though not only his neck but his face, arms, and hands were a weathered and scaly crimson. He was a tall, heavyset man who always wore extra-large blue-denim overalls that did not conceal his jumbo frame, and whose slow, deliberate movements meshed with the rhythm of his tobacco-chewing jaws. As he and my father ambled down the road toward the farm, he had trouble keeping up with his younger and sprightlier sharecropper.

Mrs. Gruene greeted them as they neared the house. She was dressed in the same overalls as her husband, but although half his size, she had three times his vigor. On this is as on almost every other day of the year, I had seen her at 6:30 in the morning, milking cows and doing other chores around the barnyard. The woman was a workhorse. Blessed with a wiry frame and good height (perhaps five feet six), she wore the passage of years at hard labor on her leathery face. I imagine she must have been a handsome woman in her youth—a Katherine Hepburn type—but the broiling heat of the cloudless summer days on a Texas farm had inflicted its damage. Not even the floppy straw hat she wore for protection could have shielded her from the harsh summers of the Texas latitudes. But her inexhaustible energy pushed her on, and we often saw her driving the Ford tractor, forking hay, milking cows, and even tackling a hog. As my parents observed, she could handle farm chores as well as any man. Yet on Sunday she could dress as prettily as any woman. And in the winter, when the work slowed down, the aroma of baking bread and simmering soups filled her home. Not surprisingly, as Mama noted with a touch of envy on more than one occasion, Mrs. Gruene was not one to sing background for her husband when it came to making decisions about the farm. She was, as Tía Lorenza often said, "*una mujer de huevos*—a woman with balls."

Papa and Mr. Gruene were examining the fence behind our house when I asked our patrón about the redwood stilts holding up the structure. With the insistent curiosity of a child, I had always wondered why the building was perched so high off the ground. In olden times, Mr. Gruene informed me, the Brazos would flood all the way to that point during periods of torrential rains, and the house had been built on tall redwood piers to avoid the waters. "But that's not our problem these days, son," he added. "Right now we wouldn't mind a little flooding."

His comment reminded me of the little game of "rain" I had been playing for the past few weeks, and I strolled to the faucet in the middle of the yard—our source of water, since we had no indoor plumbing. Filling a large jug, I pretended to be Old Man Weather carrying rain to the parched cotton fields of the Brazos Valley. With the undivided concentration of a child at serious play, I had used a screwdriver to chisel several large squares into the bare earth of the patio in front of the house, and I had carved out evenly spaced lines inside each square. The squares represented the cotton fields as seen from an imaginary cloud drifting above, while the lines served as rows. Now armed with the precious liquid, I deliberated: which field shall receive the blessings of my bounty? One inch of rain on this patch, three-quarters there, half an inch on the one beyond that, and a small deluge over the Peña plot. With appropriate gravity, I attended to each and every field, walking slowly over the terrain, making sure the cloud poured the designated amount over the parched earth, until all had received their allocation. Now, I paused and thought, there should be some good harvests all around.

≡

The Fourth of July arrived, and still no rain had washed the dusty fields of the Brazos Valley. Mr. Gruene's tone had become more somber of late: it was beginning to look as if the 1951 season would be a repeat of the last. The disastrous harvest of 1950 was still fresh in our memories. After a promisingly wet spring, the spigot had been turned off in May, and thereafter a brutal, summer-long "drouth," as the local folk called it, choked off the crop. Despite Mr. Gruene's daily homilies on the good rains just beyond the horizon, no precipitation fell, the plants wilted, and only the hardiest of bolls bloomed at harvest time. The current season had started out very much like the one before. The spring had brought copious rain, and the cotton had grown rapidly in the months of April and May. But as soon as June arrived, the rains had withdrawn, as if on cue from Tlaloc, the rain god. Tonatiuh, the sub-tropical sun, had taken command. The weeks passed and we waited while Papa and Mr. Gruene daily retraced their shuffle to the cotton field for the obligatory inspection. Otherwise, there was little work to be done—not even weeding, for weeds also depended on water.

Perhaps to escape, at least momentarily, from what seemed to be a nightmarish repeat of recent history, the Gruenes decided to take the Fourth of July off and go to the celebration being held in nearby Rockdale. They invited my older brother Alessio along, and early in the morning, the Gruenes, their daughter Ellie Mae, son Elvin, Jr., and

Alessio piled into the family pickup. The day was unusually sultry when the Gruenes left, with a reddish haze hanging over the July sky. "The atmosphere looks different this morning," Mr. Gruene remarked to Papa as he climbed into the red Ford pickup. "Maybe it's a good omen," he added. "This might be the day we've been waiting for." With that hopeful comment, he slammed the door and sped off.

By ten o'clock, the haziness began to coalesce around ragged, smoky clouds that appeared out of nowhere, their shapes and colors changing swiftly, as if they were in a rapid boil. At first they were small and ephemeral, but by noon many had grown into larger and more imposing masses, with round and woolly tops. Although the sun could barely pierce through the haze and the proliferating clouds, the day had become oppressively hot and muggy. Scarcely a breeze blew, but as I looked up, I noticed the clouds kept churning just the same.

By early afternoon, some of the cumulus shapes nearby had spiraled upward, so that the woolly, orange-hued tops seemed to be nudging the roof of heaven itself. "Cumulo-nimbus, early stage," I said to myself, recalling the weather book I had read for a class project. More exciting for me, the underbellies were growing darker by the minute. Expert weather watchers that we were, we knew that when such cloud bases turned black, it was only a matter of time before one of the towering monoliths would build into the familiar thunderhead. We also knew that once one of these thunderheads erupted, its load would drop in one concentrated area, since this type of storm rarely moves far once its floodgates have opened (convectional air-mass storms, they are called).

Our sights were particularly focused on a woolly giant that had mushroomed just to the east of us and seemed to be drifting slowly in our direction. As it approached and its outer banks blocked the sun, the air became even more still than before, giving the atmosphere an eerie feel, as if an explosion were imminent. The blossoming thunderhead continued to drift in our direction, and soon, its sooty underbelly squatted directly over us, dwarfing nearby sisters competing for space to grow and dump their own loads. The dark monolith hovered above us for about five minutes while the air grew heavier and steamier. By this time its underside, a mass of coiling charcoal and reddish-brown bands, seemed ready to burst with pent-up fury.

Suddenly, a bolt of lightning knifed through the still air, followed in quick succession by a deafening blast of thunder that reverberated for several seconds as it spread through the bowels of the cloud. The quiet following the first report was almost surreal, deepened by the smell of burnt ozone in the air. A few seconds elapsed, and then thunder crackled from another part of the cloud. As if on a cue, a gust of cool wind rushed in, and, suddenly, a round of fat, heavy raindrops began to spill out of the writhing mass, exploding like firecrackers as they struck the dry dust of the front patio. These lasted less than ten seconds, then once more, the eerie silence. Another bolt of lightning and an ear-splitting crash followed, and then the rain started pouring in torrential sheets. The barn, less than a hundred feet away, almost disappeared from our view.

For about fifteen minutes, the rain beat on the tin roof of our house with the roar of a thousand clapping hands, while Papa paced back and forth on the front porch, looking out at the gray wall of water all around us. Almost as abruptly as it started, the torrent let up and was replaced by a steady light rain that lasted another ten minutes. And then it stopped raining altogether, and, as we looked up, we could see the cloud dissipating above us, even as a new storm cell brewed a few miles to our west. A half hour after the mini-tempest had erupted, only the exhilarating smell of cool, wet pasture remained.

Papa hurried down to the rain gauge by the side of the barn. I jumped off the porch and followed him. His face broke into a wide grin as he held up his index finger for Mama to see. She was standing on the porch. As I could see for myself, the little glass tube had topped out at a point just below the one-inch mark. A sense of elation overcame me, and, intoxicated by the pungent smell of soaked dry pasture, I ran barefoot through the puddles dotting the gravel road that led to the cotton field. The miracle of rain was already evident—the cotton leaves, which only the day before had looked withered and lifeless, had now stiffened and turned their corners upward as if in a smile, while the yellow blooms, now fully open, burst with vitality.

We saw no more rain before the harvest that summer, but the storm had come at a critical moment. The roots absorbed enough energy from the rain to bring to seed all the blossoms—the bolls from which the white gold sprouted—and the yield came to nearly a bale-an-acre. We paid our debts to Gruene, with enough left over to make the trip to Colorado City, where the West-Texas cotton season awaited us. And, while Mama did not get her washer, the venture was rewarding enough to encourage the Peñas to try sharecropping all over again. But we played it safer. The next time we worked as medieros, beginning in 1953, we moved farther south to Mumford, where we harvested on Joe Milano's irrigated farmland.

Two years and two droughts after we left Calvert, we heard from friends that Elvin B. Gruene had finally bought himself an electric pump to draw irrigation water from the Brazos River.

6

FÉRICA HILL

Spanish-speaking Mexicans in the United States have long been in the habit of hispanicizing American geographical names. Besides the transliterations of "Riviera" ("Ribera") and "Edinburg" ("Limburgo"), the city of Lubbock became "Lóbica," Corpus Christi was converted to "Corpos," and Austin was renamed "Ostión." The state of Kansas became "Kiansis," while the California cities of Bakersfield and Carruthers are pronounced "Bequesfil" and "Corrales," respectively. Harlingen was radically overhauled, becoming "Jálinche," while Fort Worth was christened with "Foro Hues." Among the places linguistically transformed (or mangled, depending on one's viewpoint) is the once-famous *loma de Férica*, a grade on a highway in Central Texas that marks the final ascent from the lowlands of the Gulf Coast to the Edwards Plateau.

Named after the city of Fredericksburg—"Férica"—the notorious "Férica Hill," as we bilingual youngsters called it, was a legendary landmark among migrant tejano workers and their norteño kin who followed la pizca. Located north of Fredericksburg on U.S. Route 87, la loma de Férica was also a symbolic threshold of sorts. It marked the boundary between warm and nostalgic South Texas, which most cotton pickers fondly called home, and cold and remote el norte, the Northwest Texas high plains where the waves of Mexican pickers returned year after year in search of *oro blanco* (cotton, or "white gold"). A steep climb, about two miles long, Férica Hill was thus a gateway between the two contrasting regions, standing as a formidable obstacle for vehicles traveling al norte, and as a turbo-boost for those on their way south, toward home.

We were traveling north on Highway 87 in the rickety Harvester we called el candongo. "Candongo/a" is both an adjective and a noun. While the feminine noun-form refers to an old mule, the masculine adjective may be translated as "the cajoled." Both forms aptly served the nickname, since Papa often found himself tinkering with the old tank and literally coaxing it to start, as one would an old mule, sometimes throwing in an expletive or two. We were on our way to Colorado City, where the cotton fields on Mr. Billingsley's farm awaited us. Papa, Mama, and little sister Elia were riding in the cab, while Alessio, Plon, and I were riding in the back, inside a crude *Grapes of Wrath*–styled camper Papa had fashioned atop the truck's flatbed. The camper's frame consisted of studs about five feet tall, driven into the prefabricated metal wells along the edges of the flatbed. The studs were connected and secured at the upper end with two-by-fours, which were attached to three sloping rafters fastened to an overhead beam. Weathered one-by-twelve planks, nailed to the studs, served as side panels, and an army-green waterproof tarpaulin, pulled tightly over the rafters, provided head cover.

In this particular year, 1952, we had lingered for the summer in our hometown of Weslaco, deep in the Rio Grande Valley. We were driving to Colorado City directly, rather than hopscotching through the harvest in the Corpos area and other points East, as we usually did in other years. The distance from Weslaco to Colorado City is about 450 miles, which we negotiated in segments, since Papa was the sole driver in those early years of campaña, and he was reluctant to drive after dark. Besides, the candongo peaked out at thirty-five miles per hour, and even at top speed, we would need to travel nonstop for at least sixteen hours to reach our destination. Such a timetable was out of the question, so at dusk we pulled to the side of the road and hunkered down for the night. At dawn we all rose, limbs stiff from lying in the cramped camper, and resumed our journey. At this pace, it would take us the better part of two days to reach Mr. Billingsley's cotton fields—provided the candongo did not break down.

As we did every time we migrated, we had loaded the *tiliches* (assorted household items) onto the camper. The tiliches took up most of the space on the flatbed, but a small area in the center-rear was reserved for the three boys riding in the back, and it also served as a bed for the family at night. In one corner was the galvanized tub we used for bathing and washing clothes, along with the indispensable buckets. To this day, I can still hear the handles striking the side of the tub as the tires would hit the expansion joints on the concrete road—"click-clack, click-clack, click-clack." The tallador hung on one of the side panels. Its corrugated ridges, which Mama wore thin scrubbing clothes, shone brightly in the sunlight when we rode with the tarpaulin folded back to take in fresh air. The kerosene stove was in another corner, next to the crate full of dishes, cooking pots and pans, and the family's *molcajete*, a relic from pre-Columbian times that Mama preferred for grinding spices and making guacamole.

Also packed somewhere among the tiliches were hats, caps, ear muffs, cotton gloves for picking, and another crate full of shoes. The blankets we used for bedding were folded on top of one of the crates behind the tiny rearview window, a convenient spot for viewing the unfolding scenery as the truck lumbered forward. Resting at the bottom of the pile were two large, banged-up suitcases stuffed with all the clothes we would need for our sojourn in el norte. More easily accessible was a basket loaded with foodstuffs and home remedies, which, unlike some of the heavier crates, was not secured to the flatbed with ropes. As I looked about, I could see the box of miscellanea stuffed with knickknacks, ranging from sewing kits to an old stripped-down Philco radio with no chassis, and, of course, the trusty nigasuras my brother Plon and I used for shooting down yellow jacket nests and other suitable targets. Finally, a small toolbox for mechanical emergencies lay in a rear corner where we could easily reach it.

We had made it about halfway up Férica Hill, aware that many a clunker had fired its last piston on the dreaded grade. I had climbed on the crate with the blankets and was peering into the cab, where I could see that we were pushing fifteen miles per hour. The venerable candongo was lurching up the grade, and it was obviously straining: acrid black smoke billowed out of the tailpipe and backed up into the makeshift camper where my brothers and I were riding. All this time, Papa kept pushing and pulling on the choke, trying to keep the truck from stalling. Suddenly, we heard a loud explosion coming from the muffler, and the old Harvester abruptly expired. Papa barely had time to pull off the highway onto the shoulder before it rolled to a stop.

Then, to our horror, the truck started to roll backward, pulled by the gravity of the steep incline. Papa put the transmission in the lowest gear and slammed on the brakes, but to no avail. He pulled out the emergency handbrake, but that did not stop the slow lurch backward, either. In desperation, he flung his door open and yelled to Alessio: *"Bájate y agarra una piedra grande*—get down and grab a large rock. *¡Ándale!"* Alessio darted down and grabbed the biggest rock he could find, throwing it behind one of the rear wheels. The truck teetered precariously as it almost rolled over it, the entire hulk groaning from the strain. "Get another one!" my father yelled. Alessio picked up a nearby rock and placed it beneath the other rear wheel. This time the truck stopped in its tracks.

Plon and I jumped down to survey the scene. As it stood there, the old candongo reminded me of a wounded bull in a *corrida* I had once seen with Papa and Tía Virginia across the border in Reynosa. The beast had stood impassive and wobbly, gaping at the red flag moments before it fell victim to the matador's final thrust, the *faena de muerte.*

"¡Ah, que troque chingado!" As was his habit when he was agitated, Papa had worked himself into a lather by the turn of events. We were stranded halfway up Férica Hill on a hot August day, with little hope for assistance. Traffic along these rural highways was almost nonexistent in those days, and the few motorists passing by were too preoccupied with the treacherous grade to worry about someone else's misfortune. It was going to be Papa's responsibility to get us out of the fix. He was aware of our predicament, and this only increased his frustration—hence his reliance on time-honored expletives. This time it was going to take more than cajolery to get the candongo moving again.

Meanwhile, no sooner had the truck stalled than Elia began to cry. She was hungry, and we were running low on food. "Manuel, reach in the food basket and bring Elia the last piece of *mollete* left." I had looked forward to my favorite Mexican sweet bread for dinner's dessert, but I did as Mama asked. Papa had hoped to make it to Mason, the next town up Highway 87, before dusk, where he planned to stock up on groceries for the second leg of the trip. He had promised us some hamburgers for dinner, but that plan was now in jeopardy. It seemed we were stranded on the desolate slope of Férica Hill indefinitely, and unless Papa could fix the candongo, our only hope was the arrival of a sheriff's patrol, which occasionally cruised this lonely stretch of road.

Knowing we would be stuck on the hill for a spell, I ventured away from the truck and began to scout the terrain. I walked a short distance into the brush beyond the barbed-wire fence lining the road as far as the eye could see. It was late August, and it had rained recently, so the seasonal short-grasses were in full bloom. Férica hill lay at the juncture between arid West Texas and the more verdant lands to the east, where live oak was plentiful. On the slopes of the notorious landmark, however, the hardy juniper and yucca were the predominant varieties dotting the rocky limestone terrain, although a few stubby live oaks persisted, while clumps of cacti were visible here and there. I wandered into the junipers to explore a bit and to relieve the bladder. But as I was standing there in my compromised position, I heard the familiar hiss: a rattlesnake was shaking its *cascabeles* no more than three yards from where I stood. Terrified by the dreaded sound, the snake's menacing eyes and its slithering tongue, I bolted, pants unbuttoned, and finished urinating on the fly.

"*¿Qué pasó, muchacho?*" my father asked, when he saw me running, wide-eyed, toward the truck.

"A snake, Papa!" I cried. "A rattlesnake!"

"I'll go kill it, Papa," volunteered Plon. "Let me get it with my nigasura."

The spot where I found the snake was about two hundred feet from the truck—too far to pose any danger to us. "No," my father responded. "Let the snake be. She's no danger to us here." Having grown up on the snake-infested banks of the Rio Grande, my father was intimately familiar with the instincts of the rattler, and he knew the reptile would avoid humans if at all possible. "She won't be coming in this direction," he assured us. "Besides, we have more important things to do. Get me that wrench."

Papa had taken out the toolbox, and he was working under one of the folding panels that served as covers for the engine. (Harvesters of the early thirties did not have a lift-up hood). Alessio provided assistance. A half hour later, after removing the spark plugs and cleaning them and re-calibrating the points, Papa emerged, hands smeared with black smudge and reeking of raw gasoline. "*Ahora sí,*" he said. "Let's see if we can get this candongo started." He climbed into the cab and turned the ignition switch. The engine turned, started, and sputtered for a few seconds, but then it choked and died. "*Ándale, pinche candongo*—c'mon, you worthless old mule," he muttered, as he kept turning the ignition. The Harvester did not respond.

Finally, he got out, took off the air cleaner, and began readjusting something. He instructed Alessio to climb in and turn the ignition, but when my brother did so, we heard a loud pop and another curse from

Papa. We all rushed to see what had happened. He was bent over, holding his hands over his eyes, and there was a smell of burnt flesh in the air. Mama, who was already panicky enough over the ordeal, rushed to him and asked, "¿*Qué pasó, Francisco?*" "*Nada, nada, mujer,*" he replied, an edge of impatience in his voice. We never knew exactly what had happened, but apparently the carburetor had built up excess gas and backfired, somehow igniting the fumes present in the chamber. Fortunately, only his eyebrows and lashes had been singed. His face was a sooty red, but he had suffered no actual injury. "*Gracias al Señor*—Thanks to the Lord," Mama uttered, as she examined my old man's face and body. "*Ya, ya,*" he pushed her away, now in full control. "Everything is fine. Now, let me see if I can get this blasted candongo started."

He went back under the hood and made a couple more readjustments. "OK, Alessio," he yelled to my brother. "Try it again, and make sure you pump the pedal when it starts." Alessio turned the ignition, and the engine sputtered again, momentarily, but this time it kept running. "Keep it going," Papa yelled, as he hurriedly collected the tools and threw them in the back. He jumped in and pushed Alessio to one side, gunning the throttle a few times to clear the excess carbon build-up. He kept the engine running at medium throttle for a couple of minutes, then, satisfied with the results, he gave the order: "Everybody on board. ¡*Vámonos!*"

The rusty candongo lurched back onto the highway, the gears grinding as Papa shifted from low to first in one hasty motion to shorten the vacuum between the gears. The Harvester survived the initial shift, but it was critical to get to second, since first was much too slow to negotiate the lengthy climb, and speeding up in first would place too much strain on the engine. Papa revved the throttle in anticipation, and then, gears grinding anew, he snapped the truck into second. The engine choked and coughed momentarily, while we held our collective breaths, but it recovered after Papa pumped the pedal vigorously three or four times. We were all thinking: "This should be enough. If it doesn't stall, the candongo should make it up the hill in second, even if it takes a while to reach the top." We knew Papa would not risk shifting into third gear. "Come on, you old turtle," Plon and I yelled, "don't let us down!"

Two hours and thirty-five miles later, the evening well into dusk, we were all eating hamburgers in Mason. In a jovial mood following our brush with ill-fortune, we were joking about la loma de Férica and how we had almost started our trip back home *antes de tiempo*, before due time, and *de recula*, rolling back-asswards. A bit of legendry had just been added to the notorious landmark that had so long epitomized for tejanos and norteños what the *campañas al norte* were all about—uncertainty, hardship and, in the manner of Sisyphus, the will to carry our burden up the Férica Hill of Texas time and time again, until our very perseverance became a victory over fate itself.

POSTSCRIPT

Forty-some years later, long after Férica Hill had become a gentle, four-lane slope on Highway 87, I was chatting with two tejano expatriates who happened to work with me at the same university in California—Chuy Luna, a professor of history, and Sly Cisneros, a maintenance man. The conversation turned to our shared experiences as migrant cottonpickers, and I asked my friends about la loma de Férica. Both still held clear memories of the legendary barrier. Professor Luna recalled his family being stranded on the same spot where we were, when the family truck stalled climbing the infamous grade. The Lunas were on their way to la pizca in the Lóbica area of the Texas Panhandle.

7
HEAVENLY SATURDAY

"What'n the hell are you kids doin' here?"

The words hurled at us by the burly man behind the pass-through window of the hamburger joint sounded more like a challenge than a question, and they were followed in rapid order by the command already cloaked in that challenge:

"We don't serve Mexicans here. Now get the hell away. Beat it!"

It was a Saturday afternoon in Colorado City, and the Peñas, along with hundreds of other seasonal cotton pickers from the Rio Grande Valley and other points along the Texas-Mexico border, had descended upon this small cattle-and-cotton community in West Texas. We were in town to do the weekly shopping, go to the movies, and steal a pleasurable moment from the grueling routine we faced every day of the week except Sunday, when absolute rest was the rule. Most commercial establishments welcomed the Mexican pickers' presence, and they endured the invasion of brown shoppers who temporarily overran the business district in downtown Colorado City, much as they survived the swarms of May beetles drawn to the city lights on warm summer evenings.

For youngsters like my brother Plon and me, Saturday was a magical day. *Sábado de gloria*, the Mexican workers called it, literally, "Saturday of glory," in a rough analogy to Holy Saturday, the day before the resurrection of Christ. In the context of worker culture, the term "gloria" signified rest and rejoicing, the phrase best translated as "glorious," or "heavenly Saturday." For the cotton pickers, every Saturday was de gloria, a day of rejuvenation when our bodies healed from the week-long grind of backbreaking labor. We young ones rose from bed early every day, but on this day of recreation, we eagerly greeted the sun, jubilant in the knowledge that for the next forty-eight hours we would be free from la pizca.

La pizca: The picking. To this day the words conjure vivid images of khaki shirts drenched in salt-stained sweat (or fingers numbed immovable by cold, depending on the turn of the seasons), and of bodies trudging listlessly at the end of the work week, their strength sapped by toil that grew more arduous as the days dragged one into the other. Monday, Tuesday, Wednesday, Thursday: the pizca cycle ground forward with the weight of heavy rusted gears, until Friday arrived—sábado chiquito (little Saturday), as the pickers named it—when the prospect of the weekend's leisure settled over our psyches like a soothing lubricant.

The body felt resilient enough following the weekend respite, but the ten-hour days of hard labor took their toll. From sunrise until late afternoon, every working day we ducked whiplashing branches and pulled sharp, spiny bolls; we went hungry and thirsted for water; we breathed dust laced with DDT. And, capping it all, we endured back spasms triggered by chronic bending and the drag of leaden sacks, whose one-hundred-pound loads we hoisted on our shoulders again and again for weighing. We felt the exhaustion first in the peripheral limbs, then it gradually worked its way down to the deepest layers of our muscle fibers, until, by the end of the week, we could take no more tugging, no more bending, no more pizca. By Friday noon, the will and resilience began to flag, and only the yearning for tomorrow—sábado de gloria—kept our bodies from collapsing in protest.

I liked it when Mama came out to the cotton field at lunchtime, her basket laden with the savory dishes she prepared for us every day. We worked on Mr. Billingsley's farm, near Colorado City. El viejo Billingsley owned about a hundred acres, on which he grew cotton and raised a few cattle. The cottage Billingsley provided us was surrounded by acreage, so it was never more than a holler away from our current picking spot, and Mama could easily suspend her chores to bring us the hot lunches she cooked with such delicacy. *Carne con papas, carne con fideo, arroz con pollo*, and various other meat and chicken guisados were the daily staples that Mama simmered, norteño style, in just the perfect combination of cumin, garlic, onion, and other flavors. We ate well during the harvest, stocking up especially on beef to nourish our overworked muscles, fully aware that come winter's unemployment we would have to make do with the off-season essentials, beans and potatoes.

Sometimes, Mama would stay to pick cotton with us for a spell. "Come and help me, Mama, come and pick on my row," I would plead. She would start a few yards ahead of me and stack the cotton in little piles, which I then scooped into the sack strapped around my shoulder. It never ceased to amaze me how quickly my sack filled when Mamacita came to my aid. She had such nimble hands! Of course, at age nine I could not pull the twelve-footers the adults used. Mine was perhaps five feet long—a worn-out sack my father had patched up for my use. When full, it carried about fifty pounds. I felt a great sense of accomplishment, seeing my midget bulging with white gold, even if my bruised shoulder chafed from the drag of its full load. I always did some mental addition, visualizing how many dollars and cents the white gold would fetch when weighed on the scale at the row's end.

≡

This sack takes so long to fill. Let's see—I should be about over there, where that tall quelite weed sticks above the cotton plants, before I fill up again. Maybe another half hour, and then I'll have a chance to go back to the scales, drink a little water, and rest up a bit. I wish Mama was out here, helping. But she's been feeling sick, again. It seem like she's sick a lot lately. "Amorcito, corazón, yo tengo tentación de un beso"—*how does that Trío Los Panchos bolero go?* ". . . que se pierda en el calor de nuestro gran amor, mi amor. . . ." *I wish it would rain, and then we could go home early—run down to the river, cool my sweaty feet and try the new nigasura on those yellow jackets. It's so hot. That hurricane the radio said was out in the Gulf—I wonder if it'll send a few showers up this way. Naw, it's four hundred miles to the coast from here. But those clouds bunching over there— they look like they might build up into a shower. Are they coming in this direction? Which way is the wind blowing? Let's see where this little whiff of cotton blows. East—and the clouds are to the East, so no chance for rain, I guess.* ". . . en la dulce sensación de un beso mordelón quisiera. . . ."

Next week is my birthday. Ten, I'll be ten—September fourth, 1952. And it's gonna fall on a Saturday, too. Maybe this time Papa will buy me the bicycle he's been promising for so long—like that red one I saw at Montgomery Ward. Naw, Memito, don't fool yourself. He'll say there's no money; he always says that. Besides, Plon needs shoes real bad. He's been complaining for weeks now. Nineteen fifty-seven—how old will I be? Fifteen. Boy, it seems so far away. I wish we were there already, so I could be like Plon and Alessio, and put on those nice slacks and starched white shirt and go to the dance Saturday night. Check out Valerio Longoria. And dance with Cora. She sure is pretty, even when she's out here, picking cotton and all grimy. "Yo quiero ser un solo ser, y estar contigo. . . ." I loved the way El Trío Los Panchos sang that bolero in the Pedro Infante movie we saw Saturday. And, híjole, *that* requinto *introduction: "Ting, ting, tiki tiki tiki ting ting. . . ." Maybe someday I'll sing and play guitar like that. Wear those nice outfits. And be a handsome and brave mexicano, just like Pedro Infante. Yeah—sing like Pedro Infante:* "Me cansé de rogarle; me cansé de decirle que yo sin ella de pena muero. . . ." *God, I'm getting thirsty—and I'm so tired, too. That quelite looks so far away. I'll never get there, I'll never fill this damn sack.* "Te quiero ver en el querer, para soñar. . . ."

"Oye, Manuel!!" Papa's sharp voice pierced through the steamy air, jolting me out of my reverie. He was walking ominously in my direction, though still a safe distance away. "Get down and start picking, you little whelp, before I get over there and peel your hide! You've been standing around for a half hour. You haven't picked anything today. Get your nose down on those rows, *cabrón*! I wanna see those hands flying."

Plon, picking on a row nearby, looked at me with a smirk, and he circled his neck with his hands, tongue sticking out, signaling the noose awaiting me if I didn't start hustling. "Yeah, Papa," he added in an accusatory tone, "he's been standing there, daydreaming and singing to himself." My brother always saw me as *el consentido*—the favored or pampered one—and he got a perverse sort of satisfaction when Papa's wrath was aimed at me for a change, and not at him.

Plon was four years older than I, and he could pick a lot more cotton. He was considered an adult by Mexican cultural standards. Like our oldest brother Alessio and all the other migrant pickers, Plon had skipped adolescence. We were, all of us, considered children until puberty, usually around thirteen or fourteen, and then we were thrust into the world of adults. Although young and callow, at times even foolish, or *pendejos*, we were adults nonetheless, with all the responsibilities the term implies. At fourteen, Plon felt too old to go to school, and he was on the verge of dropping out. For the past two years he had attended sporadically, anyway, especially after a bout with nephritis, when he swelled up like a giant blister and missed two months of school. He was very sick, and we were not sure he would survive. And now, two grades behind the norm for his age, he felt embarrassed at being older than his classmates.

Plon was the black sheep of the family. Barely fourteen, he was already the tallest of the Peñas, his wiry frame having sprouted to a height of five feet, eight inches. By contrast, at the age of eighteen, Alessio stood a mere five feet, four inches, while Papa was a portly five-foot-seven. Hot-tempered, rebellious, and always ready with his fists, Plon was perennially in trouble with others—youthful peers, teachers, and anyone who rubbed his quills the wrong way, even our disciplinarian father. And although he was street-tough and shrewd, my parents considered him the least of the three brothers. For instance, one evening late in the harvest season, while sitting around the little space heater in Billingsley's cottage, my parents contemplated aloud what their three sons' destinies would be. "Manuel will be a musician, perhaps an intellectual, a man of letters," Papa was saying. "Yes," Mama chimed in, "and Alessio may yet be an artist. He is so talented with the colors." "What about Plon?" I asked. "Plon?" My father reflected for a moment. "No, my Plon will be a *marranero*—a pig-herder."

Forty years later, after a tumultuous life in which he had played many social and economic roles, including preacher and cement contractor, Plon, or José (having finally reclaimed his birth name), fled California to escape the IRS. He settled in a desolate twenty-five-acre patch of brush and mesquite outside Chorizo Springs, Texas, where he battled chicken hawks, rattlesnakes, coyotes, and other predators while rais-ing assorted fowl and livestock. When my brother Frank (Alessio), now living in California, heard about José's trip to the Rio Grande Valley to collect some piglets a friend had offered him, he wryly observed, "*Por fin se cumplió la profecía de Papá*—at last, my father's prophecy has been fulfilled. José is now a true marranero."

≋

We picked cotton on Billingsley's farm for the first time in 1948, and we returned to his fields for the next four years, before we learned that the harvests were better up north in the Panhandle, around the Lubbock area. Billingsley was different from most of the growers for whom we worked during those years of campaña. Many of the fields we picked belonged to large farming operations, and their owners remained invisible to us, using their foremen as proxies for the power they wielded over us. As a small-time grower, el viejo Billingsley was not only visible, he was unreservedly friendly with my father, and on occasion his wife would share with us leftover biscuits she baked. The cottage he provided us reflected our patrón's basic compassion. Although it consisted of two small rooms without plumbing, it was far better than most shacks we occupied during our campañas. It was fairly new and was always clean when we first arrived in early September. Billingsley kept it freshly whitewashed, and he had not only insulated it with drywall, but equipped it with electric lights and a small natural gas space heater.

The heater was especially welcome as autumn wore on and the nights grew colder; it was indispensable on cold November Saturdays. Sábado de gloria was the one day the Peñas had both the time and energy to bathe, and by early November, when the first "northers" blew down from the high plains, a bath could become a tooth-chattering ordeal without the benefit of a heater. The wash-down was part of the magic of Saturday, a weekend ritual that not only cleansed the five-day layer of grime we had collected while wrestling sacks in the dusty fields, but revived the spirit and gave us the resolve to begin the cycle afresh. By turns, starting with Papa and working down to me, each one of us entered the room with the heater and placed the portable tin tub and a bucket of warm water in front of the hot blue flames streaking out of the gas jets. The glow radiating outward thawed our shivering bodies, as we rubbed in the soap, poured water over our heads, and watched the bubbly grime curdling around us in the filling tub. Afterward, we would put on our weekend best—new clothes, preferably, or at least pants ironed smooth by our industrious Mama and shirt collars she had starched until stiff. We were now ready for heavenly Saturday.

Billingsley's cottage possessed another advantage: it was hard by the nascent Colorado River, at this geographical juncture barely forming itself as it wound through the West Texas high plains. The river bottom was breathtaking, with many granite boulders, or *peñas* (emblems of our family name), dotting the riverbed, and a thin but dense canopy of cotton-woods and other vegetation lining the shoreline. Plon and I spent many a Sunday afternoon playing in that bottom, where we particularly relished disturbing the large yellow jacket colonies high atop the trees. We had fashioned a couple of nigasuras using cut-off "Y" tree branches, strands of red inner-tube rubber, and tongues from old shoes as construction mate-rial. The riverbed contained a plentiful supply of small, smooth rocks, ideal for the nigasuras, and the yellow jackets were our favorite targets. On a couple of occasions we paid the price with painful stings on our backs, as the winged marauders identified their tormentors and chased them up the river bank, exacting the proper revenge along the way.

Farmer Billingsley paid us every Friday evening after the picking was done for the week. Papa had bought a bookkeeper's ledger in which he kept track of all the *pesadas*, or individual sack weigh-ins. He added up the daily totals and presented them to our patrón, who converted them into a per-hundred-pound equivalent. For example, the three and a half bales (7,000 pounds) the Peñas picked during the third week of September fetched $105, at the going rate of $1.50-per-hundred. That was good money, the payoff for a full week picking the first, or bumper, harvest. (There were usually two harvests, sometimes three during the season, but the yield diminished rapidly after the first.) It had taken the collective toil of Papa, Alessio, Plon, and me—with occasional help from Mama—to bring in that sum, but it was the only way to amass enough capital for the hard winter months. We knew that in a typical year we could count on no more than four or five weeks of one-hundred-dollar earnings, what with decreasing yields, bad weather, and other obstacles. Reaching the one-hundred-dollar threshold was thus cause for celebra-tion, as it brightened the prospect of meeting our goal: to save $500 for the winter of unemployment.

As usual, on this particular Friday I watched as Billingsley paid my father with crisp new bills—five twenties and a five—which Papa actu-ally let me touch and smell. I shall never forget the luxurious feel of those bills, their musky scent, and the strange excitement they evoked, one bor-dering on sexual arousal. At age ten, I was being introduced to the fetish of money. More significant from a practical viewpoint was the method of payment—cash—which signified the nature of the transaction. Paid by piece rate, the pickers were considered independent contractors, rather than employees, and Billingsley and other growers were thus able to evade the law requiring employers to contribute taxes toward their workers' social security.

As they did after each payday during the years of campaña, my parents saved as much as they could for the lean winter months awaiting us, and on that third Friday of September 1952, Papa promptly transferred forty dollars of the week's pay to Mama. She was the family treasurer. As in other weeks, however, at least half of the family's earnings was pumped into the economy of Colorado City, on food, clothes, household items, and maintenance on the old Harvester. Part of the budget was also spent on beer for Papa's parranditas (mini-binges that often turned into parrandotas—big binges), and on other incidentals such as movies or, for the older boys, ticket money for the Saturday-night dance in town. That, of course, is why the local merchants were so tolerant of the Mexican pickers; they welcomed the transfer of our sweat-stained dollars into their bank accounts.

But not the burly man behind the counter of the hamburger joint. His hatred of Mexicans overruled the logic of his enterprise—to sell as many hamburgers as possible—and he thus harbored no desire for our business.

Plon and I had just left the movies. I think we had been to a Mexican western, a *charro* film starring the idolized singer and actor, Pedro Infante, whose exploits we cheered, along with about a hundred other people in the large tent some enterprising Mexican had converted into a portable theater. The seating consisted of folding chairs set up in curving rows, an arrangement that made it difficult for youngsters like me to watch the movie while sitting behind the taller and wider bodies of adults. But the action on the screen more than compensated for the paltry inconvenience of a craning neck. After the show, we were hungry and looking for a place to buy a hamburger when we spotted the little joint with a pass-through window facing the sidewalk. Avid lovers of this symbol of American fast food, especially on a heavenly Saturday after a movie, we hurried to put in our order.

A young woman was at the window, but when the manager saw us, or heard Plon's Mexicanized English, he came over and pushed the girl

to one side. His angry face, pimple-scarred and reminiscent of rare hamburger, was enough to frighten us. He didn't have to repeat his command,
as even the always-feisty Plon was caught by surprise. We hung our heads
and scurried away. But his words had splattered over us like broiling fat—
"We don't serve Mexicans here!"—scorching themselves into our brains
forever, like a branding mark of shame.

I knew Plon was angry for a long time. Many years later, he recalled the
event: "If I had been a man, as I am now, I would have beat up that gringo's
ass." For the remainder of our lives, our attitude toward male gringo strangers would be colored by that brief but tense encounter on a sábado de gloria
in a dusty West-Texas town: a hulking white merchant's angry face, and
two Mexican youngsters retreating meekly from his blistering command.

8

BIG BUG THAT PEES

We called them *chinches*—large, humpbacked green beetles that lived among the cotton plants. The largest could grow nearly an inch in length, and to me, at least, they never looked anything but menacing. I was afraid of them.

One day, the combined families of Francisco and Benicio Peña were out in force, harvesting the cotton we grew as sharecroppers on E. B. Gruene's farm. Tío Ben and I were picking on adjacent rows when I ran into a chinche for the very first time. I had reached for a boll, ready to pluck the white gold right out of its spiny haven and tuck it in my five-foot sack, when I caught sight of the green beastie. I was initially startled and then horrified as I beheld the large insect, and I jumped backward with a shriek.

"Tío, Tío," I cried out to Uncle Ben. "Look, look, here's a creature that's really big! An *animal* that's gigantic! Come, Tío, come look at it!"

My uncle swiftly took off his cotton sack, and he rushed toward me. "What's the matter, sonny?" he asked, a look of real concern on his face. As I later learned, the first thought in his head was that it might be a poisonous snake, perhaps a water moccasin, common near the Brazos River where we were picking.

"Right here, Tío," I answered, pointing to the beetle. "What is it?"

On spotting the bug, Uncle Ben's attitude suddenly relaxed. "Oh, Memito," he said, a note of relief in his voice. "It's only a chinche. Don't be afraid."

"Well, what does it do, Tío? Can it do anything to you?"

"Not really. It just pees." Uncle Ben was referring to a peculiar characteristic of this type of bug. It releases a pungent fluid that has a corrosive effect, burning a spot on a cotton leaf when it excretes the substance.

"It pees?" I echoed my uncle's description with a note of perplexity in my voice.

"Yes," he repeated, "they pee—they put out a liquid that can burn a hole on that leaf it's perched on."

"OK," I finally said, "so why can't I hear the *chorrito*—why can't I hear the sound of the pee pouring out?"

Uncle Ben burst into laughter when he heard his nephew's droll question. When he told Papa and the others about my comments, everyone laughed in turn. My brother Alessio, always the prankster, leaned close to me and whispered, "You know why you can't hear chinches pee? Because their wiener's too tiny. You have to get right up against it—but then it might burn a hole on your earlobe!"

When Mama and Tía Lorenza heard about the "big bug that pees," they, too, laughed heartily. The incident quickly became part of our family lore, but it was several years before I knew enough about humans and insects to join in the laughter.

9
THE CURSE OF THE JASSOS

My oldest brother Frank, or Alessio, always had a mischievous side to him, which was heightened because concealed by his disarmingly quiet and mild manner. He was, as people in the barrio would say, a *chingaquedito*—not an easily translatable term, but in English it might be rendered as "one who screws you sneakily." Not that my brother was an unsavory character—far from it. It was simply that he was an outwardly harmless fellow who happened to have a slightly perverse streak in his personality. He was not averse to a prank when the occasion presented itself. My father said it came from my mother's side. Like Alessio, Agustina Jasso was *un terrón de azúcar*, as people used to say of her—a lump of sugar. But underneath her undeniably humble and sweet disposition lurked a mischievous streak, which peeked through often enough via her wry, sardonic humor. Alessio was like that, too.

My brother particularly enjoyed ferreting out and then exploiting other people's quirks, such as, in my case, the tendency to overreact to life's little emergencies. For example, one morning while playing among the weeds that surrounded our shack in Edroy, not far from the city of Corpus Christi, I accidentally swallowed a little blossom, a seed from a common weed. In a panic, I rushed into the shack to report my misfortune. Alessio was home that day, and, as I hurriedly explained my plight to Mama, he listened with a look of increasing concern. Despite my experiences with his pranks, I trusted my oldest brother implicitly, and when he demanded that I show him the offending weed, I took him outside and pointed out the blossom I had swallowed, hoping he would reassure me it was harmless. Instead—and to my utter horror—he took one look at it, opened his eyes wide in mock consternation, and rushed toward Mama, saying in a voice marked by distress, "Look what Manuel swallowed!" Then, turning to me, he said, "This is a very dangerous plant. We must get you to the doctor immediately, otherwise your intestines will begin to burst."

I was a tender six years of age at the time, while Alessio was fourteen, and his pronouncement was nothing short of a death sentence to me. My heart began to pound in my throat, and I started to hyperventilate as I tried desperately to cough up the little seed I had swallowed. I rushed up to Mama in tears and pleaded for her to take me to the doctor right away. I was thoroughly convinced I would faint at any moment and that I would never again regain consciousness.

Mama, who had been busy making tortillas for dinner, asked me to show her the dreaded weed. Again I rushed to the site by the house and pointed it out to her. She examined it, smiled, and reassured me. "Don't worry, *m'hijito*," she said, putting her arms around me, "this is a perfectly harmless plant. It's called an *amargosa* (bitterroot), and cows and horses eat it all the time. Alessio!" She screamed at my brother. "Why are you frightening Memito like that? You ought to be ashamed of yourself, you bully, for playing pranks on your little brother. You know how sensitive he is to suggestion. I'm going to tell your father about this, and we'll see if he doesn't give you a good licking and make you stop your mischievous doings."

He was actually an exceptionally intelligent and talented young man, my oldest brother Alessio. I can still recall his pencil drawings of various individuals; they were so faithful to the original that anyone could immediately recognize the likeness. That attribute, too, came from my mother. In grammar school, he absorbed the daily lessons like an ink blotter, and he had learned to read in both English and Spanish by the time he was six, according to Mama. He also displayed some musical skill, and it was from him that I learned the basics on the guitar. But he had dropped out of school before the end of the seventh grade, partly because of the family's need for his labor to help support his younger siblings. But as he confided to me many years later, he had also left school because he began to experience feelings of unreality every time he stepped into the classroom, which threw him into a state of panic. He dropped out of school by the time he was fourteen, becoming a full-time agricultural laborer and working alongside my father.

But even as he grew older, Alessio never lost his roguish sense of humor. We never enjoyed the comforts of indoor plumbing until my teenage years, when we finally remodeled the shanty Papa had bought in Weslaco during World War II, and so we always had to rely on outhouses. For sanitary purposes, the *casitas*, or "small houses," as they were called, were usually located at some distance from the shacks we occupied, and as a child, when I felt the urge to evacuate at night, Alessio, Plon, or both would have to accompany me. The moonless nights of rural Texas could be absolutely pitch-black, and since we rarely had a flashlight, it was only by lighting matches that we could find our way to the outhouse. Once there, Alessio waited outside while I went in, climbed on the platform, and relieved myself—that is, if my prankish brother didn't frighten me out of the urge first, for he was fond of planting ghoulish ideas in my head.

A favorite of Alessio's was the castration-laced warning about the cold, bony hand waiting to emerge from the depths of the sewage pit. Just as I was hunching in squat position, I would hear his trembling voice coming from the darkness outside: "Beware of the bony hand that people say dwells in the shit," he would warn. "They say it grabs you by the nuts and pulls them right offa' you—if it doesn't suck your whole body into the black pit first." Already uneasy about the inky void below me, I panicked at Alessio's warning and bolted out of the outhouse. It was only after I started bawling that my brother would finally change his story: "OK, OK," he would say, now with a tone of impatience, "don't believe anything I said. I was only kidding." But his words sounded so chilling, especially in the total darkness of those West Texas nights, that it was years before I learned to turn a deaf ear to his macabre warnings.

The Peñas were living in Hearne, Texas, working on Joe Milano's estate, when rather suddenly, Alessio's sprite began to lose its mischief. His woes started with a bad case of the flu, and then he got to a point when he had lost his spark and his *joie de vivre*. Not long after that, he began having trouble going anywhere alone, even to work in Joe Milano's fields. As I discovered for myself, he would plunge into a state of panic when he found himself in a situation he deemed without escape, especially if he was alone. It became increasingly difficult, and finally impossible, for Alessio to carry out his duties on the farm, and in the end I was chosen to accompany him for his night shift as irrigator. Even the simple company of his thirteen-year-old younger brother had a soothing effect on Alessio, and he was able to carry on with his work, as long as he didn't lose sight of me.

"*Es la maldición de los Jasso*—it is the curse of the Jassos," my father pronounced, once Alessio's condition became clear to him. As we were all aware, a couple of Mama's relatives had suffered from paralyzing fear, and from time to time Mama herself had endured bouts of agoraphobia and panic, the latter sometimes overwhelming her without apparent provocation. I can still vividly recall the night the authorities set fire to oil that had spilled into the Colorado River near the Billingsley ranch in Colorado City, where we were picking cotton in 1951. Flowing close by our cottage, the blazing river ignited the night sky, the flames reaching high above the trees that dotted the shore. Unaware of the planned fire, and convinced the world was coming to an end, Mama had panicked and bolted out of the house, running headlong away from the river. She ran so fast it took an extra effort for Papa to catch and restrain her. "*No tengas miedo, mujer*—don't be afraid, woman," he spoke to her in the firm, authoritarian voice he often used to such great effect. "There has to be an explanation for the flames. Nothing will happen to you." Her adrenaline finally under control, she returned to the cottage exhausted, and for the next few days she was exceptionally jumpy.

And now it was Alessio's turn. The doctors of the fifties were as unfamiliar with panic disorder as we were, and they kept attributing Alessio's ills to various sources—a lack of key vitamins, a troubled childhood, or, as the illness also manifested itself in gastrointestinal distress, the need for a specialized diet. But all their ministering was to no avail, and Alessio's condition kept getting worse. Finally, a Mexican *curandera*—a folk healer—recommended a change of climate for Frank, perhaps a sojourn in his ancestral home in Weslaco, as a way to snap him out of his panicky, depressed state. We were of course in no position to relocate to Weslaco—the thirty acres we sharecropped with Joe Milano were harvest-ready—but my tía Virginia, who dabbled in *curanderismo* herself, suggested Alessio spend some time with her in Edinburg. Papa agreed, and it was decided Frank should spend a few weeks with his aunt. Preparations were made, and one day Papa and Frank climbed into the 1952 Chevy sedan we had bought from our patrón and embarked on the 350-mile journey to the Rio Grande Valley.

My brother spent several weeks in Limburgo, and perhaps as a result of the change of scene, the *hierbitas* (herbs) Aunt Virginia prescribed, or the self-limiting, recurrent nature of panic disorder, he came back feeling a good deal more confident about himself. In time he recovered fully from the disorder, and he remained free of panic for nearly twenty years. In his late thirties, however, he slipped into alcoholism, and one day, in a state of extreme withdrawal, the panic returned. At that time, however, my brother followed Mama into born-again Christianity, and soon after he converted, he was once again "cured," never again to suffer the syndrome. Free of the demons unleashed by panic disorder, he could well understand and sympathize with the plight of his youngest brother, when in later years he, too, succumbed to the ravages of the dreaded condition.

POSTSCRIPT

They had to take him out of school, my nephew Benjie Peña, because he was getting panic attacks that paralyzed him with fear. He skipped a whole semester, until his condition was stabilized with medication. My daughter Elsa had gone through the same ordeal a couple of years earlier, when we had to park on the school grounds and stand ready, since at any moment she might bolt out of class. Periodically, the anxiety roiling inside her preadolescent body would build to an explosive level, and she found it necessary to flee and seek reassurances from Mama or Daddy. The two children were following their fathers' pattern, as the curse of the Jassos wound through the genealogical thread. We would always wonder: "Who will be the next victim?"

10

BREAKING WIND, BROKEN SILENCE

(A Cathartic Moment)

Pincers in his hands tightly clamped, Papa was pulling at the barbed wire with all his strength, when, suddenly, a blast of wind escaped from his straining body. I was watching while he, Pol Piña, my brother Alessio, and Mr. Taylor were fencing a plot on Joe Milano's River-Bottom Place. They were working in earnest silence, with nary a word uttered, tightening the brace around a corner ensemble. After relaxing for a couple of seconds, Papa gave the wire another hard tug, when—rrrupt!—another blast issued forth. No one reacted, least of all the dour Mr. Taylor. His face remained as inscrutable as ever.

Mr. John H. Taylor was a short, wiry African man, somewhere in his sixties, whose head was crowned with thick, kinky, short-cropped hair that had turned almost white. The younger Mexican workers always called him "Mister," or rather, "Mistuh" Taylor, though I cannot say whether the form of address was in genuine recognition of his seniority, out of mocking respect for his blackness, or, more likely, a playful juxtaposition of the two. He had a broad nose and yellow beady eyes that were almost lost in the expanse of his swollen chin. It was not a normal chin. He had fought as a foot soldier in Germany at the end of World War I, and, during one of the Allied assaults, the Germans had retaliated with mustard gas. The gas struck Mr. Taylor's face underneath his protective mask, inflicting a clean burn that ran the length of his jaw. In time, the burn healed into a blister-like ridge that looked from a distance like a well-manicured beard, but on close examination it was obvious that the ridge was a scar.

The blistered chin gave Mr. Taylor's face a ponderous, almost freakish look, which his basic personality did nothing to soften. To put it bluntly, Mr. Taylor was a curmudgeon. He was also a loner who kept his own company in a little cabin he rented across the Brazos River, in the nearby hamlet of Gauze. One never knew when it was safe to approach him, though on any morning we could expect him to be in one of his crabbed moods, when it was easier to pull hair out of his beardless chin than words from his sullen mouth. For the Peñas, his oft-repeated caveat upon being greeted in the morning, "I ain't mad but I ain't talkin'," became like an identity marker, a distillation of Taylor's crusty personality. When he greeted you with this warning, you knew it was better to stay clear of him.

Caveats aside, the younger men did not take his moroseness seriously, perhaps because as a feeble old black man he did not command fear, despite his truculence, or perhaps because underneath his prickly exterior—and occasionally peeking through his suspicious eyes—was a pixieish streak. In any case, the Peñas, the Condes, and the other Mexican youth who worked on Milano's estate often needled him about this or that—a needling he generally tolerated, especially since it was always done in a playful, affectionate way. We knew the banter was penetrating his funny bone when the trail of an impish smile crossed his face. But, when he grunted his favorite line—"I ain't mad, but . . ."—we all knew to expect no response from him other than a stony silence.

And in the two years that I had known him, I had never heard the taciturn Mr. Taylor laugh out loud—not one single time.

The wire still refused to give the slack needed, so Papa yanked it once more, adding a bit of extra muscle to his effort. For the third consecutive time, a discharge of gas issued from Papa's rear, this one trailing off with a slight gurgle. All of this motion—the tugging, followed by the anal snort, followed by the next tug—occurred in rapid succession, so that the last report was like an echo of the first two.

Be that as it may, on hearing Papa's third fart, "Mistuh" Taylor suddenly let go of his end of the wire and fell backward, legs kicking in the air and guffaws pouring out of his mouth like short bursts of small-arms fire—"Ra-ca-ca-ca-ca-ca-ca-ca . . . !" The man groveled in the dirt, twisting and turning, keeping up a steady barrage of loud peals of unrestrained laughter. It was as if he were purging himself of all the bilious humor built up from his years in the war and its ugly memories, from the endless toil and loneliness, or, perhaps, from the muffled rage of his racial oppression. The bizarre display continued for about a minute as the rest of us gaped in utter bemusement at Mr. Taylor's hysterical reaction. His guffawing was so infectious we soon found ourselves joining in, but the moment we did, he clammed up, got on his feet, adjusted his leather gloves, and, dour as ever, picked up the wire and resumed his work.

On seeing Mr. Taylor regain his composure, the other men cut short their laughter, and they also went back to the task at hand. Suddenly, all became quiet again, as if the cathartic moment had never happened. I never heard "Mistuh" Taylor let loose his mirth like that again.

11
OVER MY DEAD BODY

My fifth-grade teacher at Mumford Elementary was a lovely and vivacious young woman, Mrs. Guidry—all the more shocking to us when she suddenly launched into a tirade during our civics lesson that May morning in 1954. She had a cherub of a daughter, perhaps three years old, who often visited her mother at school. Mrs. Guidry spoke fondly of her little jewel and about her dreams that the child would someday grow up to become an outstanding citizen. Perhaps our teacher's expectations of a daughter growing up in the world of white privilege she accepted as a birthright was what provoked such rage when she heard about the *Brown vs. Topeka* decision. To Mrs. Guidry, the landmark court ruling was an assault on that privilege, and she vented her anger openly and without restraint.

"Over my dead body," concluded our teacher in her twangy Texas English, "will they force my daughter to attend school with colored people." The words exploded from her lips like bursts of pressurized steam, drenching the air with their oppressive force. Her rosy hue had turned a deep crimson as she rehearsed what the U.S. Supreme Court had done. Even to a fifth grader, it was obvious she was in an agitated state, and the class sat in stunned silence after her diatribe. I sneaked a peek at Miguel García, the daredevil in the class, to see how he was reacting to our teacher's extraordinary display of emotion, hoping his usual swagger might ease my own discomfort. But even Miguel had been caught off guard, and when he finally turned to me, he puckered his lips awkwardly and turned his gaze toward the floor.

A few days earlier, the Supreme Court had handed down one of the most important civil-rights decisions in its history, when it ruled unanimously that the "separate-but-equal" doctrine, which segregated blacks and confined them to their own schools, was unconstitutional. To Southerners like Mrs. Guidry, the decision was a galling insult. As we Mexicans were unavoidably aware, the white folks from the Brazos Valley of East-Central Texas had little affection for blacks. In towns like Bryan, Hearne, Calvert and Mumford, the hamlet where I attended school, everyone knew blacks were the "untouchables," people with whom whites must avoid unnecessary contact. The reaction to the Court decision, as personified by our teacher, was thus immediate and visceral.

My family learned first-hand about the relations between blacks and whites in the Brazos Valley when we set up residence in the town of Calvert during the winter of 1950. Being ancestrally grounded to the Rio Grande Valley in deep South Texas, we were intimately familiar with the conflictive relations between Anglos and Mexicans in that region, but few blacks had ever migrated to the border area, and neither Mexicans nor Anglos had much experience with the African Americans. For instance, only two black families called my birthplace of Weslaco home—the Joneses and the Jacksons. Both families had youngsters close to my age—John Wesley Jones, who graduated with me from high school several years later, and Leon Jackson, who was two or three years older. Both John and Leon were fluent speakers of Spanglish, the bilingual dialect common to the South Texas barrios, and so they fit in easily with the Mexicans of Weslaco. Perhaps because they represented an exotic but minuscule "African" presence in the community, and because both youths were handsome, athletic, and intelligent, the two were well liked and admired, at least by the Mexicans. The Anglos seemed not to be threatened by the two African American families in their midst—both boys went to the integrated Weslaco High—though neither John nor Leon hung out much with Anglos.

But in January of 1950, when we found it necessary, again, to leave our ancestral home, on the advice of friends we headed for Calvert, where we soon came to terms with Elvin B. Gruene to become his sharecroppers. Most important for the lesson on race relations I was learning, I once overheard Mr. Gruene confide to my father that he was glad we had come along. In his early sixties, he was getting up in years by then, and running the farm by himself was becoming ever more difficult. The recent victim of a stroke, our patrón had lost some of his mobility, and he was increasingly dependent on others to carry out the work around the farm. Despite all that, Mr. Gruene hesitated to hire "colored people" for anything other than menial tasks such as hoeing and picking, because, as I heard him tell my father, "You can't depend on colored people; they're too lazy and unreliable." Apparently, he considered Mexicans to be a notch above blacks in intelligence and thrift, at least to the extent he came to rely more and more on Papa for the expertise he had gained from long years as an all-around farm hand, or, as he inelegantly put it, as an "ox at the plow."

Elvin B. Gruene's farm was adjacent to a much larger estate, owned by an absentee landlord, a Mr. Teasdale, whom I remember as a jaunty older man from three or four occasions I caught a glimpse of him. Once, I saw him drive up to the main house in an expensive car, dressed in a dapper pinstriped suit and fedora hat, and accompanied by an attractive, well-dressed woman, considerably younger than he. Most surprising, given the state of racial relations in the Brazos Valley, was her identity: she was what Mexicans call a *cuarterona*—literally a "quadroon," but to Mexicans, anyone somewhere between black and white yet possessing such African markers as kinky hair and full, fleshy lips. According to workers on the ranch, Teasdale lived in the Houston area, but he maintained a *casa chica* on his estate. In the Mexican vernacular, a *casa chica*, or "small house," refers to the secondary home of a married and usually well-to-do individual, one run by a live-in mistress, as was the case with Teasdale's cuarterona.

The Teasdale establishment maintained a large labor force, the bulk of which until recently had been African American. Since the Second World War, however, the blacks had been moving to northern cities like Chicago and Cleveland, and they had been displaced by Mexicans migrating up from the Rio Grande Valley and northern Mexico. The Peña boys had friends, the Escalóns, who lived at *la hacienda de* Teasdale, and once, when Elías Escalón and I were exploring the grounds, we discovered a gallows-like frame in one of the barns. The frame, we were told by an old Wash Jones type who lived on Teasdale's hacienda, was "where niggers used to be whipped for disobedience." I never confirmed whether the Faulknerian codger's story was true, but in Calvert itself the practice of separating blacks and whites in public places was still rigidly observed in the early fifties. Indeed, long-time residents recalled that not so long before, blacks had still been required to yield the sidewalk to approaching whites.

Not all farmers shared Mr. Gruene's low opinion of African Americans' labor skills. When we moved from Calvert to nearby Mumford in 1953, we went to work with the youthful Joe Milano, a personable second-generation Italian who whisked around his estate in crisply starched khaki outfits and spit-shined shoes. Considered a "good boss" by his workers, Milano owned a much larger establishment than did Gruene, and he employed a number of blacks, some of them in supervisory roles as crew leaders. But neither Milano nor any of his peers in or out of agriculture would ever have considered sharing their intimate social space with the African Americans. Even a man like Joe Milano, who was seen as progressive by all who knew him, still saw the "Negro" as distinctly inferior, someone who could not conceivably deserve to live as an equal with him and whose children could not possibly enjoy the same privileges as his. The Milano offspring, Josephine and Joe, Jr., acted accordingly. They displayed an aloof attitude toward the black domestics who groomed the immaculate grounds of their manorial house, while the latter treated the children of the "boss man" with the proper deference. In his fundamental beliefs, then, Joe Milano was in harmony with Mrs. Guidry and Mr. Gruene. An integrationist conception of equality would have been as unthinkable to our new patrón as it was to the other two.

The politics of race, and especially the notion of a racial pecking order, influenced the Mexicans of the Brazos Valley both as to their views of themselves and as to their perception of the blacks. Quite simply, the Mexicans saw themselves as superior to their African American counterparts. Both groups were wretchedly poor, and economically there was little to distinguish one from the other. On Milano's estate, for example, my family lived for a while in a cluster of scattered shacks called Boone's Place, which housed both Mexicans and blacks. Yet the social contact between the two groups was minimal. The case of the Peñas and their evolving attitude toward the blacks is instructive in this respect. While we lived on Joe Milano's farm, we worked alongside the blacks, and we actually maintained cordial relations with them. Nevertheless, I learned soon enough—and this without any specific prohibitions from my parents— to keep my distance from the children of Slogam, an African American who lived a stone's throw down the dirt road at Boone's Place. Nor did my older brothers ever visit the recreation spots frequented by Slogam's oldest son, Charlie. Charlie, Alessio, and Plon might work side by side in the fields, but on Saturday night, the black and brown boys went their separate ways.

In truth, like the other Mexican workers in the Brazos Valley of East-Central Texas, the Peñas quickly absorbed the prejudices of Anglos like Mr. Gruene, and we thus shunned socializing too closely with the African Americans. To put it bluntly, the Mexicans thought of the African Americans as slackers who generally possessed a low level of thrift, intelligence, and motivation. Our prejudice notwithstanding, there were always blacks who disproved the prevalent stereotype. Certain black individuals did command our admiration and, sometimes, our affection, as was the case with the enterprising Sammy Hines, who had long worked on Joe Milano's estate and also with the prickly old codger, Mr. John Taylor. Hines was considered by everyone on the estate as one of the best all-around workers, and Mr. Taylor's irascible but impish character made him a favorite among the younger Mexican workers. Of course, as I learned soon enough, the blacks themselves entertained no particular fondness for the Mexicans, either, and they probably saw us as no better than themselves—if not worse.

My brother Alessio's attitude was perhaps typical among the Mexicans. He attributed certain bad habits to the extra black hands who were hired by both Gruene and Milano to chop cotton. According to Alessio, they killed an inordinate amount of time after arriving on the field in the morning, sharpening hoes and loitering around the *cabeceras*, or rows' heads, before they finally settled down to work—at their own leisurely pace. They spent the next several hours lethargically going through the motions, while not a sound escaped from their lips. Then, around three in the afternoon, someone would start a singsong monologue, which others quickly took up. Soon a whole chorus of call-and-response was under way, while the pace of hoeing slowed even further. But that, Alessio would say, was the style of the blacks. Nothing was going to push them to quicken the pace of their work. They were, as everyone knew, "lazy and shiftless."

Although the Anglos of the Brazos Valley were not as hostile to the Mexicans as they were toward the blacks, they still viewed us with condescension. As they did with the African Americans, they generally avoided intimate contact with us, although the taboo against such contact was not nearly as rigid when applied to the Mexicans. Interethnic commingling was common enough among Mexican and Anglo youth in the schools, if not beyond the boundaries of the school ground. By the 1950s, the racial categories devised by the Anglo-Americans generally, in which whites and people of color were assigned their respective, segregated spaces, had evolved sufficiently to designate the Mexicans as "white"—or at least white enough to deserve admission into the Anglo schools. Such had not always been the case. Until the 1940s, in many places throughout Texas the Mexicans were segregated along with the blacks, while in yet other communities there were three separate schools for the respective "races." Thus, in 1954 the whites-only elementary school in Mumford did include Mexicans, and they made up about half of the student body. Beyond the sixth grade, students were bused to the larger school district in nearby Hearne, where the black students were likewise segregated from the Mexicans and Anglos.

We Mexicans might have felt privileged to attend school with the whites, but Mrs. Guidry's defiant stand against the Supreme Court ruling forced me to confront dilemmas I had hitherto felt intuitively but had never resolved. As an eleven-year-old son of migrant cottonpickers, I was keenly alive to my stigmatized status as a Mexican. After all, not so long ago, in West Texas, I had been denied service at a hamburger stand, and the angry words of the manager, "We don't serve Mexicans here," still smoldered in my subconscious. I was also aware that beyond the school ground, contact between Anglo and Mexican children was almost nonexistent. Many of my schoolmates were children of the growers on whose fields our families toiled, and boys like Danny DiNiro and Joe Cassini had their way of letting Mexicans like Miguel García and me know that we were not their social equals. Once, DiNiro barely avoided being slugged by Miguel when the former called the bean tacos my friend had brought for lunch "wetback food." Only the intervention of the teacher on yard duty prevented Danny from getting a licking from my street-tough friend. Thus sensitized to the whites' sense of racial superiority, I could sympathize with the plight of the blacks. I too had felt the sting of racial hatred.

Mrs. Guidry's defiant stance against the court mandate was a pointed reminder of just how difficult the project of racial integration and,

Mumford Elementary

ultimately, equality for people of color would be. The specter of white backlash, already written on my teacher's contorted face, spoke with blunt eloquence to the reality of racial antagonism and the whites' awesome power to dictate the terms of our existence within their midst. Mrs. Guidry's message was clear: submit to our domination and live relatively unmolested lives; resist our power and face our wrath. No court decision was going to change this fundamental arrangement—at least not in the short term. Then again, the institutionalization of racial inequality was so entrenched and so powerful in its subtlety that outbursts like the one we witnessed from Mrs. Guidry were seldom needed to enforce (and reinforce) the racial hierarchies present in Texas and elsewhere in the South. The ideologies perpetuating these hierarchies effectively instilled in all of us a sense of the in-born superiority of the white "race," and we children of minorities were forced to model ourselves as best we could on the ideals dictated by our white superiors.

In other words, as members of powerless minorities, we Mexicans and African Americans knew our assigned places in the dominant society. Only an act as blatantly upsetting to the social order as the Supreme Court decision could force all of us to confront the gross inequalities present in our everyday lives, and thus, for different reasons, the Guidrys and the Peñas were profoundly disturbed by the court's radical action. Mrs. Guidry perceived the decision as a direct affront to white privilege. We saw it as a double-edged sword—a sign of better times for blacks (and perhaps Mexicans, too) but also as a potential trigger to white backlash, which could have ugly consequences for both the African Americans and us. In the early fifties, few of us—black or brown—possessed the vision or the spirit of resistance of a Rosa Parks, despite our repressed hopes for a "true realm of freedom." That realm would remain beyond our grasp for at least another decade, just as the fulfillment of its promises was fraught with turmoil even at the beginning of the twenty-first century.

In subscribing to the subtle, though sometimes overt, ideology of white supremacy prevalent in the larger society, the Mexicans inescapably devalued the blacks. In the racial dichotomy devised by the dominant society, we occupied a somewhat anomalous position between the superior whites and the inferior blacks. As my friend Neil Foley wrote in *The White Scourge*, the hybrid Mexicans "walked the color line," fracturing the essentialized distinction between the "pure" white "race" and the "debased" black. But we could not help comparing *ourselves* to the white, Euro-American model, and, reminded often enough of our own racial and cultural "shortcomings," we found ourselves wanting. Only much later would I come to understand why I and so many of my friends tried in vain to act and to be like the whites, and why we settled in the end for a dual or bicultural identity, with all the contradictions inherent on such a dualistic cultural border.

But at age eleven I only knew that who I was—a Mexican—carried with it both a stigmatized sense of "Otherness" and my own denial of my ancestral culture, and that was a dilemma I could not ignore. Thus, while the case of *Brown vs. the Topeka Board of Education* contained the promise of a better future for blacks and other ethnic minorities, the hatred written on Mrs. Guidry's face was a frightening reminder that our fate in a hostile Anglo society ultimately rested on her willingness to change, not on rulings coming down from Washington.

And so, in my efforts to rid myself of the stigma attached both to my culture *and* to my lowly status as a farm worker, I engaged in behavior damaging in the long run to my self-esteem. Like many Mexican children, I tried to model my behavior on that of my Anglo classmates, with sometimes painful results. As a youngster coming into adolescence during the years we lived in the Brazos Valley, where the Anglos exercised their power with both benevolence and arrogance, I yearned to be respected, if not accepted, by those Anglos. Thus, in groping for a social face, I at times felt shame over my ancestry, particularly as I developed an interest in girls. On more than one occasion I spurned the attention of adolescent Mexican girls, simply because they reminded me of the wretchedness I had experienced among our people. I sought, and occasionally gained, the interest of the Anglo girls, only to be disappointed as invariably (and as adolescents are prone to do) the girls soon found someone who was more appealing than me.

In the sixth grade, just as I was reaching puberty, I developed an intense crush on my very attractive teacher, Mrs. Jameson. I engaged in the wildest of chimeras as I tried in vain to reconcile the conflicting forces raging inside and around me—the seductive power of the subject of my forbidden desires, the hormonal flames exploding within me, the machismo already deeply ingrained in my male identity, and, juxtaposed against it all, the powerlessness of my life as the son of Mexican farm laborers. In the end, the crush on Mrs. Jameson could only confirm for me the state of racial relations governing my life. On one hand was the commanding presence of the white majority, as majestically inscribed in the body of my voluptuous teacher; on the other was the futility of my desire, as symbolized by the abandoned shack where I engaged Mrs. Jameson in my transgressive fantasies.

Many years later, as the black civil rights and Chicano movements transformed the social landscape and the light of social change painfully dawned on the people of Texas and the South, I wondered whether Mrs. Guidry had ever undergone a change of heart. Perhaps, in the manner of Governor George Wallace, she, too, had renounced racism late in her life. I also wondered whether her cherubic daughter had transcended her mother's hatred of blacks. Had she come to represent a new vanguard of racial reconciliation, or was she but another link in the ancient genealogy of white supremacists? For my part, I would spend years searching in vain for personal redemption, even as I abandoned my dreams of admittance into the intimacy of Anglo social circles. But it would not be until my induction into the Chicano Movement in California in the early 1970s and, later, my eye-opening education at the University of Texas with the heroic Chicano scholar, don Américo Paredes, that the voices of my ancestors would lift me out of my confusion. Along with so many of my generation—the Chicano Generation, in the words of my historian friend Mario García—I discovered that one can learn to endure and indeed revel in life on the border between two warring cultures.

But on that May morning in 1954, I was still an innocent captive of age-old racial hatreds and supremacist politics. My fifth-grade teacher's harangue against integration was thus a grim, though only half-consciously perceived, reminder of my own precarious existence at the margins of the dominant Anglo society. It would be years before I finally buried the foul carcass of racism Mrs. Guidry had hung on me.

SECOND
STROPHE Where the Ox
Does Not Plow

12

WHERE THE OX DOES NOT PLOW

My father wanted to take us al norte to pick cotton. We had beaten that path too many times over the past twelve years, ever since I was about five, and I was fed up with it. The harvest began in July in the Corpus Christi area, moved east to the Brazos Valley and Waco, and thence to places in West Texas like Colorado City, Tahoka, and Plainview before it ended in early December. Until now the whole family had journeyed together on those migrant treks, except for Imelda, who was married in 1947, although hard times often forced her and her husband Noé to join us. But my brother Plon, or José, as we now called him, had married recently, and my oldest brother Alessio (now Frank) had finally landed a steady job at Pike's Lumber, and he would no longer be making the trip. So this time my father proposed to take what was left of the family—Mama, little sister Elia, and me. My legs quivered as I stood in front of him, but I held my ground: "I am not going to pick cotton or anything else—ever again!"

I had always been afraid of my father. When angered he could be a violent man, and he had never hesitated to use the thick wide belts he favored on his children, especially in earlier years when he had been stronger and more vigorous. I shall never forget the time Plon and I missed the school bus because we had been arguing instead of getting ready. We were sojourning for the winter of 1949 on a farm near the hamlet of Edroy, Texas. That morning, Plon and I walked the belated mile across the plowed fields to the bus stop in a cold February mist, only to retrace our steps in fear, knowing Papa's fury awaited us at home. We received the lashing of our young lives, and of course, we never missed the bus again. Only once or twice afterward was I the recipient of the old man's belt—so powerfully did this early licking impress itself upon me. The lesson of obedience had been permanently learned.

And now, on the eve of my seventeenth birthday, it took all the courage I could summon, but I was determined to make known my displeasure at the prospect of another campaña. The treks following the cotton trail across North Texas had always been disruptive and humiliating. They were disruptive because they inevitably kept me from getting to school in September as "normal" kids did. Until the ninth grade, I had never enrolled before the first day of December, when the harvests were generally over. Too often, I had struggled to catch up with the other children, especially when I advanced to the middle grades.

The adjustment from middle to high school had been particularly traumatic. As usual, I was out picking cotton when classes began, and it was only after I threatened to quit school that my parents took me out of the fields and sent me to my sister Imelda's in Weslaco. They remained in The Texas Panhandle town of Plainview, finishing the harvest. I joined the ninth-grade class in the middle of October, well after the start of the fall semester, and to my distress, I was completely mystified by the algebra that the rest of the students seemed to have mastered so well. It took many hours of brain-numbing study—not to mention all the fitful nights dreaming about cascades of unsolvable numbers—before the breakthrough solution finally liberated me from my misery. I discovered that absolute equality must obtain between the right and left sides of the equation marked by the "=" sign, and that whatever one does to the left must be matched by an identical action on the right. (In the equation, "$3x=12$," to isolate "x" one must divide both sides by three: Ergo! $[1]x=4$.) Achieved totally without the teacher's help, the algebraic solution was a defining act of self-mastery. It was of the same order as learning to read Spanish on my own at age five, or discovering at age fourteen the functional role of diminished sevenths in the romantic boleros I was so fond of singing.

The migrant treks were humiliating because the poverty of our lives was harshly exposed every time we crammed into the hovels the growers provided for us. Lacking indoor plumbing of any kind, let alone the amenities of cultivated life, the hovels were painful reminders of our lowly status. Yet despite my loathing for farm labor, I was glad we never had to attend school while we lived in such miserable conditions. While the local children were in the classroom, my fellow young migrants and I were in the fields, backs bent, tugging sacks full of cotton and learning the time-honored American lesson of hard work, if not always thrift. On occasion, when school patrols came around to check for truants, we were told to hide among the taller plants until it was safe to come out and resume our picking. In later years, I came to the realization those patrols were a sham: no one was going to deprive the growers of their Mexican pickers at the height of the harvest. After all, wasn't it a West-Texas superintendent who had confided to education researcher Herschel T. Manuel that it was up to the "white population" to "keep the Mexican on his knees in a cotton patch?" To officials and farmers alike (sometimes they were one and the same), the need for Mexican labor did not "mix well with education."

We finally ended our campañas al norte in 1957, the same year I threatened to quit school, with the cotton harvest in West Texas. That year is also memorable for the detour we took through the Midwest, where we worked in the summer on a truck farm near Aurora, Illinois. We harvested vegetables for a couple of Greek immigrants, brothers John and Ted Theoharakis. This was the only time the Peñas ever visited the Midwest or picked such exotic and, to us, inedible crops as Swiss chard, turnips, and kohlrabi. The work was monotonous, but not nearly as backbreaking as the drag of a one-hundred-pound sack full of cotton. Besides, Ted Theoharakis had a dreamy fourteen-year-old daughter, Ana, who picked alongside us and made the days interesting for me. Although I was too shy to approach her, I always fancied she had taken a liking to me, and I spent a good part of that summer in chimerical reveries about the romantic times we would spend together in some nebulous future. Just before we left, Ted bought a new truck to haul his produce to the Chicago market, and he had a sign painted on the door, "Ted Harkis Produce." When I asked him why he had anglicized the name, he gave me a lesson on acculturation: "We're in America, Manuel, and we should try to fit in."

After the 1957 harvest we returned, more or less permanently, to the barrio of my birthplace in Weslaco. We lived for a while in the three-room matchbox Papa had bought for $500 in 1942. He held the best-paying job of his life during the Second World War, buying tomatoes for a canning company, and he saved enough capital to pay cash for the house. But that was before I came along. Almost from my infancy, the family had resorted to itinerancy, as my father's financial miscalculations and bouts of alcoholism forced the Peñas into the migrant-labor stream. And so, except for brief visits we made to the Valley in the winter months, the old shanty remained vacant during the years we roamed el norte. Exhausted by the years of vagrancy, my parents had decided after the 1957 harvest to try and lay anchor once more in the old homestead.

The house my father bought during the war was not all that different from the shacks we occupied during our campañas, and it was a persistent reminder to me of our chronic poverty. But thanks to my brother Frank's new job at Pike's Lumber, eventually we grafted a larger building onto the old frame, this one with indoor plumbing, electric lights, and—especially gratifying to me—smooth drywall interiors that we painted in bright yellows and aqua-greens. By contrast, the old shack had nothing but bare, unpainted planks for walls, which, as if their stark ugliness were not enough, provided little shelter from the chill winds that sometimes swept the Valley in the winter. However, to save on construction expenses, the south wall of the original structure was preserved, though it too was insulated with drywall. Finally, to cover the wooden floorboards, we installed a burgundy linoleum, with bright flower designs.

Papa broke down, at last, and bought a few household necessities for the finished house—a much-needed refrigerator, a couple of cheap but newer bedroom sets, and the wringer-type washing machine he had long promised Mama. He also bought a sparkling new, white enamel Norge gas range with an oven and polished black control knobs that I thought were absolutely classy. For me, the gleaming knobs stood as symbols of our entry into modern, civilized living *and* of our emancipation from our greasy camp stoves and their association with the primitive life of the campañas. But he refused to buy living room furniture, and we had to settle for an old couch a neighbor sold to us for ten dollars.

We had no art works or crafts for interior decoration, but Mama did hang some old photo enlargements of Imelda, Frank, and José in the living room. And, on a coffee table I had built in a ninth-grade woodshop class, she lovingly placed a sleek black panther made of shiny glass—a "TV lamp" popular in the fifties. She had bought the lamp on installments several months earlier when she learned we were going to rebuild the old shanty. She also put up a miniature handicraft I had cherished since I first gained the light of consciousness, long before I knew about Hansel and Gretel. It was a little weather box in the shape of a brightly colored cottage, with a thermometer and a swiveling T-shaped pole mounted upside-down, on which was perched a witch on the left, and, on the right, a boy and girl. Sensitive to barometric changes, the pole rotated, so that when the days were fair with high pressure, the children came out, and when lowering pressure threatened inclement weather, the witch would take her turn outdoors. And, to lend the homestead a bit of her personality, Mama surrounded the place with a few of the *matitas* she loved but had never been able to cultivate—rosebushes, jasmines, and *coyoles* (canna lilies). Finally, in the back patio she planted a peach tree to complement the gnarled mesquites antedating the barrio itself.

With our home now furnished with the rudiments of civilized living, at least by barrio standards, I felt a little less exposed when a teacher occasionally paid a visit or when friends dropped in. Resting on trapezoidal concrete piers, the new house was adorned with wood siding, which we painted a bright aqua blue that in later years reminded me of the Mexican folk-Baroque styled houses in the barrios across the border. Ours was typical of other homes in the neighborhood—two small bedrooms, a living area, and a small kitchen. We could not have had more than seven hundred square feet of living space, but even this was a vast improvement over anything we had occupied during the long years of campaña. More importantly, it eased some of the shame I had endured when we had nothing for beds but blankets on the floor and crates for a kitchen table.

The permanent move to Weslaco allowed the family a sense of stability, and I quickly began to form lasting friendships with the more settled young men of the barrio. Most of my new friends came from working barrio families, such as the Ayalas and the Ramírezes, but there were a few, like the Rodríguezes and the de la Rosas, who lived in *el lado americano*—the more prosperous, Anglo part of Weslaco, where a few upwardly minded mexicanos had recently begun to settle. Finding myself in a socially uplifting circle of friends, I gradually acquired from them an appreciation for the tokens of a respectable, middling-class lifestyle, even if these were not always within my means—brand-name clothes from Levine's menswear, Turtle-Waxed cars, band banquets, and genteel parties with sweet-smelling girls. I also gained the confidence to engage in acculturative activities such as band, choir, and the Key Club. These had been beyond my reach when we were transients—both because I had never been encouraged to participate and because the shame I felt over my wretched living conditions discouraged me from socializing with classmates beyond the school grounds.

Surrounded by young men and women brought up according to the norms of the *gente decente*—middling-class Mexican Americans who practiced a lifestyle based on genteel notions of civility—I began to shed the rustic culture of my fellow transients, just as I overcame the reclusive habits of my days as an isolated migrant. Perhaps nothing symbolized my cultural transformation more than the increased use of English for everyday communication and my deepening bias against things "Mexican." In particular, I began to distance myself from the emblems of my childhood culture—the hardcore, working-class *pachuco* style of dress, with its zoot-suit pants and mawkish hairdos, and the music of the migrant workers, the thumping accordion style known as *conjunto*.* Most significantly, as I absorbed the genteel and more Americanized habits of my newfound friends, I realized that this was the social life I had always striven for, even if I had been only vaguely aware of its existence somewhere beyond the circles of poverty surrounding me.

Contributing not a little to my sense of belonging to a stable community was the birth of the Matadors, a group I organized with Henry "Quique" Ayala, whom I had known since early childhood, and Eddie Ramírez, one of my new friends. The Matadors improved rapidly as we spent many hours practicing our music, and we were often called upon to sing for weddings, talent shows and Ty Cobb's live variety program on the local TV station, KRGV. At this time I also began to play occasional jobs with Eugenio Gutiérrez, a musician and erstwhile neighbor my family had known for years. Gutiérrez at one time had led a professional recording band, or *orquesta*, but he was by now a declining man given to drinking, and although he still considered himself a proud member of the gente decente, he had resorted to playing at small barrio weddings and even cantinas. At my father's request, he had taken me under his tutelage and taught me how to play Mexican dance music on the guitar. He hired me when I became adept enough to play the boleros, *polcas-rancheras*, *danzones*, and the occasional fox trot that formed his orquesta's repertoire.

---

*Thirty years later, proud of my working-class roots and fully aware of the conjunto's cultural importance, I wrote a book, *The Texas-Mexican Conjunto*.

Having thus been transformed by the more refined world of the gente decente and my exposure to a culture well removed from cotton sacks, outhouses, and the rustic conjunto, I loathed the idea of another campaña—of uprooting myself and plunging once more into the sordid life associated with migrants and farm labor. This time, it would have taken more than a beating from my father to change my attitude.

"Cabrón," my father threatened. "I am still in charge here, and you will go where I say. And believe me, I can still give you a tanning you won't soon forget." Papa's voice still had the drilling edge that had once made me cringe. But deep down I knew it was an empty threat. It was June of 1959, Papa was approaching sixty-five and anxious to get on Social Security, and I could see the chronic fatigue of poverty etched into his face. A life of grueling work and hard drinking had taken its toll. It was clear he didn't want to go anywhere either. "We shall see," he said, as he stepped out, "but if we don't go on campaña, you'll have to work at something. You don't earn enough from your music."

We finally convinced my father to abandon his plans for one more trek al norte. Mama wondered if it would be such a good idea now that José was married and gone, and Frank had a steady job at Pike's lumber yard. "Besides," Mama reminded Papa, "they say the *máquinas* are replacing hand pickers, and I hear it's getting harder to find good fields to pick." "*Quizás tengas razón*—perhaps you're right," Papa finally admitted. At Mama's urging, he decided to contact el viejo Moore, a farmer in the Weslaco area for whom he had once worked. Moore grew a little cotton and some tomatoes, and he agreed to hire my father to cultivate, fertilize, and do general preparation for the harvests. Papa accepted Moore's offer despite the meager wages, which were barely enough to buy food for the family. But things brightened when Moore offered me a job me as an irrigator. "El viejo Moore wants you to start tomorrow," my father told me. Irrigating didn't seem so bad—I had done it during the years we lived in the Brazos Valley—and I was relieved to learn there would be no trip al norte.

Just the same, the prospect of returning to farm stoop labor was as humiliating as ever. "This is the last time I work in the fields," I told my father in a defiant last stand. "Next summer I'm gonna find me a decent job." "As long as you contribute something, son," he replied, his voice becoming softer. "You'll have to work, even if it's in the fields." He understood my aversion to farm work—he hated it himself—but he had long ago resigned himself to the drudgery. Deeply ingrained in his work ethic was the conviction that the Peñas were all doomed to a life of menial toil, which Papa believed to be the curse of the family lineage despite my brother Frank's new job and his own success as a produce buyer during the war. Thus, with a tone of resignation, he added, "It is the lot of our people, m'hijo, to spend our lives in toil. As my own father used to say, '¿A donde va el buey que no are?—where can the ox go that he won't have to plow?'"

"Well," I replied with a defiant edge in my voice, "this ox is different; he'll find a place where the ox does not plow."

I knew Papa was proud of the good grades I received in school, and that he dreamed I would be the one son who broke the dropout cycle so deeply rooted in the extended Peña family—and in all the barrios of South Texas, for that matter. Except for cousin Enrique, Tía Virginia's oldest son, none of my relatives had ever gone beyond the eighth grade. Symptomatic of the state of things in our barrio, every month of May the administrators at Lincoln Elementary held an elaborate graduation ceremony for the sixth graders and their proud parents. School officials were perfectly aware that at least half of the all-Mexican student body would become dropout victims of the treks al norte. My father painfully realized that I represented the last hope for academic success among the men of the Peña family, but he also had to demonstrate the authority he still exercised over his children. Hence his threats in the face of my intransigence.

I was working in farmer Moore's fields when the Matadors were offered a job performing at one of the new, ambitiously luxurious hotels in the budding resort area in South Padre Island, on the "Gulf-of-Dreams" coast about fifty miles east of Weslaco. The hotel was called the "Sea Island," and for years it was the most glamorous in the area, until it was absorbed by one of the big transnationals. Thanks to our agent Bob Dixon's hustle, the Matadors were offered work on Friday and Saturday, two performances each evening, for a total salary of one hundred dollars—a stupendous sum to us, which we split evenly (with a token amount, ten dollars, going to Dixon). By this time the Matadors had acquired a regional reputation, and our musical selection was diverse and professional enough to impress the management at the Sea Island. They brought us in for an audition, liked the flair of our performance, and hired us to entertain in the hotel's Outrigger Club.

The contrast between the Outrigger Club and the streets of Weslaco was striking. To begin with, besides the Matadors, the only Mexicans at the resort were the cooks and housemaids. Then there was the restrained luxury and genteel, bourgeois manner of the sun-bronzed Anglos who patronized the Outrigger, which seemed light years removed from the carnivalesque bustle of the barrio. The vacationers would have considered exotic and perhaps bizarre the raw cries of barrio *tamal* and *menudo* vendors, the vulgar *palomillas* (adolescent cliques), and the cacophonous conjunto music blaring out of open windows. The yawning divide between the two social extremes was punctuated by the discrepancy between my life as entertainer in the high-toned Sea Island and as irrigator in the mucky fields of farmer Moore. (Despite my new job as entertainer, my father insisted I fulfill my obligatios to our patrón.) The surreal transformation I experienced switching from one occupation to the other stunned me every time I stepped on the stage of the Outrigger, and I constantly dreaded fainting while performing—so inadequate did I feel to the task of entertaining such a dazzling group of socialites.

But the same juvenile self-doubt that led me to feel like an artistic imposter also spurred a sense of bravado—as it did to my partners—and the rough luster of the brash young Matadors seems to have carried the day for us. The Anglo vacationers took us to heart.

The summer of '59 was not the last time I worked in the fields—later, I toiled in the California orchards until 1965—but it did mark a turning point in my life. It was then that I made the irreversible though only half-conscious commitment to escape the drudgery of farm work and the poverty that until now had been my patrimony. My emancipation from the agricultural fields and the legacy of exploitation, shame, and deprivation they had bequeathed to the Peña lineage would come about in piecemeal fashion. Yet while my body remained captive to the degrading effects of menial labor for several years to come, the spirit had been liberated the moment I proclaimed to Papa my intention to quit the cotton fields forever, and to find a place where the ox does not plow.

13
THE MATADORS

The name was emblematic—Matadors. It was chosen by our agent, local disk jockey Bob Dixon, who felt the group's name should reflect our "Latin" ancestry. Henry "Quique" Ayala, a childhood playmate of mine, was the lead singer, Eddie Ramírez sang baritone, and I provided the high tenor and guitar accompaniment. The Matadors had begun as a larger conglomerate of singers and instrumentalists, when we went by the more Americanized name of "The Rocking Kings." Leo Sosa, from nearby Donna, had brought us together in 1958. The rock-and-roll wave had swept the Rio Grande Valley, and several groups made up of Mexican American teenagers sprang up, all hoping to follow the path Ritchie Valens (Valenzuela) had blazed to the top forty charts.

Bob Dixon discovered us at a sock hop, when we were still known as The Rocking Kings. Radio station KRGV, whose studios were in our hometown of Weslaco, used to sponsor these teen dances at the American Legion hall, and we had been invited to perform during intermission. Dixon, who worked at KRGV and its sister station, KRGV-TV, was immediately impressed, and he offered to become our agent. He had no experience in the live entertainment field, but he knew some people in the radio and television industry he thought could open some doors for the Kings. Since no one in the group knew anything about show business, we felt fortunate to find someone who would guide us, and we made an informal agreement with Dixon to represent the group. We never paid Dixon more than a token sum for his efforts; but to his credit—and despite our high school band director's accusation that he was out to exploit us—he hung with us as a sort of cheerleader, if not actually an agent, until the Matadors dissolved. More importantly, he treated us evenhandedly and with easy familiarity, never betraying the sort of prejudice toward Mexicans then rampant in the Anglo community.

The other groups in the Valley sang mostly "doo-wop" songs, but the Matadors were more eclectic. Especially after the transforming year of 1959, when we changed the name and pared down the motley ensemble to a more manageable trio, our repertoire quickly expanded. We explored a wide variety of genres, ranging from jazzy Four Freshman songs to Mexican trío boleros, and even a few rancheras and a corrido or two. In other words, the Matadors were bimusical, the result of our exposure to both American pop music and the Mexican-Latino styles common to the local dance orquestas in which Henry, Eddie, and I earned part-time cash. These orquestas, with names like Eugenio Gutiérrez, the GGs, Leo Salazar, and Oscar Guerra, were modeled after the American big bands, but they all played their share of Mexican and Latino music because that was what their Mexican American patrons demanded.*

Money was always in short supply, since the Matadors never gained enough popularity beyond the Rio Grande Valley to draw the big purses. We therefore scrimped on equipment and clothes, particularly in the early days of the group. I had to make do with a cheap Harmony guitar and a toy-like, twenty-watt amplifier, and we wore inexpensive matching shirts from CR Anthony that a sympathetic high-school teacher purchased for us. Despite the cash shortage, as our popularity increased other benefactors began to come forward with clothes and equipment, and that is how Henry, Eddie, and I eventually acquired a more professional wardrobe of formal jackets and tuxedo pants. I shall never forget the first time we wore the shimmering maroon coats, matching bow ties and cummerbunds, snow-white tuxedo shirts and cuff-links, and the luxurious black pants that Baum's Menswear in McAllen all but donated to us. (I think we paid about $35 for each uniform, which we paid in installments.) Our first performance with the new outfits was at a gala celebration to mark the grand opening of the plush McAllen Civic Center. The glamour of the event, garments that felt like crisp new dollar bills, and the enthusiastic

---

*For a comprehensive history of this important ensemble, please see my book, *The Mexican American Orquesta* (Austin: University of Texas Press: 1999).

applause we received were enough to make us momentarily forget who we really were.

The Matadors were all children of poverty—the grinding kind experienced by Mexicans in Texas, with its heavy dose of Anglo racism and its oppressive practices. Yet we were all native sons to this soil. The Ayalas, Peñas, and Ramírezes were no *fuereños*—late immigrant "outsiders" recently arrived from the Mexican interior. Our ancestral families had settled the lands straddling both sides of the Rio Bravo—or, as the Americans renamed it, the Rio Grande—in the 1740s, when José de Escandón led a band of Spanish-Mexican settlers into the northern wilderness. By comparison, the Anglos were newcomers to the lower Texas border, their presence in large numbers dating no further back than the 1920s. But neither Henry nor Eddie or I appreciated the significance of our birthright as natives—indeed, we were secretly ashamed of our ancestry. Like Du Bois's "Negro," we were victims of a "double consciousness," looking at ourselves, necessarily, through the Mexican eyes of our parents, but also—and more damaging to our self-esteem—through the supercilious gaze of an Anglo society bent on reshaping our identities. And so, we obstinately identified ourselves as Americans, even as we yearned to escape the hellish bicultural border on which we seemed trapped.

As biculturals straddling the boundary between two cultures in conflict, we had seen up close both kinds of life—the Mexican and the American. We did not have to go across the nearby international border to witness the former. The barrios where Quique, Eddie, and I lived were etched into our consciousness, with the dusty unpaved streets (or muddy, depending on the season), weather-beaten houses, and inescapably Mexican character all forming part of our bedrock identities. The Matadors were intimately familiar with the street talk of the palomilla and the conjunto music on the radio. We knew the curanderas and their herbal remedies, and we had deadened our hunger with the barrio staple, *tacos de frijoles*. We even had ridden the early-morning *troques* that carried the weathered brown faces to pick vegetables and citrus fruits. Yes, we knew the barrio well.

But our indoctrination at Weslaco High, through our participation in band, choir, clubs, and other high school activities, was inescapably transforming us into Americans, even if hyphenated, as in Mexican-American. We thus engaged in the myriad "*chingaderas* [follies] imitating the way of the Anglo patrón," as playwright Luis Valdez put it, that were so much a part of Mexican working-class life in the Valley. We claimed George Washington, General McArthur, Clark Gable, and the martyrs at the Alamo as our heroes, just as we subscribed to the Anglo-Texan myth of bigness—the notion that things Texan are cut on a grander scale than anywhere else in the world.

The Matadors were keenly aware of the goings-on across the Southern Pacific tracks, where all the americanos lived. That was the part of Weslaco where the streets were paved and the most prosperous businesses were located, and where Donna Reed houses with white picket fences and well-kept St. Augustine lawns were the norm. It was also where the real power in the community resided. As anthropologist Arthur Rubel was discovering in our hometown at that very moment, a few Mexican Americans had actually begun to encroach on the americano side, setting up residence there, but the racial and class divide was still pretty much unbridged.* However, by the end of the twentieth century the exodus of Anglos from Weslaco was almost complete, as they fled to other parts of Texas in the face of the growing tide of Mexican immigrants sweeping the Valley. The flocks of "snowbirds," or "winter Texans"—retired Anglos fleeing the northern climes—were the exception.

Our knowledge of that part of town was gleaned through our attendance at Weslaco's only high school, which of course was located in the heart of el lado Americano, as people would say of South Weslaco. The school was at least nominally integrated, but in the most intimate social gatherings, the two ethnic groups maintained a strict segregation.

Despite the class and ethnic divide, recurring romantic liaisons between Mexican and Anglo youth—carried on secretly, of course—provided fodder for lively teenage gossip. Usually, word of these liaisons never came to the ears of adults still steeped in old ethnic prejudices, but these adventuresome adolescents were laying the groundwork for the more enlightened race relations of the next generation of civic leaders. When a teenage relationship occasionally was uncovered, especially one between a poorer Mexican boy and a well-to-do white girl, matters could get sticky. Such was the case with Henry Ayala, who was considered a prize catch by any of the girls at Weslaco High, whether Mexican

---

*See Rubel's ethnography of Weslaco, *Across the Tracks: Mexican Americans in a Texas Town* (Austin: University of Texas Press, 1965).

or Anglo. Notwithstanding his family's lowly social standing, Quique's proud bearing, good looks, and sexual magnetism attracted the girls' attention, and his breach of interethnic dating taboos threatened once or twice to precipitate a crisis.

Yet of the three Matadors, Quique was perhaps the most scarred by the effects of poverty. His father, Matías Ayala, was a day laborer who struggled perennially to feed his wife and five children. In fact, Quique was jokingly known as *hambres*—famines—because he seemed to be perpetually foraging for food. Unlike my father and Pablo Ramírez, who struggled as well but took risks and weathered many reversals during their long lives, Matías Ayala moved timidly. His caution was driven by his pessimism. As he often lamented to my father, "No, Chico, for the lucky ones around here it's suck, suck, and suck; for poor goats like us it's nothing but 'baa, baa, baa.'" On more than one occasion, his family found itself on the edge of real hunger.

More so than Eddie or me, Henry yearned to be as "mainstream-American" as the middle-class Anglos who controlled Weslaco High. But poverty and degradation had been his legacy: the large Ayala family lived in a cramped three-room shack that always impressed me with its darkness and the smell of crowded human bodies. We never talked about it, but I knew Henry loathed his living conditions. Until recently, when we built our new house, I had lived in equally wretched surroundings, and this commonality, as well as the close friendship of our families, solidified our bond. Even if we often feuded, Quique and I shared the love and social intimacy of brothers, just as we shared a stubborn pride and a desire to escape the stigma of our ethnic poverty. And this pride kept us from joining the exodus of Mexican students fleeing from the schools; we were determined to prove ourselves as equals to the Anglos by playing and winning at their own game.

Very few of us ever set foot in Henry's house. He seldom went there himself, preferring to spend his time at Tía Lupe's. His father's sister, Tía Lupe was a bit better off. Though raised with her brother in an impoverished family, she had an instinctive appreciation for middle-class respectability common to the rural gentry of northern Mexico—the norteños—and she lived in a modest but tastefully furnished home a few blocks from Matías. Her husband Casimiro, an enterprising small businessman, ran a cantina and dance hall next door, as well as a taxi service, and he had been able to provide his wife and adopted son, Casimiro, Jr., a comfortable life by barrio standards. When Henry was meeting anyone but the Matadors, he used Tía Lupe's as his address.

A wiry five-feet-seven-inches tall, Quique was a talented and exceptionally handsome lad with abundant sex appeal. He had an excellent ear for music, a vibrant tenor voice, and a journeyman's skill on the trumpet. He was a *criollo*—a descendant of Spanish-European stock—and he secretly enjoyed being likened to the actor Tony Curtis, his shiny dark hair and intense yellow-green eyes a magnet for all the girls of Weslaco. Ever since I had known him as a youngster, he had cultivated an air of studied nonchalance punctuated with episodic fits of rage. His role model was the actor James Dean, and it was not unusual to see Henry at dance parties, his back against the wall, arms crossed, glossy hair combed neatly back, with a serious look in his cat-green eyes. While the other young men vied for the attention of the girls, Henry simply stood there with his brooding look, seemingly oblivious to the furtive glances the girls cast in his direction. Only after an appropriate interval of self-display would he drop his pose, pick out one of the party beauties, and join in the rhythmic festivities.

His good looks could get Quique in trouble, as happened when a group of pachucos—working-class toughies—chased him out of nearby Donna at knife-point because he had captivated one of that city's choice daughters. On another occasion, we were roughed up in neighboring Mercedes because he was after one of that city's beauties. But his worst ordeal came when the band director and taskmaster, the oft-awarded Marion Busby, discovered the lad was using band trips to tighten his grip on one of the Anglo belles of the Green-and-Gold pride of Weslaco. When Busby found out about the liaison, his short fuse exploded: he was not about to risk his reputation over a Mexican kid's willful disregard for the community's unspoken ban on interethnic romance. He would put a stop to this outrage at once. It was a Monday, after a weekend trip to band competition. School had let out for the day, and the Matadors were milling about the band hall, getting in a little practice, when the martinet stormed in and, in the stern voice he used to such great effect, summoned Henry into his office. Eddie and I knew immediately Henry was in for the hazing of his life.

The irony in Henry's dilemma was manifest in the dichotomy that cut through his life like a machete: "racially," he was unequivocally "white," but ethnically he was "Mexican." But the greater irony lay in Busby and the Anglo community's refusal to see past Henry's ethnicity. As the joke circulating during that time (collected for posterity by folk-lorist Américo Paredes) so inelegantly but effectively explained matters: in New York City or Chicago, a young man like Henry might pass for a "passionate Spaniard," but in South Texas he was just a "fuckin' Mexican." So ingrained was the stereotype that the Anglos were willing to let the ethnic label—"Mexican"—cancel their notions of "race."

Interestingly, the early Anglo settlers of the Southwest did make a distinction between "Spaniard" and "Mexican" based on color and status, but by the 1930s, antipathy toward the "Mexican" had intensified so much that skin color had become irrelevant. Paul Schuster Taylor, the Berkeley economist-turned-ethnographer, saw this antipathy in the Anglos of neighboring Corpus Christi, whom he found to be so steeped in the lore of Anglo superiority over the Mexican that in their behavior, the past "lives vividly in the present."* That is why, as Paredes pithily observed, even a blue-eyed German-Mexican youth could be expelled from a swim-ming pool for speaking Spanish in—of all places—the heavily German town of New Braunfels, in Central Texas.

This was the dilemma the young Quique and other Mexican Ameri-cans like him faced, and their only possible escape was to deny their ethnic inheritance.

The other member of the Matadors, Eddie, was the group jester—a breezy, lighthearted, and tough-skinned fellow with many friends. He was so popular in the high school band that he was elected president of the Green-and-Gold in his senior year. Although not as handsome as Henry, like the latter he was a Spanish-Mexican criollo—a tall, lanky charmer who could dazzle even the Anglo girls, and who at least once broke down the ethnic divide and lured one of the band's beauties, a twirler, into an intimate rendezvous. As the most "Mexican," racially, of the Matadors, I could only envy Henry and Eddie for their prowess over girls from "the other side."

Of the three Matadors, Eddie was the most prosperous. His father, Pablo, was a self-employed trucker who hustled fruit and *braceros* (Mex-ican contract-laborers) up and down the Valley and beyond. Although he had absorbed his share of setbacks, Pablo managed to provide his family

---

*See Taylor's classic study, *An American-Mexican Frontier* (New York: Russell & Russell, 1971 [1934]).

a sturdy, white-washed frame house in the barrio, and he had furnished it with all the basic luxuries of domestic working-class life. Eddie was the offspring of Pablo's second marriage, to Concha, a loquacious woman with middling-class aspirations who kept nudging her children to reach beyond the barrio experience. The youngest, Arnie, eventually became a physician. Eddie had a good ear for harmony if only an average baritone voice, but he was a gifted trombone player. His band uniform was draped with the medals he had won in solo competition, and Concha had dreams of her son making it in the big time. Her expectations were particularly high when it came to the Matadors, and she entertained the fancy that we would someday become famous, even more so after we signed on with a recording label from Houston.

The Matadors did indeed work hard at their craft, spending many hours learning new songs and perfecting their tone and harmonization. At Bob Dixon's suggestion, one day we went to his drummer-friend Jimmy Nichols's recording studio and cut a demo tape that everyone involved with the group agreed was one of our best performances. Dixon sent the tape to Houston television personality Larry Kane, an old acquaintance of his. Kane turned the tape over to Jimmy Duncan, A & R (Artists and Repertoire) man at Backbeat Records, who was so impressed with the crisp performance that he arranged for an audition. In May of 1959, the Matadors and Dixon traveled to Houston, where Duncan heard us live and was once again impressed. He signed us to a company contract on the spot. A month later, we arrived in Houston and spent the next nine days living in a motel, while we worked daily on the four sides Duncan had selected for us to record.

One of the songs we recorded, a rock-and-roll piece titled "Handsome," actually reached the top-forty playlist in several radio markets, including Baltimore, St. Louis, Houston, and, of course, the local area. In the Valley itself, we became instant celebrities, and many of our classmates were a bit awed by our newly acquired notoriety. But except for Concha, our families seemed oblivious to the publicity.

Hardened by life's endless stream of reversals, our relatives were skeptical of quick-fame-and-fortune schemes. As Imelda's husband, Noé Rodríguez, would joke, "A mí se me hace que éstos no llegan a jacales pandos—Methinks these upstarts won't make it past the last shack [in the barrio]." Further alienating our families was our choice of music. Bent

The Matadors, 1960

on proving our worth as performers in an American music market, we delved further and further into musical styles alien to the people in the barrio—songs by the Four Freshmen, for example, whose style was decidedly highbrowish, even by Anglo standards. Perhaps irked, and puzzled, by our excursions into such esoteric music, my brother Plon was in the habit of poking fun at the Matadors, putting on his own little "show" every time he saw the three of us dressed for performance. "And now, ladies and gentlemens [sic]," he would say, in an exaggerated Spanish accent and with a loud tone dripping with sarcasm, "for your listening ears, a Bobbie Dixon discovery—the Ma-taters!—oops, Matadors."

Thus, even as our popularity in the Valley climbed, no one from my family or those of the other Matadors offered any encouragement, much less any attempt to intervene and help us exploit the financial possibilities suddenly unfolding for us. The skepticism of our relatives seeped into our consciousness as well, and it had a dampening effect on whatever conceits the Matadors might have harbored. In any case, our opportunity to chase after real stardom was squashed before it ever got off the ground.

Backbeat proposed a concert tour for the Matadors in early October of 1959, hoping to capitalize on the budding new hit. But the band marching season was at its peak, and the Matadors all played leadership roles in the Green-and-Gold pride of Weslaco High. Marion Busby immediately objected. "You're not going anywhere," he insisted, and with unerring psychological calculation, he added, "unless you don't give a hoot for the reputation of this great band. If that's the case, then the Green-and-Gold is better off without you." Totally disheartened but loyal to the end, the Matadors yielded to Busby's pressure. "You can always go on your tour in December," our taskmaster concluded, by way of demonstrating his "fairness." But the propitious moment had come and gone. By December, "Handsome" had long disappeared from the top-forty charts, and our brief tenure as celebrities was history. Finally, dashing any hopes for future success was the sudden downturn Backbeat Records experienced in 1960. The release of our second record was postponed and eventually canceled as the company focused its resources on established artists like Bobby Helm. The Matadors had squandered their only opportunity to crack the big time.

The Matadors continued as an organized group for a few more months, and it was actually at its professional peak when we finally quit singing together. But we were beginning to squabble among ourselves and get on each other's nerves. We had spent endless hours in close contact over the preceding three years, and the raw edges of our egos were beginning to show, in particular Henry's and mine. The two of us had always carried on a tacit rivalry, and now, despite Eddie's pranks and efforts to mediate the widening rift, we argued about everything from costumes to musical selection. In May of 1961, when Henry and I graduated, he and Eddie (who had graduated in 1960) decided to go al norte to Chicago, where, it was rumored, fabulous jobs were going begging in the factories. Infamous for its poverty wages, the Valley seemed like a hopeless pit, and Henry and Eddie were eager to escape. Besides, the Matadors had reached a dead end.

Shortly after graduation, Henry, until then a nominal Catholic, converted to the Church of Jesus Christ of Latter-Day Saints, and he eventually made his way to Utah and Brigham Young University. He married into a white Mormon family and became a school psychologist, thus fulfilling his greatest ambition—to escape poverty and the blight of his ethnic stigma, and to live as a respectable citizen in middle-class, white America. Eddie married a childhood playmate of mine, la Nena, and joined the Air Force as a trombonist. He was shipped to Anchorage, Alaska, where he played his horn for twenty-two years and put an extra eighty pounds on his lanky frame. In the end, "Sasquatch," as I now teasingly call him, parted with la Nena and Alaska, and he returned to the Valley where he sought for years to recapture the lighthearted comedy he had played out as a high school prankster.

After Henry and Eddie left, this Matador hung on for a couple of months in Weslaco, working at a service station (my first job outside of agriculture and music), before I too bolted and made my way to California. I did not see Henry again until 1968, and Eddie remained out of sight for twenty years. I returned to Weslaco after six months in California, and the following year I attended school at Pan American College in nearby Edinburg, majoring in music. Then, in 1963, I again fled to California—this time permanently—to be near María, a tender lass from nearby Mercedes whom I had met during a Matador performance. Her family had moved to the Golden State in 1960, in search of better job opportunities.

Of the days of glory with the Matadors, only a copy of the Jimmy Nichols tape survived in my possession, a precious token of a transforming moment in my odyssey from the cotton fields to the halls of academia.

14
HITTING THE BIG TIME

There must have been at least five thousand teens in the cavernous arena, screaming *en masse* with the introduction of each act on the stage below. The young Houstonians were attending The Larry Kane Show, the Oil City's local version of Dick Clark's nationally televised program, American Bandstand. The loudest shrieks came when Bobby Helm was announced. His song, "My Special Angel," had recently been number one on the hit-parade charts, and Larry Kane was reminding his youthful fans that the idol of the moment would be making his appearance shortly. "Hank" Ayala and the Matadors was one of the opening acts, and the three of us waited nervously for our turn.

It was the middle of September, and one of the forty-five-rpm singles we had recorded earlier that summer had just been released. The lead cut, a medium-rock tune titled "Handsome," seemed to be gaining airplay in its early life on the hit-parade playlists. Our appearance on the live Larry Kane Show was to be the christening event for the Matadors' maiden record, with the large and rambunctious crowd in attendance serving as a festive backdrop. Jimmy Duncan, composer, A&R director, and all-around negotiator for Backbeat, had arranged to bring us up from the Valley for Kane's weekend show, and we had driven to Houston with Bob Dixon, our agent/manager. "This is it, fellas," Dixon told us. "This is the opening we've been waiting for. We're gonna make a big splash in Houston, and then we're gonna hit the big time. All we need to do is keep our cool and strut our stuff."

We had arrived in Houston for our recording debut in June of 1959, on a typically steamy summer day. Against the longest of odds, the Matadors had taken the first step toward the "big time": we had signed a contract with Backbeat Records, the company that catapulted Bobby Helm to the number-one spot on the national charts. And now, at Jimmy Duncan's request we were in Houston to record a minimum of four sides, the equivalent of two forty-five-rpm disks. The disparity between the rural provincialism of the Valley and the urban worldliness of Houston was so pronounced it overwhelmed our sense of scale. The galaxy of night lights and the dizzying bustle of downtown Houston's workaday streets were as alluring as they were frightening, and at our tender ages, seventeen to nineteen, we felt as if we were actors in some country-rags-to-city-glamour fantasy hatched in Hollywood.

When we arrived, we checked into the LaRita Courts, an economy motel somewhere in the city's industrial district, a short distance from Backbeat's studios. The room had two double beds, and Henry—"Hank," as Backbeat had dubbed the Matadors' lead singer—immediately claimed one for himself, leaving Eddie and me to share the other. "It's better if you sleep away from us, anyway," joked Eddie. *"Allá duerme con tus pinches pulgas—*Sleep over there with your fuckin' fleas." *"Chinga'o, vato*—Goddammit, dude," he added, a note of disbelief in his voice. "How did we ever get here, man, us three *vatos rascuaches*—low-life dudes?" "Because we're damn good, man," replied Henry in his perfectly fluent English.

Like most Texas-Mexicans, Eddie lapsed into Spanglish when bantering with friends like his singing partners—a speech style maligned by linguistic snobs that alternates between English and Spanish, often within the same breath. Spanglish was the language of the barrio, and, despite its low repute, it captured poignantly the conflicts we faced straddling the boundary between two cultures. There was always a trace of Spanish intonation when Eddie spoke in English—though not when he sang in that language. He had, as our Anglo teachers reminded us often enough, an "accent." Henry, on the other hand, had spent endless hours mentally rehearsing the speech patterns of Anglos, mastering them so well that he seldom tripped over the usual pitfalls, such as the mispronounced long "e" or the short "i." That is why Jimmy Duncan was so impressed with Henry's and the Matadors' talent: as accomplished bilinguals, we were perfectly fluent singing both in English and Spanish. Before the Matadors, few popular singers had ever done that. And now here we were, we thought, poised at the edge of stardom.

"*¿Sabes qué, vato?*"—"You know what, dude?"—asked Eddie, with his usual braggadocio. "We're gonna kick some ass! Let's get on with the show, baby!" The Matadors were in need of Eddie's daredevil toughness at that moment. Deep in our guts, serious doubt, and even fear, lurked about our ability to compete at this level of the entertainment business, known for its callous treatment of would-be stars. We were confident enough making the rounds of the talent show circuit in the Valley, but Houston's blank-faced masses were as intimidating as its urban glitter was seductive. Despite our fears, one driving force kept us from buckling under the pressure—our determination to prove that these three *vatos* were not going to droop tails and scurry back to the safety of the barrio.

We stayed in the LaRita Courts for nine days, courtesy, we were told, of a self-made and reclusive tycoon named Marcus Taylor, who supposedly owned Backbeat Records. We never met our benefactor, but it was whispered among people in the know that he was a "Negro" masquerading as a white man. It was further rumored he had exotic habits, such as bringing in "belly dancers from Arabia" for wild parties in his suite in a fancy Houston hotel. And, of course, he kept a beautiful blonde, whom he drove around in that symbol of the nouveau riche, a Cadillac. Finally— and this was whispered in the most conspiratorial tones—because of his color, Taylor reputedly used white men like Jimmy Duncan as fronts to maneuver his way through the intrigues of the racist and cutthroat recording industry. All of this information seems to have traveled from ear to ear, perhaps more as urban legend than fact. Certainly Jimmy Duncan, who, presumably, was intimately acquainted with the tycoon— if he existed at all—never mentioned his name to the Matadors. In any event, we never actually learned who controlled Backbeat Records, and in time we came to doubt the tycoon's very existence. For all the talk about "the Negro who passes for white," the company might have been the property of a corporate group.

The routine for the nine days we sojourned in Houston was established the morning after our arrival. After the novelty (for us) of a daily shower and fastidious attention to toiletries, we would walk to the diner across the street for breakfast. The ham and eggs were delicious, as were the grits that came with them. The diner's special Louisiana hot sauce gave the breakfast a lively zing I can still savor to this day. The shapely waitress with smooth alabaster skin, pitch-black hair, and dark mysterious eyes fired my imagination. I ached for her so intensely I could almost taste her sexual fluids. The total anonymity of Houston unleashed the most carnal of desires, even as it loosened the threads of restraint that checked our behavior back home in the barrio, and on one or two occasions I almost felt bold enough to pitch a romantic proposition at the waitress with the mysterious eyes. But I was the scrawniest of the Matadors, and in the end I gave up, convinced that not even the power of my tía Virginia's potions could have delivered her to me. Besides, she was not especially friendly to us, and the fear she might rebuff me ultimately squelched my lecherous fantasies.

During the first few days the Matadors were in Houston, we walked the four or so blocks to the studio after breakfast. Rehearsals began around ten o'clock in the morning. But during the final days, the preparations moved to Jimmy Duncan's, a middle-class retreat somewhere in one of Houston's better neighborhoods. He was the author of Bobby Helm's "My Special Angel," and three of the songs we were learning were also his compositions. The last, a slow rock-ballad titled "Betty Jo," had been composed by Henry. He had written it for an Anglo heartthrob of his, a popular cheerleader at Weslaco High and one of the few beauties who steadfastly, though coyly, resisted his advances.

We met a remarkable young man during our stay in Houston—Bobby Doyle, a pianist-guitarist with a voice of velvet but who had been blind since birth. Doyle and his partners, bassist Kenny and drummer Bill, were also under contract to Backbeat, and the company was using them as utility sidemen on our recordings. They played their instruments and sang some of the background vocals for us. "Boobus," as we took to calling Doyle, became an instant friend of the Matadors, and his natural humility, his encouragement and extraordinary talent made our task easier. For even as we adjusted to the daily routine and learned quickly enough our musical assignments, we found it difficult to rid ourselves of the basic sense of inadequacy we felt in the unfamiliar culture of the recording industry.

But the Matadors were a determined trio, and, despite our visceral fears, visions of fame and glory kept darting before our ambitious eyes.

We were therefore game to any challenges awaiting us in the fiercely competitive world of the big time. Besides, our undeniable talent gained the respect of Duncan, Doyle, and the others involved in the preparations. When the day came for recording, we were ready, and although initially anxious, we plunged into the task at hand with enthusiasm. We had no trouble performing to Duncan's and Backbeat's expectations.

≡

"Used to see them on the corner—hum, hum, hum—
making such an awful roar—hum, hum, hum—
with their noses on the window—hum, hum, hum—
at the local candy store.
Handsome. . . ."

The sound of Hank's voice, with the Matadors humming in the background, cut through the noise of the crowd as our song came over the loudspeakers. Our turn had finally come and, hornets buzzing in our bellies, we rushed up to the stage amid the crowd's cheers. My legs felt wooden and prosthetic as we trotted out and positioned ourselves in front of the TV cameras. All the while the scene had the surreal quality of a dream: the rows of swaying bodies in the stands seemed frozen in time, even as my ears registered their deafening screams. I could feel my fingers moving over the guitar frets and my lips articulating the words, yet the action all around me had a mechanical, even anesthetic quality about it. Everything moved at a glacial pace.

But the whole act on the stage was mechanical, literally, for the Matadors were not actually singing. For the first time on a stage, we had no need to sing or play, since the prerecorded "Handsome" was being piped through the loudspeakers. We were, in fact, lip-synching. Like the noisy audience before us, we had become listeners to our own music, and the burden of delivering the perfect live performance was lifted from our shoulders. All we had to do was pantomime. A strange and highly focused sense of exhilaration overtook me as I became fully conscious of the predetermined "perfection" of our performance. I found myself actually exulting in the moment: We had achieved the ultimate triumph; we were in the big time, and suddenly it all seemed so easy.

The screaming teenage girls, the surge of adrenaline, the dazzling lights and TV cameras, and the crush of autograph seekers played in our memories long after we left Houston. It was, to revisit the old cliché, a once-in-a-lifetime experience. But the Matadors did not yet know this, nor the fact that we would never again exult in the rush of such a climactic moment. Nor could we have fathomed the lasting impact that our exposure to the recording industry and its pressurized big time, no matter how fleeting, had already wrought on our still-tender egos. We would grow that much stronger as we came to recognize the measure of our accomplishment: three *vatos rascuaches* who had risen to the challenge of the big time—a world radically alien to the microcosm of the barrio, with its circles of friendship and reciprocity. Few of our peers would ever face, much less rise to answer, such a challenge.

15
THE NIGHT I LOANED
KENNY FIVE DOLLARS

As soon as I entered the Mother Earth Restaurant, I recognized the sonorous bass voice, chocolate-rich and velvety, oozing through the intercom. And then I saw him. He sat erect in front of the piano, swaying back and forth as he delivered the lines of the romantic ballad he was singing: "She wore bluuuue velvet. . . ." It was Bobby Doyle— the same Bobby Doyle the Matadors had befriended in Houston, when we were preparing for the recording session we hoped would launch us into the entertainment big time. I was surprised at how little he had changed.

Because he was blind, he did not see me approach the piano bar. I spoke to him: "Hello, Boobus," using the nickname we had given him back in 1959. "Manool," he replied in his clear, resonant bass, instantly recognizing my voice and using the nickname he had made up for me.

I had not seen Bobby in nearly twenty years, nor had I thought much about him for a while. But I had recently returned to my native soil after a fifteen-year absence, enrolling at the University of Texas in Austin to work on a Ph.D. in Anthropology. One day, I was reading the *Austin American-Statesman* when I saw an ad for the Mother Earth Restaurant. "Bobby Doyle at the Piano Bar—6:00 to 8:00 P.M.," the ad read. Could this be the same Bobby Doyle? I wondered. I decided to find out.

After he finished at the piano, Bobby joined me at the bar, and we drank beer and reminisced about our days in the big city. We were all very young and inexperienced, back in the summer of 1959, but Bobby was a highly talented artist, and we admired him enormously, especially since he was so unpretentious and so willing to make friends with three backwater Mexicans from the Rio Grande Valley. He had sung backup for the four sides we recorded for Backbeat Records. As we reminisced about those days, Bobby reminded me of the night, six months after we met in Houston, when The Bobby Doyle Trio visited the Valley to play at the Holiday Inn in McAllen. He had called the Matadors that night and asked us to come by and jam with his group.

"D'you remember lending Kenny, the bass player, five bucks that night?" he asked. At that moment I did not and, indeed, had forgotten that after the job we had all gone across the border to the red light district in Reynosa, Tamaulipas. But as Bobby refreshed my memory, I began to recall some of the events of that evening. I remembered someone from Bobby's group wanting to bed down with a prostitute at one of the cantinas.

"Was that the same Kenny who was playing bass with you when we met in Houston?" I asked.

"Yeah," said Bobby, "same Kenny. He was broke that night, when we went across the border; we hadn't got paid for the gig yet. And you loaned him five dollars to screw a hooker he liked."

At that moment the scene crystallized in my mind. Yes, I remembered, I had played a dance job with Eugenio Gutiérrez's band the previous weekend, when I had earned twelve dollars. Lending the five dollars had put a big hole in my wallet, but I felt it was important to leave a good impression with Bobby and his friends. We always felt like that way about Anglos who were friendly with us. We wanted to leave them "with a good impression," as if each one of us, as Mexicans, were somehow representative of the whole race. "Think badly of me," was the thought in the back of our minds, "and you'll think badly of all my people." That's how sensitive we were to the Anglo perception of us.

"Well," I said, "at least someone had a good time that night. I hope he didn't catch the clap."

"I don't think so," Bobby chuckled, now realizing that I had no idea who the man we were talking about was. "But he can afford a lot more expensive women now. You know that after he left my trio he went on to crack the big time in a big way."

"What do you mean?" I asked.

"Don't you remember? The guy you loaned the five bucks to was Kenny Rogers."

16

CALIFORNIA DREAMIN'
(Glimpses of Eden)

I dreamed in my youth
of being a movie star;
and one of those days I came
to visit Hollywood.

On arriving at the station,
I bumped into a buddy,
who offered me an invitation
to go work on the "traque"
[railway].

When I got fed up
with the traque,
he invited me again
to the harvest of tomatoes
and to thin beets.

And I earned some
little trifle,
and I left for Sacramento.
when I had nothing but zilch,
I had to work on the cement.

On that infamous pulley
more than a few gave up;
and I—how could I bear it?
So I quit to go wash dishes.

It's the type of honest work
that many Chicanos do;
although with the hot water
the hands swell a bit.

The coach is about to leave,
we are speeding up.
eyes that saw you leave,
when will they see you return?

Good-bye, dreams of my life,
good-bye, movie stars;
I'm going back to
my homeland
even poorer than I came.

—"El lavaplatos" ("The Dishwasher"),
an old Mexican Ballad

This was California, finally. The sun was setting in a blaze of burnt orange as we approached the state line on highway U.S. 80 connecting Yuma and San Diego. I could hardly wait to see again the state so many of my fellow tejanos celebrated as a modern-day Jauja—the mythical land of Cockayne, where pesos grew on trees and the streets were paved with caramel. California—the name rolled off the tongue like a rhythmic drum cadence, sounding English and Spanish at the same time. It was the dream-land of Guy William's Zorro (zip, zip, zip!) and the great Spanish grandees who had ridden on their roan stallions; the place where the forty-niners struck gold and transformed sleepy hamlets into roaring boomtowns. It was Hollywood and James Dean, Marilyn Monroe, Tony Curtis, and all the glamorous names and places Texans dreamed of. This was the Garden of Eden, with its endless bounty and the promise of a new life, if not fame and fortune, for every Texas-Mexican displaced by the máquinas—the mechanical cottonpickers that had stripped thousands of families of their livelihood.

My brother José and I had been riding in the crowded Trailways bus since early the previous day when we left Weslaco on our way to Gilroy, in the Bay Area. José had reconciled with his young wife, Lula, who had left him in the Rio Grande Valley and migrated with her family to California months before. He invited me to come along, and, fed up with working at a Billups gas station for $25 a six-day week, I agreed to make the trip with him. It would be the second time I had been to the Golden State. In 1958, the Peña family had worked the summer fruit-and-grape harvest in the San Joaquin Valley, and I returned to Texas with a good impression. The ninety cents an hour was far better than the wages back home, and the trees and vineyards provided the kind of shade absent in the Texas cotton fields. Best of all, the usually arid heat of the San Joaquin Valley seemed balmy in comparison to the steam houses that were the Rio Grande and Brazos Valleys.

And now, fresh out of high school in 1961, I was about to return to California. The road sign read, "Yuma: 36 miles, San Diego: 216." "We should be in California by nine o'clock this evening," I thought. A sense of excitement rippled through my body, and I felt quite certain that romance, adventure, and thrilling new discoveries awaited me just beyond the Yuma desert.

≡—

We arrived in Yuma just after mid-day, when the thermometer outside the Wells Fargo Bank registered 105 degrees. Alonso's 1953 Chevy was leaking copious amounts of transmission fluid, and his youngest child Armando, barely a year old, had uncontrollable diarrhea. I was feeling miserable and slightly faint; what the doctor diagnosed as a "nervous stomach" had been acting up for months, and I had reached the point of depression. Alonso's sister María was making the trip with us. She had ridden the Greyhound all the way from Fresno back to the Rio Grande Valley on the pretext of helping her brother Alonso drive the nineteen hundred miles from Mercedes, Texas, to Wrangler City. In reality, she had made the trip to persuade me to come back to California with her.

As we sat in the shade of a scrawny tree, waiting for the baby to be seen in the nearby clinic, I gazed at my sweetheart and, momentarily oblivious to my current miseries, my thoughts drifted to the night when had I first met the perky lass. It happened at a dance where the Matadors had performed back in '59. We had sung during intermission at a *quinceañera*, the Mexican version of the traditional coming-out party for fifteen-year-old debutantes. When the orquesta resumed playing after the break, Henry and Eddie were quickly claimed by a pair of beauties while I stood around, hoping to find someone who would dance with me. I spotted María at the far end of the American Legion hall where the celebration was being held. Apparently, none of the local *románticos* had yet descended upon her, and she seemed to be waiting for someone to ask her onto the floor. From across the hall she struck me as quite attractive, so I circled around the mass of dancers whirling counterclockwise in the traditional tejano style, just to get a closer look at her.

She did not see me approach, engaged as she was in conversation with another girl. She was obviously quite young (soon to be fourteen, I later found out), but there was an air of maturity about her and a confident tone in her voice, unusual for someone of such a tender age. A *criollita* (with some Jewish in the mix, I would later learn), she was blessed with a smooth, perfectly shaped oval face of pearly complexion, an exquisite nose, and luminous hazel eyes graced by aristocratically arched brows. A head of dark, luxuriant hair draped her slender shoulders, both framing and pronouncing her delicate features. Taken in by her Mediterranean beauty, I asked her to dance and held my breath.

"I'm too tall for you," were the first words she directed at me as she sized me up.

Flustered but undaunted, I pressed on. "Well, why don't we try it, anyway?"

She took a closer look, seemed to recognize me, and finally consented.

"My name is Manuel," I said to her as I took her hand. "Hi," she said, "I'm María." And with that I led her onto the dance floor, where I discovered to my delight that she was an excellent follower. Her petite body felt light as a feather as I led her through various maneuvers in time to the polca-ranchera the band was playing. My dancing skills paid off, though being a member of the popular Matadors probably didn't hurt. María was instantly impressed—not by my less-than-handsome looks, as she would later remind me, but by my dancing—and our relationship was off to a gliding start. In fact, she was so pleased to find a good partner that she made a suggestion after the polca ended: "I have some flats in the car, and if you want to, I can wear those instead of these heels. Then I won't feel like I'm taller than you."

Low-heeled shoes now covering her dainty feet, we swirled round and round the counterclockwise floor for the rest of the evening, dancing polcas, boleros, and danzones, all the while talking and laughing. When we finally said good night, my heart was already aflutter over the spunky young criollita with the feather-light movements, infectious laugh, and Spanish-Mexican charm.

I found out she was from nearby Mercedes, and since it turned out I already knew her father Octavio and brother Alonso (members of the GG Orchestra and both well acquainted with Eugenio Gutiérrez, my music teacher), a mutual feeling of intimacy quickly blossomed between us. More fortunately for me, my acquaintance with Octavio García made it a bit easier to slip under the vigilant eyes of Mama Eva and gain permission to visit María at the García home, albeit strictly as a "friend of the family." Over the next few months, the friendship between us warmed, while deep within the folds of my heart, María's name was already being permanently etched.

But my future father-in-law moved the family to Wrangler City, near Fresno, California, in January of 1960, six months after María and I had met, and the budding romance was prematurely nipped. I did not see her again until my second sojourn in California, in August of 1961, when José, Lula, and I migrated from Gilroy to Crestview a few miles from Wrangler City. I did not stay long in the Golden State, however, and it wasn't until I returned for the third time the following year that my future bride and I were finally committed to a lasting romance. When I left yet again for Texas after the '62 summer harvest, we kept in close contact while

I attended Pan American College in Edinburg. Then things went awry. Mama was diagnosed with cancer and had to undergo surgery, and I began having problems with my "nervous stomach." My condition deteriorated after a bout with the Asian flu, and, in a depressed state, I had written and told María to forget about me. But she was persistent.

And now here we were, together again, stuck in Yuma with a disabled car and a sick child. The land of Jauja never looked grimmer.

≡

We had done pretty well that summer of '63, harvesting seedless Thompsons for the raisin crop all around the Crestview area at ten cents a paper tray. Fully recovered from my recent bout with nervous stomach (or "irritable bowel," as medical science eventually labeled this disorder of "undetermined etiology"), I felt stronger than I ever had in my life, and I was able to work steadily despite the oven-like heat of the San Joaquin Valley summer. I had even sent Mama and Papa a little money, and saved a few more dollars for my college education.

We had picked for Alvin Berry and Yasufumi Komoto, for the affable Kenji Sakamoko, and also for Frank Wilde, a Wash Jones type straight out of Faulkner. The dapper and unfarmer-like Mr. Suddjian had also hired us to harvest his crop, as did a couple of other small raisin growers who year after year brought in the same basic crew for the raisin harvest. Toño Jáuregui acted as contact man and crew leader, and working alongside him was his brother Cuco and a couple of his preteen boys. The Jáureguis' sister and her husband also picked with us, as did Manuel and Arabella Rodríguez, along with the flock of kids they had born. Arabella's nieces, Queta and Manuela Garza, as well as their pretty sister, Élida (the object of a few of my romantic chimeras), were also part of the little army. Their cousin José Garza and his wife Delia picked with us as well. My brother José, his wife Lula, and I had first joined the raisin brigade during the 1961 harvest.

That year, we had no place to stay when we arrived from Gilroy, but Toño Jáuregui let us use a decrepit trailer house he had junked in the back of his lot. Jáuregui and most of his little crew of pickers lived in a barrio called Tombstone, just outside Crestview. Where the name came from I was never able to ascertain, but some said it was a cynical reference to the "Wild West" character of the settlement—a collection of mostly run-down houses and lean-tos lined along pothole-filled, unpaved streets, pretty much forgotten by city planners. It was seldom patrolled by local law enforcement agencies. Saturday-night brawls among drunken revelers were common, although no one took much notice as long as no serious injuries resulted. Járegui's trailer house was no more than eight feet by ten in size, so it barely accommodated José, Lula, and their two small daughters. Built of metal, it was particularly hellish inside when the temperature climbed over one hundred degrees—which happened regularly during the summer.

I was thus forced to sleep in an old jalopy my brother bought when we arrived in Crestview. But I was an eighteen-year-old not yet dis-accustomed to the hardship of the campañas, and besides, the proximity of my love light in Wrangler City more than compensated for the inconvenience of living out of a car. When I returned the following summer (1962), however, José and Lula had rented a three-room shack down the street, and I then shared a tiny bedroom with my brother's two small daughters, Imelda and Linda.

As I discovered when I returned to California in 1961, the task of picking grapes can seem deceptively attractive, even romantic, especially as portrayed in the old Gallo wine commercials. Contented yeoman farmers and their robust workers bustled cheerfully across the TV screen, harvesting the biblical crop amidst the fertile fields and balmy weather of the Napa Valley. Soft winds rustled the grapevines and caressed the untiring bodies of the smiling laborers, evoking an idyllic scene worthy of the next vacation. Come and loll in leisure, the commercials beckoned, drinking cabernet while plucking grapes in the Eden of the West.

In the San Joaquin Valley and its torrid temperatures, picking grapes was not exactly as pictured in the utopian scenes of the Gallo Vineyards. Well, perhaps during the first hour—when the air was crisp and redolent with the fragrance of ripening fruit, dewy vines, and fecund soil—one could be lulled into a dreamy, almost nirvanic state. The body was fresh and resilient, the morning cool and moist. But when the sun rose high enough above the cloudless horizon to aim its blazing rays on the exposed earth below, the dreamy state quickly turned into a sweaty struggle. By then, deep into the daily grind, we ducked whiplashing vines and spit out mouthfuls of sand; scraped knees on the rough ground and brushed off scores of black widows; and most dreadful of all, we braced ourselves for the yellow jacket nests certain to be hidden in every row we picked.

Kenji Sakamoko had a heart of velvet, as did Frank Wilde. Unlike other local farmers, who squeezed every ounce of exploitation they could from the overworked Mexicans who tilled and harvested the orchards and vineyards of the Great Valley, Sakamoko and Wilde were exceptionally generous. I always thought they must have been farm workers themselves in another life. Sakamoko, a thin fellow with eyes wrinkled in a perpetual smile, was a kindly middle-aged man who would have found it unthinkable to fire anyone for slacking off on the job. On the contrary, he did everything to make the toil as bearable as possible. Once, in the dead of a very cold winter, when we were working by the hour pruning the frozen vineyards, he lit a fire and invited us to take a break so we could warm up our numb bodies. I always thought of him as a reluctant petty capitalist, someone who would have been far happier on a communal farm. He did not have within him the ruthless instinct to expropriate every penny of labor power his workers could yield. Other growers understood his "weakness." I heard one neighbor criticize him as incompetent, a slacker whose lackadaisical approach to farm management was bound to bring ruin to the plot his parents had bequeathed him.

Perhaps the neighbor was correct, at least from the point of view of a petty capitalist. In time, as the agribusiness economy of the San Joaquin Valley was increasingly consolidated into the hands of a few family empires and corporate farms, men like Sakamoko, Wilde, Berry, and even the industrious Komoto faded into obscurity. Their puny farms languished or were swallowed up by more ambitious and efficient capitalists, men with names like Roswell, Stuttgart, and Sartoian, all of whom had started with little, but came to build empires and amassed sizeable fortunes in farming.

The Sartoians are a case in point. Even in the 1990s, old-time pickers in Crestview still remembered how reluctant the Mexicans were when it came to picking raisin grapes for "los Arminios," as they called the Sartoians. While their kinsman was achieving legendary status as an author, "los Arminios" were building their fortune on the backs of the Mexicans. And they did it in classical capitalist style—by exploiting the old labor theory of value down to the minutest tasks. As every picker knew, you had to work twice as long in the Sartoian vineyards to earn your ten cents on the tray. The Berrys and Wildes were not particularly vigilant when it came to the volume of grapes on each tray, and workers often spread them as thinly as possible, as long as they didn't violate the principle of the "full tray." Not so with the Sartoians: every square inch of paper had to be filled, and thickly, too. They tolerated no spaces where only a single layer of loose grapes covered the paper rectangle—let alone empty corners, no matter how small. If that happened, the picker was subject to docking—getting something like seven cents for a less-than-full tray, rather than the customary ten. They were that stingy.

"Los Arminios" were therefore the employers of last resort, when the picking got scarce and things turned a little desperate. Yet while the Sartoians may have exploited their Mexican workers to an extreme, they were simply responding to the logic of capitalism. As every grower knew, corporate buyers, shippers, other middlemen, and anonymous "market forces" inevitably siphoned off their shares of capital, severely limiting the farmer's profit margin. But as every grower also knew, labor was the one critical element he could control: the higher the worker's production and the lower the wage, the higher the margin was for the grower. Thus, those who practiced this axiom of "free enterprise" most efficiently were the ones who prospered in the face of fierce competition from the growing number of corporate farms.

≡

"Amorcito, corazón, yo tengo tentación de un beso. . . ." It was sure nice to hear Los Panchos play that bolero on XEW Saturday night, on the drive back from the dance job with Octavio Ruelas's band. I'm glad the old '53 Chevy don Arturo Ballí sold me has a radio. Amazing, how you can pick up a radio station all the way from Mexico City in California late at night. El Trío Los Panchos—they sounded so beautiful, so familiar after all these years, and yet—well, so painful. A few good memories—the Matadors and those all-night parties, the serenades at dawn. And so many years dreaming of the good life, and of all those lovely chicks I never got anywhere with. Los Panchos. So many sad memories, too—the campañas, the aching back and sore body from picking all that cotton. God, I can't take this anymore. The goddamn Japanese farmer told me I was too slow, and that he was gonna have to let me go. Hell, I just couldn't get the hang of it—how to *pick those Emeralds for packing. Clean here, clip there, and before you know it, ten minutes are gone. I don't blame the Jap for firing me. Still, I'm glad José told him to go fuck himself and quit, too. At least I didn't have to wait around. And, anyway, I've had it with this fuckin' heat, and the dirt that gets into every sweaty pore of your body. I wonder if we'll find other work tomorrow? "Yo quiero ser un solo ser, y estar contigo. . . ." El Trío Los Panchos. Boy, the Matadors could do that song just like them—maybe even better. If only we had gotten a break. Jesus, Memito, you gotta find something else to do. How long has it been? Since you were six—you've been out in these rotten fields since you were six. And you swore to Papa we would never get caught in these sweat factories from hell again. Nineteen fifty-nine, wasn't it? Yep, that's when the Matadors were swinging at the Sea Island. I should go over and talk to Art Ballí, Jr; maybe he can fix me up at Kinney Shoes. Why can't I get a job like that, working in a nice air-conditioned building, in a shirt and tie? What am I afraid of? It can't be that hard, selling goddamn shoes. I mean, it can't be any harder than sing-ing at the Outrigger Club. "Compañeros en el bien y el mal, ni los años nos podrán pesar. . . ."*

≡—

My face was on the television screen, the camera focusing in for a close-up. I was watching my own appearance on the Luis Gómez Show on Channel 47. As was customary, the program had been taped on Thursday evening, to be broadcast on Sunday morning. I was singing one of my specialties, a romantic bolero, with Alonso García pounding out the piano accompaniment.

José and I were working for the affable Randolph Kuhn, who, like many growers of the time, had his own little packing shed on the farm he operated. We were hired to pick peaches, but sometimes Kuhn would pull my brother and me out to help with the chores around the pack-ing shed. We unloaded the full crates hauled in from the nearby orchard, emptied them on the conveyor belts for sorting, loaded the trucks with the market-bound fruit, and performed other assorted tasks. One of the other workers told Kuhn I was a singer, and that I would be appearing on television later that Sunday morning. Kuhn seemed impressed, and he asked me if this was true. When I answered "yes," he asked whether

I would like to watch myself on television. At eleven in the morning, he brought José and me into the family living room, where Mrs. Kuhn and their lovely daughter joined us, and we all stood around the TV waiting for one of the Kuhn workers to display his artistic side. Mrs. Kuhn did not ask us to sit down, and it was obvious to me why she did not extend the invitation: José and I were covered with grime from head to toe, and the dust would have soiled the flowery pastels on her sofa.

"Here's Carmen Cristina, the Lark of the Valley, to sing 'Tú sólo tú.' Let's give her a big hand!" Luiz Gómez, the host, was announcing one of the Valley's better-known talents. Carmen Cristina's parents followed their daughter on the show. The venerable old couple, known as Los Morenos, had been among the pioneers of Mexican American music, cutting their first record for Columbia in 1937. Dressed in their charro outfits, they warbled one of don Luis Moreno's heart-wrenching rancheras. "And now, here's Manolo, singing one of his specialties for us, the beautiful bolero, 'Solamente un vez—You Belong to My Heart.'" Gómez always addressed me as "Manolo," never by my birth name, and now, deep into his performance mode, he was bursting with camera charm, mixing his broken English with Spanish while the applause from the studio audience could be heard in the background. "And I see that he brought his trombone with him this time. Let's give Manolo a big hand!" My image flashed on the screen, and there I was, crooning my heart out for the folks of the San Joaquin Valley.

The face on the television screen seemed alien to me, as if it were someone else singing, not me. In fact, the whole scene seemed unreal— the television images, the motley group of viewers in the Kuhn living room, the stark difference between the scrubbed, well-groomed singer dressed in coat and tie and the grimy "I" who was taking it all in. A vague sense of déjà vu came over me, as my thoughts drifted back a few years, to when the Matadors were singing at the Sea Island Resort Hotel, on the shore of the "Gulf of Dreams." Standing amid the genteel decor of the Kuhn living room, I felt the same sense of disconnectedness and grotesque transformation I had experienced at the Sea Island, when it seemed as if there were two different selves locked up within my body— one performing at the ritzy Outrigger Club, the other flinging mud in the slushy fields of Farmer Moore.

"You're a very good singer." Mrs. Kuhn's voice echoed in my ears, jolting me back to the present. "Thank you, ma'am." I suddenly felt embarrassed at being seen in such a grimy, unkempt condition, especially by the lovely Kuhn girl, who added after her mother, "Yes, and you look very nice on TV." I left the room as quickly as I could, turning down a glass of lemonade Mrs. Kuhn had offered. I loathed the sordid life I was living as a lowly farm worker, and I wondered once again whether I would ever escape the curse of the ox.

≣

You really have to get a better job than this, Memito. Laying peaches to dry—what's a guy like you doing here? Jesus, I'm beginning to think Papa was right—maybe you are a fuckin' ox at the plow, and we'll never get out of this hell hole. . . .

≣

We were desperate. The peaches were slow to mature and the raisin season was at least six weeks away, so José and I got into his dusty, drab-gray '50 Plymouth and went scouting for work. "Tumbleweed," Jose called the jalopy, after the banged-up nag he saw in a western movie, whose speed and perseverance saved Audie Murphy from a barnful of trouble. We had wandered some thirty miles away from home, well beyond the orchards of the east side, when we came across a crew chopping cotton near the hamlet of Far Point. "You got any work?" José asked the foreman. "Sure." "How much do you pay?" "Dollar-ten an hour." "Órale, we'll take it."

We could tell immediately by the men's speech and general demeanor that the crew was made up of *fuereños*, immigrants from deep in the Mexican interior. "They're probably *mojados*," José observed, "working here illegally." That was of no particular consequence to us—or so we hoped. Growing up in Texas, where native Texas-Mexicans and norteños formed the vast majority of the farm labor force, we had only occasionally run into fuereños in the cotton fields, and then mostly as temporary braceros. Once we had even "adopted" a young fuereño from the state of Guanajuato—Pénjamo, as my father christened him, after the city by the same name.

Pénjamo stumbled into our camp outside Corpus Christi, scrawny and disoriented from days of walking without food and little water. He had made his way across Mexico to the border, and he had then braved the treacherous walk across vast stretches of snake-infested chaparral and cactus between Laredo and Corpus Christi. Papa and Mama immediately took him in, and he joined us on our campaña to West Texas, where he picked cotton with us until December. Pénjamo worked feverishly hard, as if he were trying to prove his worth as a laborer, and when we finally parted with him, his hustle had earned him a job on a farm for the winter. By then he was twenty pounds heavier and a couple of hundred dollars richer, thanks to Mama's guisados and the free room we had provided him. Pénjamo's full-throttle work habits, and those of braceros we had seen, convinced us that fuereños were desperate people, willing to work twice as hard and at half the wages just to be allowed to work in the United States. We were glad they were scarce in the cotton fields.

The crew José and I joined reminded us of Pénjamo. The men worked fast—at breakneck speed, to be exact—and they soon left me so far behind that they finished the row we had all started together, then another, and actually began to catch up with me from the rear. The men seemed bent on pleasing the foreman, perhaps fearful of being fired if they slowed their pace. I tried as best I could to match their frenzied tempo, but by the end of the day, the fuereños had caught up to me from behind at least two or three times. (José was a bit more successful at keeping them within striking distance.) The next morning I could hardly move from the beating my muscles had taken the previous day, but I went back to the cotton fields anyway, ready to face the grind one more time. "This has to be worse, by far, than pulling a one-hundred-pound sack full of cotton," I thought, as we sharpened the hoes and prepared to start hacking at weeds.

The pace immediately picked up where it had left off the day before. Not one to shy away from confrontation when he perceived injustice, José called out to the little group of three or four who were leading the charge.

"Hey," he yelled at them in Spanish. "What the hell do you think you're doing, killing yourselves at this pace? You guys are not chopping by piecework; this is hourly work. You're not gonna get paid one cent more per hour, even if you bust your asses."

"We came here to work," one of the choppers responded, and he kept on racing ahead.

"You're an idiot," José yelled at him, now in a fighting mood, "a pendejo."

Upon hearing José's verbal attack, the fuereño seemed uncertain as to whether to respond in kind, charge at his challenger, or to ignore the insult and keep working. He paused briefly, and then, perhaps weighing the consequences, he raised his hoe in a wide arc and resumed his hurried rhythm.

By and by the foreman came around. He, too, was a Mexican, who appeared to be a legal immigrant, probably from the same region as the crew he supervised, West-Central Mexico, as were most of the Mexican workers who migrated to California. He had apparently been watching us from somewhere off the field. "I'm gonna have to let you go," he said, addressing me in particular. "You're not keeping up with the rest of the crew."

"You know what?" José intervened. He was still steaming over what he felt was the servile, morose attitude of the fuereños. "You can take this hoe and shove it up your ass. And if you don't like it, let's take care of business like machos. Don't think for a moment you scare me just because you're the fuckin' foreman." He had squared his slender shoulders, my always feisty brother, as if he were ready to come to blows with the man standing in front of him.

The foreman, who was considerably beefier than my brother, glowered at José but said nothing. Only his trembling lower lip betrayed the fury churning inside him. He seemed ready to charge forward, but he turned around instead and walked toward his pickup.

"Here's your fuckin' hoes!" José yelled after him, as he threw his implement in the foreman's direction. "You know what to do with them." "*Vámonos*," he said, turning to me. "We're not slaves of these cabrones. We're Peñas; we don't have to take shit from anyone."

"What about our pay? We busted our asses for a day and a half. "

"Fuck it. Let's get out of here. "

This has got to be the last year this ox pulls the plow. College starts next week, and maybe by next summer things will be different. Maybe I can still sell shoes, or even work at a service station. Anything but this, Memito. For María's sake. Now that she's your wife, she deserves better than this. You know she doesn't expect to be married to a farm worker the rest of her life. She's much too proud for that. OK, maybe I can teach guitar at that

Gospel Music store. The salesman—what was his name? Sal Struthers—he really liked the way I played that Gibson ES 335 he had on sale. What a guitar! He even offered a space at the store for me to teach my students, if I ever decided to do that. I should drop in and see if his offer's still good. Yeah, that's what I'll do. Maybe.

17
WE ARE NOT BEASTS

The surge of adrenaline started in my bowels and, with lightning speed, overwhelmed my mental faculties. I could count on one hand the number of times I had experienced this kind of rage, with its jolting effects. It happened that rarely. In the flick of an insect's wing, and quite independently of my volition, my body had mobilized for violence: it was ready to strike out and inflict injury. Somehow, though, the instinct for self-preservation prevailed, and the conscious mind, having been momentarily bypassed, recovered enough to deflect the response. Instead of striking the man with the shovel in my trembling hand, I hurled the angry words at him: "We are not beasts! Why do you yell at us like we were a bunch of oxen? You have no right to treat us like this!"

My brother José and I worked for Herbie Kuhn during the fruit-tree harvests of the early sixties. Like his cousin Randolph, Kuhn ran his own packing operation, H. R. Kuhn Packing Company, which also processed fruit for some of his fellow growers. As agricultural employers went, Kuhn was probably no worse than his neighbors in the way he treated his Mexican laborers. He was usually abrupt in his managerial style, and he spoke in clipped phrases delivered almost in a monotone. But it was enough to make his Mexican workers jump into action. The second summer we worked for him, however, he opened up a bit with José and me, especially after he took us out of the orchards and assigned us to the packing shed. On a couple of occasions, he and I actually engaged in conversation, and it was then that I got a glimpse of his more humane side. He seemed interested when I shared with him my hopes of going to college, and he told me of his own son's educational aspirations.

"As a father," he said, "I wouldn't mind turning over this operation to him someday. It's not such a bad way to pull in $25,000 a year [a tidy sum, in 1962 dollars]. But farming takes a lot of commitment and patience. You have to put up with a lot of crap, and sometimes you have to be more ruthless than I care to be. I don't know if my son would wanna go through all that. He plans to become an engineer."

I felt better about farmers after my talks with Kuhn. He seemed genuinely interested in sharing with me the challenges and uncertainties of farming, and during those moments of face-to-face talk, I thought I understood why the patrones could at times be so callous toward their workers. Their own feelings of insecurity in the face of a capricious industry turned at least some of them into tyrants. "That's why," Kuhn once told me, "not just anybody can be a farmer. It takes guts, and you certainly can't afford to be a bleeding heart. You gotta be level-headed in this business, and you gotta be tough with everyone—your creditors, the co-ops, the workers—with everybody, even yourself."

Herbie Kuhn was momentarily startled by my outburst, even as I continued my tirade. He had ordered us to dig holes to transplant potted vines, and, upon inspecting the work of one of the men and finding it unsatisfactory, he started to berate the defenseless fellow, who looked awkwardly at the ground while the patrón dressed him down verbally. I had never seen our boss get this worked up, especially about something as trivial—or so I thought—as a poorly dug hole. Not that Kuhn had flown into a rage, but the edge in his clipped speech was like a drill boring his displeasure into the head of the dazed little man standing before him.

I stood by silently, holding in my resentment, but the instant he uttered the question, "Can't you stupid people follow simple instructions?" something snapped in my head, sending the surge of adrenaline storming through my bloodstream. I had taken the question very personally, as a direct affront to my intelligence and that of my people. The sight of the ashen-faced mojadito, standing timorous and small against the hulking presence of our patrón, brought crashing into my consciousness the gross inequality I had constantly witnessed between my people and the americano bosses. For an instant, the rancor I had always harbored but never expressed was riveted on the white man standing in front me, his large, beefy torso bulging under the blue-denim shirt he wore. My accumulated anger screamed for action, and I wanted to lash out and cave in the patrón's skull. But the fear of violence immobilized me, and the wave of rage was deflected and ultimately dissipated in the torrent of expletives I sputtered toward the object of my hatred.

Once he recovered from the surprise verbal attack from the scrawny little Mexican, Kuhn looked at me not so much with anger as with perplexity. I fully expected him to do something drastic in the face of my mutinous behavior—perhaps fire me on the spot, especially since he had just unloaded his wrath at someone himself. Instead, he shook his head, turned around, and muttered, "I don't have time to fart around with you. Get back to work, all of you." And with that, he walked away. Although brief, the episode lodged in my brain, partly because of its enervating effects—once it was over, my knees turned to butter, and I felt as if my energy had been siphoned out. But it also registered in my consciousness as one more in a long list of indignities I had experienced as an ox at the plow, and I wondered, once more, "When will it end?"

José and I actually had it out with Herbie Kuhn at least twice more. But he never fired us, and we never walked away. To this day, I do not know why he tolerated our insubordination, or even why we stayed on. Most growers would have given us the heave-ho. In the end, however, we left not out of defiance or dismissal but at the prospect of better wages elsewhere. In 1963, we heard other growers had begun to raise the hourly wage to $1.25, while Kuhn was still paying $1.10. When José asked him for a raise, he refused. "OK," said my brother, "I guess this is it; we're going where they pay $1.25." "Good luck," said Kuhn, in his clipped, unemotional tone, and with that he turned around and went about his business.

We never again worked for the H. R. Kuhn Packing Company, although I never forgot the patrón's unflappable response to my outburst. In contrast to my impotent shrieks, he had remained cool and in control of the situation. For me, Kuhn's reaction underscored his own dictum on the need to be level-headed and tough in the ruthless business of farming, just as his gruff, no-nonsense attitude toward his workers seemed the *sine qua non* for survival in such a brutal occupation. Ironically, in his dealings with his own workers many years later, José, then in business himself as a cement contractor, very much reminded me of Kuhn—a chance association of communicative styles, no doubt, since my brother was not particularly fond of his old boss or the way he had treated us.

18

THE GARDEN OF EDEN
(Ballad of the Ox)

Octavio García, my new father-in-law, was listening to a Spanish-language station on the hand-sized transistor radio he carried in a pocket of his overalls. He, his other son-in-law Esteban Treviño, and I were laboring with about a dozen other fellows in eye-blinding sweat, laying out the freshly cut peaches to dry on the asphalt. The drying yard sprawled at the heart of the large orchard, so the peaches were fully ripened and still oozing syrup when the women cut and arranged them on the wooden trays, which we laid in rows atop the asphalt. After a couple of days or so in the blazing California sun, the sweet, meaty fruit would turn into *orejones*—dried, ready-to-eat "peach ears."

"Ya son las dos de la tarde con cuarenta-y-cinco minutos, hora correcta, y la temperatura ambiental registra ciento-cuatro grados Farenheit," the disk jockey was informing us in his crisp, resonant voice: "The correct time is 2:45 P.M., and the current temperature is one-hundred-four degrees, Fahrenheit."

"Yeah," I heard someone say, "where he's sitting it might be a hundred-four. Out here in the middle of this orchard it must be one-hundred-twenty." "You know what they say about California," another worker chimed in, "it's the Garden of Eden."

It was indeed hot on that July afternoon in 1965, but I was a youthful and rather scrawny twenty-two-year-old, so the heat did not particularly faze me. But Octavio was in his mid-sixties, and he was decidedly over-weight. I looked over at him to see how he was tolerating the oven-like heat of the dry yard where we were toiling. He wore a long-sleeve flannel shirt under his overalls, and for head cover he had a tropical helmet, or "Sahara Cop" hat, as we called it. Underneath it he sported a large red bandana that stuck out of the helmet and hung over his eyes, ears, and the back of his neck. Wrapped around his dripping-wet collar was yet another bandana, this one blue and, like the red one, adorned with polka dots. His sad, owlish eyes peered through the sweaty rags covering his fat, ruddy face, and, as always, he worked at a deliberate pace—not slow enough to catch the foreman's attention, but certainly not fast enough to set any production records.

"His fellow musicians back in the Rio Grande Valley were right on target when they nicknamed 'Elmer,'" I was thinking. "He does look, walk, and act a little like Elmer Fudd—even to the point of being, like Elmer, a mite testy at times."

It was a Monday, and Octavio and I had played with the GGs the night before in Modesto, ninety miles up the Valley on Highway 99. Saxophonist Octavio "Elmer" García had started the GGs Orchestra back in Mercedes, Texas, in 1950, before he moved the family permanently to California ten years later, in search of better job opportunities. It was a family band—Octavio on reeds; his son Beto, now the bandleader, on trumpet; another son, Alonso, on piano-accordion; his daughter María on electric bass; and I on guitar. Carlos Almaraz, another tejano expatri-ate, played the drums. We had arrived home in suburban Wrangler City, where wholesome Western values were "a way of life," at 3:00 A.M., and by 6:30 in the morning we were at the Crestview Ranch, where we would toil for the next ten hours, less a thirty-minute recess for lunch.

Despite his sweat-soaked face, Octavio looked none the worse for the late hours he had kept that weekend. When he heard the time announced on the radio, he paused, reached into his overalls, and pulled out the pocket watch Esteban had given him, to check it for accuracy. He nodded in satisfaction and put the watch back in its place, then he reached for the canteen hooked to a loop on his overalls and took a long swig. Octavio did not like to drink from the fruit can the rest of us used to draw the stale drinking water from the Igloo barrel, so he usually brought his own. When I asked him, "¿Cómo te sientes?—how do you feel?" he looked at me through his horn-rimmed glasses with his owlish eyes. "Better 'n you," he replied, and then resumed his deliberate pace, all the while listening to his transistor radio. Despite his obesity, he was a remarkably sturdy man, who would play his saxophone with the GGs until he was eighty-five, and reach the age of ninety-four before death finally robbed the old patriarch of his indomitable will to live.

≡

He may have been poor, but Octavio García was no *animal de uña*, or "clawed beast," as middling-class Mexicans—the gente decente—referred to the lowly, and sometimes hell-raising, proletarians who toiled in the pits of agriculture in Texas and elsewhere. Besides his part-time career in music, Octavio had spent much of his working life switching between farm labor and the more respectable occupation of carpentry, and so he could not lay claim to a blue-blood pedigree. But his mother, Florencia Sáenz de García, a criollita who descended from good Spanish stock (rumor had it that the blood of Sephardic Jews flowed through her veins), was a woman of some education. She had been a teacher in her native Camargo, Tamaulipas, and she had inculcated the values of the gente decente in her oldest son. Those were the values handed down among the semi-educated descendants of the original settles of Nuevo Santander, who considered themselves people of good breeding.

Octavio absorbed from his mother the virtues of a "respectable" life-style, and, despite his lowly status as a farm worker, he struggled stubbornly to live up to the norms of the "decent people" he claimed as his peers. Perhaps nothing captured this discrepancy in Elmer's life more poignantly than the transformation that occurred on Friday nights. As usual, he would drag home from the orchards in his soiled work rags, but after a cool bath and lavish attention to toiletries, he would put on his slick GGs uniform. Ready to perform, he emerged a different man, the image of Elmer the downtrodden field hand banished from view, at least while he entertained the revelers who merrily danced to his music.

My father-in-law was born in 1901, in the town of Camargo, a leap and a jog south of the Rio Grande. Camargo was one of several *municipios* surviving from the days when Nuevo Santander, tucked in the northeastern corner of New Spain, was founded in the 1740s by don José de

Escandón and his band of colonists. The future patriarch was brought to the Rio Grande Valley in 1909, and he eventually became a naturalized American citizen. He lost his father, Bernabé García, shortly after the family arrived in Mercedes. The elder García was a victim of Texas Ranger "justice," shot in the head by one of the *rinches*, as the tejanos called the famed lawmen, while he was sitting in a cantina, unarmed and drinking with friends. No one knew why the Ranger sought out Bernabé and gunned him down, but Sulema, Esteban Treviño's wife and the oldest of Octavio's daughters, claimed the rinche was interested in his wife Florencia, and the only way he could have access to her was by rubbing out her husband. Whatever the Ranger's motives, the homicide took place in 1909, when tensions between Mexicans and Anglos ran high in South Texas. It was a time when the lords of the territory did not consider the killing of a Mexican as a particularly noteworthy event—especially when it happened at the hands of a Texas Ranger. No investigation followed the untimely death of Bernabé García.*

Although poor, Octavio García was perhaps typical of the more or less gentrified Border people of his generation—as was his wife, Eva Ayala. Both had deep roots in the lower Texas-Mexico Border area, and Octavio, in particular, had steadfastly maintained the norteño gentry's sense of *mexicanidad*, as this "Mexican" lifestyle was handed down through his maternal line. As Octavio and other norteños practiced it, mexicanidad included such social conventions as an abiding respect for one's elders, which went hand-in-hand with an exalted view of Mexico's imagined heritage, as personified by revolutionary father figures like the heroic pair Miguel Hidalgo and Benito Juárez. The norteño gentry's lifestyle promoted an observance of social propriety and good manners, ranging from personal and domestic orderliness to the proper forms of polite speech, as well as the tacit acceptance of men's superiority over women and the need to protect the "weaker" sex from its own folly. Also included was the valorization of large families as promulgated by Mexican Catholicism (and as epitomized by the Mexicans' "mother," the Virgin of Guadalupe). Octavio's sense of mexicanidad also harbored a somewhat fatalistic view of life, as embodied in the belief that fate is cruel and earthly happiness

*See don Américo Paredes's chilling account of Ranger "justice" against tejanos in his classic book, *With His Pistol in His Hand* (Austin: University of Texas Press, 1958, p. 27).

transitory—though this belief was tempered by a stoic grittiness toward life's adversities.

Yet another value of the norteño gentry that Octavio held was a romanticized memory of *el rancho*, one not so different from Americans' view of the ranch, where sturdy, virile men struggled against a capricious nature to earn their survival and learn the virtues of self-reliance and thrift. Indeed, at one time, during the Great Depression, Octavio and Eva had managed a five-acre ranchito outside Mercedes, where they raised various livestock and chickens for sale and barter. Set against this exalted view of hard *vaquero* work on the ranch, however, was a deeply held disdain on the part of the gente decente for stoop labor—especially wage farm labor—albeit in don Octavio's case this value had been deeply compromised by his lowly status. Finally, as a resident of the United States, and perhaps hoping to climb someday out of the economic cellar, Octavio had learned to speak English by attending American schools and actually going as far as the eighth grade. In this regard he had made at least one critical concession to the acculturative pressures coming from the dominant Anglo society: early on he cultivated a lifelong taste for American big-band music, of the Glenn Miller-Tommy Dorsey variety.

Eva Ayala had even less education than her husband, having gone only as far as the third grade in her native village of Los Herreras, Nuevo León, not far from the Texas border. Simple in her personal tastes and of humble disposition (except when provoked), she shared her husband's social decorum, self-respect, and attitudes regarding the proper order of things. But she differed from Octavio on two critical issues: her steadfast resistance to the pressures of Americanization, and her views on the rights and responsibilities of womenfolk, which were driven by her iron will. To put it bluntly, she refused to be subservient to male authority. Her fortitude was put to the test at least once, when the Garcías' home in their ranchito near Mercedes was invaded. Several men broke open the front door in an attempt to exact revenge on Octavio, who had won a small-claims suit against one of them. When the first intruder entered the house, doña Eva greeted him with a blast from the family shotgun, blowing away one of his knees. Octavio, meanwhile, was cowering in the bedroom, afraid to confront his enemies. His assistance was not needed, however; the invaders did not stay around for a second discharge from Eva's shotgun.

Octavio and Eva Garcia, Mexico City, 1940s

Thus, while she tacitly acceded to Octavio's role as head of the García family, Eva Ayala reserved the power to take matters into her own hands and, when necessary, to contest any important domestic decision. And most emphatically, she was not about to tolerate any semblance of abuse from her husband. Once, knife in hand, she confronted Octavio and chased him out of the house when she found out he was messing with another woman. *"Te mato, hijo'e la chingada*—I'll kill you, son-of-a-fucked one," she threatened. Doña Eva's strong character, allegiance to the middling-class values of the *gente decente*, and her dogged determination to raise respectable children served the younger Garcías well as they struggled to find an acceptable place in American society.

Octavio and Eva's children followed their parents' examples, in particular that of the patriarch, and sharing his intense cultural pride, they were loath to find themselves at the bottom of the social ladder. More Americanized than their father, they worked hard to climb out of their poverty, and every one of the seven children born of Octavio García and Eva Ayala succeeded in rising above the indignity of farm labor, much to the satisfaction and pride of the matriarch. But Octavio, who lived most of his life in a world still ruled by prejudice against his people, never had the opportunity to climb that ladder, although his eighth-grade education was an undeniable achievement for someone of his generation. And so, while one by one his children struggled out of the hard poverty he had bequeathed them, Octavio himself endured the shame of manual labor all of his productive life, especially in California, where he had been migrating since the mid-forties to labor in the fields. He was, as Francisco Peña would say, an ox at the plow, exploited and pushed this way and that by the growers who hired him as an expendable piece of brute labor power.

≣

Now deep into his retirement, his sad, owlish eyes gazing into the distance, Elmer still vividly recalled the days when he toiled for growers like Pete Roswell, who watched hawk-like over his laborers with high-powered binoculars, lest they slack off and cost the patrón precious wages for unperformed labor.

"We used to work even more hours than people do now," he was recalling, in his unflappably calm, basso voice, "eleven, twelve hours a day. And Roswell watched every move we made, except when he was distracted by some other business. We didn't get a break until noon, and, since we started so early, by ten o'clock we could get pretty hungry. So one day, we couldn't see him anywhere, and we were all so hungry, see, and we each pulled out a taco from our pocket and stopped to eat while we stood on the ladders. We were pruning a peach orchard. It was the dead of winter, and cold as a freezer. A little while later, Señor Roswell came around and said, 'You, you, and you—you're fired. *No comer en trabajo.*' He had hid somewhere and was spying on us with his binoculars all the while we were eating. But he didn't fire me; I never knew why. Maybe he didn't see me eating."

"Did he have any trouble replacing the workers he lost?"

"*N'hombre, cállate,*" Elmer could now say with a sardonic laugh about those bitter days. "Those were hard times—no welfare or any kind of government help, you know—when la gente was hungry and desperate for work. The Roswells and the Stuttgarts could afford to push us around any way they wanted."

He had pulled out the pocket watch Esteban had given him years before he died of cancer—the watch with the dent on the back plate, where a bullet from a German soldier's rifle, aimed at Esteban, had boomeranged while the two infantrymen fought face to face in a battle during World War II. Stroking the smooth glass face of the watch, Octavio became pensive as his mind wandered back into the mists of time, when fortunes were being amassed in the San Joaquin Valley—fortunes made possible by the sweat of workers like Octavio García and Esteban Treviño.

Esteban Treviño was a lamb of God—or at least as close to sainthood as any mortal I have ever known. Gentle as a summer evening's breeze, Esteban had only two goals in life: to love his wife Sulema and to toil as hard as he could to deliver his children from the grinding poverty that had been his lot. A native of the Rio Grande Valley, he was a quiet, self-effacing man who did not speak much, and when he did, it was always in a low, almost plaintive voice. "My husband never raised his voice at anyone," the fiercely articulate Sulema often recalled, with a tone of sadness in her voice. "People took advantage of him, because he was poor, and because he was a humble Mexican.

"Once, we were working in the cotton fields of Huron, and he got sick, and they had to take out a kidney at the Veterans' hospital. We were living in a migrant camp, in a one-room tin shack, hot as an inferno—Esteban, myself, and all the kids, and my husband was convalescing. It was right at the end of the harvest, and the *migra* raided the camp at dawn, and they pulled Esteban out of bed, and the wound from the operation opened up and began to bleed, because they were dragging him around as if he were a sack of potatoes. They were going to deport him. 'We're gonna send you back to Mexico, wetback,' one of them said to him, in a real spiteful voice, like he was some kind of criminal. 'He's an American!' I yelled at them, 'Let him go! He's a veteran of the war; he is sick; he was just operated on at the Veterans' Hospital!' But they wouldn't listen to me, and they kept dragging him toward the paddy wagon, where they were loading the mojaditos. I rushed into the shack and started looking frantically for his papers—anything to prove to them that he was an American. I found his discharge papers, I think, and threw them at the migra agent. 'Here are his papers,' I told him, 'Is this the kind of treatment he deserves? This man risked his life so you could be safe in your homes.' I was so angry."

Her eyes red and misty with chronic rage, Sulema continued, "They finally let him go, but that's how they treated us—all because my husband was a meek little Mexican. I remember, just before he died, he gripped my hand and said, 'I only regret that I never amounted to anything in this life.' There were tears in his eyes, my poor Esteban, and I told him, 'You worked like an ox all your life, and you supported our children, and we have educated all of them. You have nothing to be ashamed of.'"

Octavio was still deep in thought as he stroked his late son-in-law's pocket watch. We were sitting in the plastic lawn chairs on the front porch of his little stucco house—the one he and Eva had bought when they moved from Mercedes, Texas, to Wrangler City, with the money from the sale of the five-acre ranchito.

After a long pause, he finally spoke: "We used to work at Ponderosa Ranch; Stuttgart owned it by then. He was no big thing in those days, nothing like the giant outfit they have now. There was a *campito*—a row of tin-roofed shacks, one-room shacks. Mostly people from Mexico lived in them—mojaditos, you know, 'wetbacks.' I think there were only two or three families from Texas. We lived in the last one, right by the fig orchard. And Stuttgart kept back a certain percentage of the wages until the end of the harvest, when we were all supposed to be paid in full. He did it—or so we were told—to make sure the workers didn't just take off and leave in the middle of the harvest. But I remember this one year—1949, I think it was. When we were just about finished, the migra raided the campito and took all the illegals with them and deported them to Mexico. Just before the end of the harvest, and all these mojaditos were deported, and they never got the wages they had coming to them. That's how Stuttgart made his fortune. Roswell and the other growers did the same. And now, you know, they're all big shots in the community—big donors at your university and for this and that. But they made their fortunes by robbing the Mexican workers of their wages."

≋

It was the last paycheck he would earn working at Crestview Ranch. I gave Octavio a ride that day to pick it up because the water pump in his 1960 Chevy station wagon was broken down. Nothing much seemed to have changed since the last day I had worked there, in 1965, except that the old crew leader, don Erasmo de la Garza, had died (as had Esteban Treviño), and one of don Erasmo's sons had taken his place. But everything else seemed the same—the pungent smell of rotting peaches littering the muddy rows of trees; workers climbing up and down the twelve-foot wooden ladders that creaked with the weight of men and their loaded buckets; the heavy thud of the tractor engine as it lurched forward, pulling the flatbed trailer with the bins; the steamy atmosphere of the irrigated orchard, reminiscent of a sauna; and, of course, the sprawling dry yard at the center of the "Garden of Eden," where María and Eva had once cut peaches while Octavio and I lay them out to dry. On this day, a dozen or so women were hunched over the cutting machines under the open-air shed, while an equal number of men placed the trays loaded with sliced peaches on the hot asphalt top. It was September of 1972, Octavio was only days away from his seventy-first birthday, and he had been forced to quit working.

"The doctor told me the skin cancer was going to get worse if I kept working in the sun," he was telling me. His ruddy face was blemished with scars now—some new and still raw, some old and scabby—from the skin cancers the doctor had burned. But even at age seventy-one, *canas* (gray hairs) were sparse in his rich, dark head of hair. "So I guess this is it. I didn't have your education, and all my life I've had to work, as my *compadre*—your father—said, like an ox at the plow. But this is it, Meme, this year's it for this ox. No more pizca, no more *chinga* [back-breaking toil] for this beast of burden—too old now, and too worn-out."

As we pulled into the heart of the orchard, where the dry yard, tractor and utility sheds, and general foreman's house were located, Octavio and I turned and exchanged glances briefly. Catching sight of the women hunched over the cutting machines in the open-air shed and the men placing the trays loaded with sliced peaches on the broiling asphalt top, we both seemed to be experiencing the same *déjà vu*, momentarily reliving the days when we had labored under identical conditions. More significant for the two of us, here in this sprawling "Garden of Eden," our careers as beasts of burden had come to an end. For him the time was now; for me it had been seven years before, when I, too, had collected my last check. Unaware that it would be my last summer in the orchards, I had stood in line, waiting to pick up both María's paycheck and mine, fully expecting to return for the next summer's harvest. I did not, as I finally summoned the courage to try my hand at teaching guitar; and still later, other occupations would become available—as social worker, youth counselor, and eventually, with Ph.D. in hand, as university professor.

And so, with no fanfare or celebration, I had thrown off the yoke that for years had confined me to the orchards of misery. I had cast off forever the emblem that had long identified the Peña lineage: the ox at the plow. But when I stood in line that September day in 1965—my birthday, coincidentally—I did not know that the day previous had marked the last time I would work with my hands in the soil and the sweat in my eyes.

POSTSCRIPT

I was visiting Silverio M.'s crew today, when one of the patrones showed up. Word of his arrival spread quickly through the orchard as soon as his truck pulled up: "¡Ahi viene l'agua, ahi viene l'agua! [here comes the 'rain,' i.e., trouble]." He was fuming. Too much good fruit was being left on the trees, too much was bruised, and the pace was too slow. As he darted from one tree to another, he barked orders in his broken Spanish: "Watch the color, watch the color! Don't bruise the fruit! "Apúrele, pronto." The workers scurried about with their ladders, noticeably quickening the pace of picking. After a few minutes hassling the men, the patrón walked up to me. "You have to put a little fear in their hearts once in a while," he confided, "otherwise production slacks off." Not much had changed since the days I had toiled in these very same orchards.

—Manuel Peña, "Writing Mexican Worker Culture:
Folklore, Machismo and Everyday Practice"

In 1986, now armed with a Ph.D. in anthropology and fully transformed into the man of letters Papa had once foreseen, I returned to Crestview Ranch to harvest—not peaches this time, but the folklore of another generation of oxen at the plow.* By then, however, most tejano expatriates had graduated to better jobs outside of agriculture. The new laborers were almost all undocumented male fuereños from West-Central Mexico. And, like their tejano predecessors, they were, without exception, uneducated and impoverished.

In a new, "postmodern" world, celebrated by many as irrevocably driven by high technology and a mobile and affluent work force, the microcosm in which the farm workers at Crestview Ranch labored formed a bizarre intersection of two incongruous cultural economies. One, represented by the culture and work routine of the men themselves—unskilled and decidedly low-tech—seemed singularly archaic and "dismodern" (rather than postmodern); the other, symbolized by the high-speed computers in the ranch's corporate office, testified to the global reach of American agriculture in postmodernist "late capitalism." Ironically, even as they labored in the most degrading of conditions and earned wages that barely sustained them, the workers were thoroughly convinced that their employers could not possibly afford to pay so many of them (five hundred, at the peak of the harvest). They consequently believed that the patrones must resort to drug smuggling to meet payroll demands.

As I moved among my "informants" (as anthropologists used to call "the natives"), I realized that in the bowels of this "Garden of Eden," the ox-at-the-plow metaphor was still vividly evoked. The workers' predicament was a reminder to me of the long road my people had yet to travel before they could reach the elusive "realm of freedom" for which so many members of my generation—the militant Chicano Generation—had agitated. Remembering the walkouts, demonstrations, pickets, boycotts, and other concerted political activity on behalf of farm workers, I wondered: was escape from the crippling fields ultimately possible for these, my Mexican brothers, in a society which still saw them as suitable only for sweat labor?

---

*Please see my articles, "Class, Gender and Machismo" (*Gender & Society* 5[1]: 1991) and "Writing Mexican Worker Culture: Folklore, Machismo and Everyday Practice" (*Western Folklore* 65 [1 & 2]: 2006).

19
BALLAD OF A CHICANO
(The Ox Buries His Yoke)

The Americans were coming,
They were whiter than a dove,
from the fear they had
of Cortez and his gun.

Gregorio Cortez was saying
with his pistol in his hand:
"Don't run, you
cowardly rangers
from just one Mexican."

"The Ballad of Gregorio Cortez"
(early twentieth century)

The present-day Chicano . . . is very much involved in
demanding his rights as an American citizen, but he also
exhibits a high regard for Mexican customs and traditions.
These concerns are manifest in a revived interest in his folk and
popular culture, especially in the folk ballads of the past.
—Américo Paredes, *A Texas-Mexican Cancionero* (1976)

You hurried up the musty stairs in the old administration building, and when you reached the third floor, you felt short of breath—not from exhaustion but from nervous agitation. You had been mulling over the interview awaiting you at two o'clock this afternoon for some time, and although you had promised not to get worked up about the ordeal, you had been unable to dispel the queasiness in your gut. But you couldn't quite put your finger on just what it was that unnerved you about meeting with these young "Chicanos" at Fresno City College. Your heart was racing by the time you walked down the long hall to the small office where the students were waiting for you.

By now you knew about the "Chicano Movement," and you had seen students who called themselves "Chicano" protest on behalf of César Chávez's farm workers and other causes. But they seemed so, well, angry and militantly anti-American. And they flaunted their Chicanismo with zealous arrogance, as if their slant on what a Chicano should be was the only acceptable way to express pride in one's Mexican roots. Their attitude offended you, in a way you could not quite explain, other than as an intuition that their valorization of the indígena *roots of Mexican culture was as superficial as it was misplaced. But you had only observed them from the sidelines, so to speak, and you had never been called upon to confront their strident cultural style. Until now.*

It was your friend Arroyo who set you up for the job interview. He had liked your personal style ever since he interviewed you for the job as counselor for the Neighborhood Youth Corps. The interview itself was an interesting sequel to your recent experiences at the Welfare Department. You had been pressured to resign from your job as a case worker for advocating too vigorously for the rights of farm worker applicants. It was all very fresh in your memory, the whole series of events still provoking anxiety mixed with satisfaction. Several unemployed workers had been denied welfare assistance, and they had complained bitterly to you. With their permission, you had taken their cases to Steve Gold, lawyer for Fresno Legal Services, an advocate for poor people. When your supervisor found out about your actions, you had been given an ultimatum: stop rabble-rousing or resign. You chose the latter, and eventually all the applicants won their appeals.

In a stroke of good fortune, one of the appellants was a farm worker who happened to be on the commission that oversaw the operations of the local anti-poverty agency, which was, like Legal Services, a product of Lyndon Johnson's "War on Poverty" initiatives. When he learned you had been squeezed out of your job at the Welfare office, he suggested you apply for the opening at NYC. "I'm on the personnel committee," he said, "and my friend Arroyo's the chair. I can work on him, and he can work on the others."

The interview had gone well, and you were offered the position as counselor. Arroyo had been persuaded by your presentation and, especially, by your stand against the Welfare Department's campaign against the campesinos. *He was so impressed that, when an opening for a student counselor position came up at Fresno City College in the Educational*

Opportunity Program (another of LBJ's "War on Poverty" initiatives), he urged you to apply. He was the Program director.

"This is where you belong, Manuel," he said. "I think you can make a real contribution at City College. The only thing you'll need to do is come in for an interview with our *comité. It's an advisory committee made up of students. We're democratic here, and we believe in giving students a voice in the hiring process. I don't think you'll have any problems.*"

Why do I feel so upset, as if my whole life were being turned upside-down? Here come those Chicano students again, marching and carrying those angry flags with the black eagle screaming against the blood-red background. *"¡Que viva la causa! ¡Que viva la raza!"* I hear their defiant voices, and they sound like hammers in my head. Somewhere, deep down, I feel as if I should share their anger and be out on the street marching with them, but I'm a responsible, law-abiding American, and I can't stomach their protesting. I'm standing with my music classmates, and some of them are openly taunting the marchers. The lovely Kathie is saying something to the girl standing next to her. Yes, I can make out her words: "They're communists, you know, they're communist sympathizers. They want to destroy our country, starting with the farmers." And she had been so friendly with me. What would she think of me if I told her, "I know why they're demonstrating. I've slaved in your farmers' orchards and vineyards. I know what it's like." She could never understand. Even I can't understand what's going on anymore.

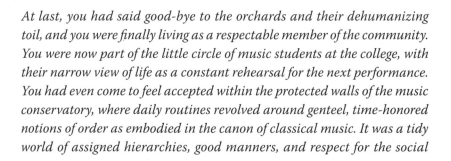

At last, you had said good-bye to the orchards and their dehumanizing toil, and you were finally living as a respectable member of the community. You were now part of the little circle of music students at the college, with their narrow view of life as a constant rehearsal for the next performance. You had even come to feel accepted within the protected walls of the music conservatory, where daily routines revolved around genteel, time-honored notions of order as embodied in the canon of classical music. It was a tidy world of assigned hierarchies, good manners, and respect for the social

130 } *Where the Ox Does Not Plow*

and political institutions that made possible the recreation of the now-sacrosanct canon—the music of Bach, Mozart, Beethoven, Brahms. These were the venerated icons who represented the highest cultural and aesthetic ideals of Western society.

Some of your classmates were actually friendly to you, although you couldn't help feeling a bit put off when they needled you about the "Mexican accent" that crept into your spoken English, or when they reminded you of your Indian features. But there were only two or three Mexican students in the music department, and perhaps forty or fifty in the whole college, and that suited you fine. In a tacit, self-defensive way, you hoped the minuscule presence of the brown students would go unnoticed, and that they would quietly melt into the sea of white faces. Your peers' middle-American life-style seemed the perfect haven after all those years of living at the margins, and you had come to share your new classmates' unspoken pride in the core American values embodied in hard work, civil manners, obedience to authority, and deep respect for American democracy. For the first time in your life, you were actually living the lifestyle your teachers had subtly inculcated in you from the first day you set foot in Edroy Elementary. This whole way of life seemed so uplifting, and so remote from the brutalizing effects of the campañas from which you had finally escaped. Comfortable with your new status, you had drifted into the social and political complacency of the conservatory.

But that complacency was short-lived. Doubts about your political acquiescence and disinclination to question the "American way" first surfaced in 1966, when the blacks set Watts on fire. José was visiting you one day when the news came on, blaring out the latest in a series of African American insurrections. Graphic video footage of the burning buildings in the black neighborhoods of Los Angeles lit up the screen. "Burn, baby, burn," said José, as he took in the fiery scenes, while drawing out the words in a slow sneer. It was the slogan militant blacks had adopted in their crusade of violence against the white society that for centuries had denied them their humanity. "José," you protested, "those people are engaged in some pretty violent stuff. How can you approve of that?"

"Burn, baby, burn," repeated your brother, his words dripping with perverse pleasure at the conflagration exploding on the screen. "There he goes again," you thought of your rebellious brother. "I'm sure no one in the Peña family would ever condone the kind of senseless burning taking *place in Watts." Except José. Of course, you argued with him, the blacks are oppressed, but there are other, less violent, means of bringing about progress. "Burn, baby, burn," repeated José, now in a kind of mock trance. "There's no other way,* carnal," *he finally added. "The nigguhs are gonna burn down your America."*

At that moment you suddenly disliked your brother. Something about his defiant tone rattled you, triggering feelings you wished to keep repressed and evoking images of a time when you had been at the receiving end of oppression, and when you, too, had experienced the urge to burn down America. But such thoughts seemed horrifying now, especially since you were finally beginning to share, however meagerly, in the bounty for which you had worked so hard for so many of your youthful years. To put it bluntly, you felt like a true native son of America, at last, and José's violent words put you on the defensive.

≡

As you drove to your appointment at City College, your mind wandered back to that still-vivid scene in 1968, when the Chicano students had marched at Cal State in support of César Chávez. You recalled the open disdain some of your fellow students had expressed for your brothers and sisters, taunting them as they marched by the music building. Your class-mates were not particularly "political," at least in the sense that they would ever have questioned the way governmental and civic institutions pro-duced and reproduced the social order. But their patriotic instincts seemed to have been stirred by the overt challenge posed by the Chicano militants to America's democratic order, and they openly voiced their displeasure. As you looked into their faces, you knew what the music students were thinking: what are these Mexicans doing, demonstrating? We let them into America, didn't we? They should be grateful to this great country for the opportunities it offers them, but instead, they are trying to tear it down. You wondered if they thought of your example—the scrappy little Mexican who had worked hard and earned his place among the "silent majority" who did not complain, demonstrate, or criticize their great country.

Yet even as you reflected on the good life you now enjoyed and on your identification with these young, patriotic men and women, deep down you knew something was askew, and the presence of the Chicano marchers was a reminder of a repressed anger hiding deep in the recesses of your Mexican core.

It was inevitable, perhaps, that your newfound attachment to "mainstream" America would sooner or later come unhinged. The Chicano protesters and the continuing farm-labor strife, daily headlined in the local news, were visceral reminders of the life you had lived in the not-too-distant past, and whatever peace of mind the dignified setting of the music department had afforded of late, the turmoil on the TV kept jarring your tranquility. The black insurrection, the war in Vietnam, the hippie and war resistance demonstrations, the Kent State shootings, the Chicago Seven, the budding Chicano Movement—all kept intruding into your consciousness as you tried to attend to the business of getting a degree to support your wife and first child and to move up in life.

But try as you might to shut out the turmoil around you, you could not ignore the violent fissures tearing the nation apart, pitting the radical voices demanding change against the conservatives who fiercely defended the old ways. You instinctively sided with the radicals—or at least their progressive sympathizers—because you knew the old ways were those of white privilege and harsh times for your people. Besides, you had long been taught at home that "liberals" were the only Americans who cared about minorities. Yet you could not get yourself to come down on the side of the voices for change, because a part of you clung stubbornly to the lessons you had been taught in school. Defend American democracy, your teachers had impressed upon you, and its equality for all. Cherish individual initiative, and remember the importance of hard work and honest living. Obey authority, and respect our hard-won American institutions. Adherence to these time-honored principles, you were taught, would be rewarded with success, happiness, and the good life.

The good life: after all those years of struggle and frustration, it seemed to be within your grasp, and you didn't want to sacrifice it for some crazy revolutionary slogan like "Burn, baby, burn" or "¡Que viva la raza!" Torn between the radicals and the conservatives, you took a moderate stance, paying lip service to the ideas of civil rights and change, but favoring a "go-slow" approach.

Then you found yourself graduated, and suddenly, you were outside the protected walls of the music department, with its distinctly conservative and elitist culture. You ended up working at the Welfare office, where you quickly confronted, in the faces of the bedraggled poor, the past you had left behind. Your new friends at Welfare, a group of hippie-styled discontents, influenced you. They were an unconventional lot—Kitt Whitby, Bob Slice, Carrie Rosca, Rhonda Kreveck—social and cultural rebels whose quixotic irreverence toward the "Establishment" offered a powerful, almost subversive, alternative to the orthodox values of conventional, everyday Americans. Many of the line workers in the Welfare office shared your friends' rebellious behavior, in sharp contrast to the older supervisory staff, who were much more ingrained in the ways of institutionalized morality—"honesty," "hard work," "thrift," "self-discipline." That staff and the whole welfare system had become the symbolic targets of the workers' disdain for orthodox American morality. Slowly, your radical friends began to erode the veneer of genteel conservatism you had absorbed in the music conservatory, even as they reawakened your basic distrust of American institutions.

At first, you resisted your workmates' alienated voices, their cynical views of capitalist democracy, and their hedonistic radicalism with its drug culture and contempt for traditional American sobriety. But you grudgingly admired their unconventional lifestyle, and when you discovered some of them were gay, you felt a stronger attachment toward them, not because you shared their sexual orientation, but because their status as moral outcasts resonated strongly with your own sense of alienation. In time, you became more and more like Kitt and his friends, and, like them, you became a rebel working within a system you saw as callous and morally corrupt. You were deeply offended by the Department's treatment of the broken spirits who day in and day out flooded the intake office where you worked. They were subjected to the most intense and degrading personal scrutiny imaginable before they were approved for, or denied, public assistance. Your anger grew daily, the more you participated in the degradation of the poor, especially your own people.

But yours was a sullen, passive form of resistance. Like your new friends, you had no specific politics of social redemption, and your anger was transformed into existential angst. (Camus, Sartre, and Ionesco were the literary models most in harmony with your state of mind, as was Freud, especially in his Civilization and its Discontents.*) You took no part in the demonstrations and other acts of resistance exploding all around you. And still troubling you, though you knew not why, was the attitude of* *the young Chicanos who were becoming increasingly more militant in their claims to be the true representatives of your heritage.*

Disillusioned, in the end, by the brutal power of the welfare system, you mounted your own little act of sabotage, which ultimately cost you your job. You then fled to the more progressive atmosphere of the Neighborhood Youth Corps. But socially reprogramming the young, alienated, and mostly black and Chicano dropouts who were your wards at the NYC was a dispiriting effort. No one wanted them—not the schools, not the employers, and certainly not the community at large—and you felt as if you were stuck in the ruts of a system oblivious to the plight of these outcast children. Images of your Texas past kept haunting you—images of children in the barren fields who had also been pushed further and further into the margins by an educational bureaucracy seemingly designed to keep them, as one Anglo superintendent put it, "on their knees in a cotton patch." The job Arroyo offered seemed like a welcome escape from the thankless task you faced as counselor to the youthful pariahs.

Except that you were not yet ready for the Chicano militants awaiting you, and the deep spiritual wounds they were about to inflict.

≡

You lingered outside the closed office door for what seemed an eternity, but the long-haired young man, dressed in well-worn bell-bottom jeans and Che Guevara T-shirt, finally emerged and beckoned you to follow him. He was decidedly curt, and you immediately disliked him. You were put off by his manner, which tightened the tension building in your gut even more.

Once inside the cramped office, the first object to catch your attention was an oversized poster of a young Chicano dressed in military-style fatigues and a black beret. He stood out against the silhouettes of a crowd on the march, red flags featuring the farm workers' black-eagle emblem waving in the air. The poster reminded you of the garish billboards you had often seen on the sidewalk outside Benitez' Teatro Nacional on Texas Avenue back home in Weslaco. Drawn in stark, angular lines and bold colors, the billboards advertised the latest flicks showing in Weslaco's own Mexican theater. The young Chicano's face dominated the poster, its features drawn, billboard style, in strong, jagged lines. His mouth was open as if he were in the process of screaming his defiance, giving him a menacing appearance. He seemed ready to do violence. Serving as an exclamation point were the words emblazoned in black at the bottom of the depicted scene: "¡QUE VIVA LA RAZA!"

The comité consisted of five young men, all wearing shoulder-length hair, Emiliano Zapata mustaches, and stern brown faces. They sat casually in metal chairs around a small conference table. Their long hair and mustaches, their revolutionary T-shirts adorned with UFW pins and other movimiento *trinkets, and their air of militancy gave them a belligerent look, as if they had all been cloned from the same radical Chicano-hippie model. Their whole manner of dress and comportment seemed the epitome of the urban-guerilla-revolution style, and you felt intimidated. After they all greeted you with the obligatory Chicano handshake (the conventional clasp, followed by the locking of fists, and then the clasp again), the comité chair asked you to sit down while he and the others took another glance at your letter of application. Finally, the leader put down the letter and, stroking his bold mustache, he asked the first question.*

"Can you tell us what activities you've been involved in to help the Chicano community?"

Somehow, you knew this was going to be the first question asked, and you had been rehearsing your answer. "Well," you replied, trying to remain as cool as possible, "I haven't been marching in the streets, but I got fired at the Welfare department for trying to help farm workers." You had felt good about your actions in the Welfare office; they were the most altruistic acts you had ever engaged in, but they sounded self-serving now, and you knew the students were not impressed. There was an uncomfortable moment of silence, and, feeling a need to redeem yourself, you spoke out: "Look, I may not go around shouting, 'I am Chicano!' but in my own way I have tried to help my people. I know where my roots are."

The student leader pressed on:

"Have you heard of MECHA—Movimiento Estudiantil Chicano de Aztlán?"

"MECHA? No, I'm afraid I haven't."

"Do you know about MAYO [Mexican American Youth Organization], or UMAS [United Mexican American Students]?"

"No, I guess not."

"What about El Plan de Aztlán? Are you familiar with that?"

"I'm sorry, I don't—look, it's been some time since I finished school, and

I've been out in the world, trying to make a living and support a family. I guess I'm not up on what's going on at college campuses."

"Hm, hm. Have you heard of El Plan de Santa Barbara?"

The whole interview seemed to have turned into an interrogation, and the questions disturbed you and threw you off balance, especially since you could almost feel their contempt for your ignorance of things that were obviously important to them. You regretted never having filled out the application you had received to join the Mexican American Political Association, since that, at least, would have given you a measure of political legitimacy. The silence following each question was unbearable. The high-pitched hoarseness the speech therapist had told you was the result of tense throat muscles had almost paralyzed you, making it obvious you were flustered.

And still they probed:

"Have you ever marched with the farm workers?"

"I haven't. Look, I may not be aware of some of these things you're asking me, but I believe I have the background and sensitivity to help Chicano students."

The leader looked at you thoughtfully, and for a moment he seemed detached. Then he spoke, with a tone of conviction:

"We don't question your sincerity. But an awareness of el movimiento is important in understanding what we're trying to do. We need someone who understands the oppression of Chicanos. The jive about assimilation and equal rights for all Americans is gabacho propaganda. That stuff about Chicanos earning their rights fighting in World War II and Korea—that was puro pedo [bullshit]. We know the Chicano is no better off today than he was twenty years ago. Look at what happened at the Chicano Moratorium, in Los Angeles; look at what's happening everywhere, with our carnalitos, and the way they're being pushed out of the schools. LULAC tried to accommodate the gabacho, and so did the G.I. Forum, but accommodation doesn't work. The only way we are going to take control of our lives and reclaim Aztlán and our cultura is by involvement in la causa—by confronting the gabacho. And we need individuals with commitment, who are aware and willing to work for the community by doing whatever it takes to liberate our gente."

His words tore into your soul like hot lances, and you felt anger and guilt and then resignation. You looked at the five young Chicanos out

Student protesters, 1975. Courtesy Manuel and Lupe Olgin.

of your wounded ego, and you wondered whether they were capable of
expressing love and joy. Their unrelentingly harsh faces seemed incongru-
ous with their youth, their chronic anger beyond healing.

　　"Have you heard of the Crusade for Justice?"

　　"No. I'm sorry, I guess—no I'm afraid I haven't. . . ."

Waiting impatiently for the red light to change, random thoughts racing
through my mind. MECHA . . . MECHA . . . MECHA. . . . AZTLÁN . . .
AZTLÁN . . . AZTLÁN. The angry slogans jab at my heart like obscene
gestures. I am Chicano, I am AZTLÁN! *¡Yo soy Chicano! Ustedes son*
Chicanos. Vosotros sois Chicanos. ¡No! Son pochos, cabrones. ¡Hijos de la
Chingada! POCHOS . . . POCHOS . . . POCHOS. . . . We are all Chicanos,
Pochos—cultural bastards, *hijos de la chingada.* Members, all of us, of that
bastardhood Carlos Fuentes christened the order of *LA CHINGADA—*

sons of the fucked one, sons of the Indian mother. *CHINGADA*—the bastard snake-of-a-word that coils around our Chicanismo and imprisons us in its folds. Can we ever free ourselves from its poisonous influence?

Their word. My word. Our mother-fucking word. Today, they *chíngale* me with their self-righteous pronouncements, and their assault on my ethnic credentials, but tonight, in my drunkenness I will vent my wrath on these self-appointed crusaders for Chicanismo: *¡Vayan mucho a chingar su madre, cabrones!*

Why are you so angry, Memito?

Because their mightier-than-thou ethnic display offended me, godammit. It was self-centered and arrogant, and it's an affront to my people's custom of humility and courtesy. And, besides, I have as much right as they do to being a Chicano. Hell, when I first came to California these vatos couldn't even speak Spanish. *¿Y sabes qué?* At home in the Rio Grande Valley we already called ourselves "chicano," when these *californios* were still "Spanish." Hell, even the super-Chicano poet, Ricardo Sánchez, called my valley a "Cauldron of Chicanismo." But we didn't flaunt it, we didn't shout it from rooftops, and we had no need for fuckin' trinkets or pretentious handshakes. And one more thing: I lived through the kind of poverty these punks can't even imagine.

But I was also a good American, and I mastered English, even as I retained my flawless command of Spanish, and I pulled myself up by my *guarache* straps and became educated. And I learned to appreciate Beethoven and Strauss (Richard, s'il vous plait!), and I read TRB's liberal views and argued with my intellectual friends that all human activities are reducible to a struggle between the ego and the id. Can these fuckers do that? And they had the gall to question my identity and my "commitment": "We need someone who is aware, *ese*." *Puta burra*, what do those punks know of "awareness?"

No, my man, that's not why you're angry. You're angry because the very reason for our existence has been questioned by these young vatos. Their unshakeable righteousness has shattered our complacency, hasn't it? And let's face it, they've exposed the madness lurking beneath this docile face we've used to maneuver among white Amerika. You know the madness well; it's the pounding in the skull, and the fire in the bowels that our hero James Baldwin described so well. Yes, that's why we wept when we read that passage, and why, like Baldwin, we knew that once we had experienced the raging fire in our gut we would never again be innocent bystanders in the pillaging of our identity.

And now, these young militants have jarred you out of your self-satisfaction. They have shone the light of consciousness on you, and shaken your faith in the gabacho and his corrupt system. You have come to a dreadful realization: You have been living a deception. Yes, yours is a counterfeit identity, Memito, foisted upon you by Anglo-Amerika. Unwittingly, you have been a participant in the assault on your ancestral identity. Let me refresh your memory.

Leave me alone! That voice I hear—it's not my voice. It lives inside me, and I hear it constantly, but it's an alien presence. I'm tired of struggling with it. Who is it? How can I silence it?

Listen to me, Memito. I am the voice of your past. Once we were one voice, one being, in harmony with our ancestors. But your true identity has been stolen, hidden from you by the gabacho masters who waged an incessant campaign against your ethnic birthright, while I was exiled to the purgatory of your consciousness. That campaign began with your well-intentioned teachers, who sought to transform you into a patriotic American, thereby turning you against your heritage. You remember those principals, Mr. Turner and Mr. West, who were so zealous they resorted to extreme measures in guaranteeing your transformation—punishing you physically for speaking Spanish on the sacred grounds of their schools, as if that tongue were an agent of defilement and you its dirty instrument.

And today, your memory relives those bitter but repressed moments, when your teachers stood in front of the class, letting slip their contempt for your people even as they celebrated their own heroes—Sam Houston, Davy Crockett, Jim Bowie. And they barely concealed their scorn when they sneered at General Santa Ana's stupidity (caught napping and captured by the heroic Houston, thus ensuring freedom for Texas), while you could only laugh in resignation, as the teachers kept right on demonizing Santa Ana and his minions. Long live Sam Houston! Long live Davy Crockett! Down with the tyrant Santa Ana! Down with Mexicans!

No one told you, of course, that Davy Crockett and Jim Bowie were ruffians, and that Houston was a jingoist bent on capturing Texas from Mexico from the first moment he stepped on Texas soil—the first in a tide of illegal aliens from Amerika who overwhelmed the Texas-Mexicans. And no one told you of the theft of Mexican lands by thugs like Mifflin

Kenedy and Richard King (remember the mighty King Ranch?). Nor was there a trace in the history books about the reign of terror inflicted on the tejanos by the hated rinches. *The rinches. Yes, they were the shock troops employed by the gringos to soften Mexican resistance against the Kings, the Kenedys, and all those who came, not to share your land but to possess it. You were not aware, then, that the gringo's land, on which your family toiled from sunup to sundown, had once belonged to your ancestors. No one told you that bitter truth—not even your own father, for his own outrage had grown numb from exhaustion and self-denial.*

And you—in your desperation to be Amerikan, you had denied your birthright, and your real identity was banished to those corners of your mind where the traces of a distant childhood yet flickered—faint reminders of that other reality, the world of your ancestors. There, in that childhood, you listened, enthralled, to the stories Papa told you, such as the one about the Creek of the Cannons and the one about Gregorio Cortez, the Rangers' nemesis. You had relished Mama's guisados, tacos de frijoles, and all the foods that nourished your Mexican roots, while you listened and became part of the music of your people—the corridos, Lydia Mendoza's canciones, Narciso Martínez's conjunto polcas, Los Montañeses del Alamo. In that childhood, you had learned to read Spanish while listening to Papa read out loud El Heraldo de Brownsville, *and then you had learned that other language, English. "Made in USA"—those were the first words you decoded, and you thought "USA" meant "used," completely innocent of the way the USA was using and abusing your people. Life was a stream of innocent experiences then—the daily lessons of survival, still under the guidance of your parents, still in the ways of your ancestors.*

You could not have known then that the ways of those ancestors were already under siege by the Amerikan invaders. Your parents clung to those ways, because they were a marginalized generation, excluded from the good life enjoyed by their patrones at the expense of their Mexican laborers. But even in Francisco Peña and Agustina Jasso's time, Amerika had pushed her roads and rails, the farms and cities, deep into the old tejano *villages, and the gringos had invaded by the thousands, bringing with them the machines that disemboweled the earth and uprooted your people. Arrogant and contemptuous of your culture, the Amerikans did not hesitate to crush your people when native heroes like Aniceto Pizaña and Gregorio Cortez struck back in self-defense. Dispossessed of their lands and their spirit broken, the Mexicans became the beasts of burden—the oxen at the plow, as Pancho Peña called them—who built Texas and the Southwest by the sweat of their brows. And, while they fattened the wallets and the stomachs of their gringo patrones, they struggled to feed and shelter their own.*

And now, here, in this interviewing office, which reeked of Chicanismo, you saw in the faces of these five proud militants the resurrection of your repressed identity. They were your alter egos, but, unlike you, who are still in denial of your indigena-mestizo heritage, they were in full possession of their sense of collective history and their alienation in a hostile Anglo world. But the re-discovery of your primordial identity was too painful, the experience too shocking. Shaken by the encounter with the "Other-that-is-I," you recoiled, even as you began to feel as if some cruel fate had conspired to make your life a mockery by forging a soulless mutant out of you. You were the product of two alien cultures—indígena and European—fused grotesquely together to create a cultural schizophrenic. Identity impacted upon identity: an American anomaly. And we must bear this anomaly together.

I stood by the book stack, transfixed, reading the man's account of the drama as it unfolded on that day in 1901, over seventy years ago. The vivid details leapt out of the page: In my mind's eye I saw Gregorio Cortez, the peaceable farmhand, shooting the sheriff in self-defense. I witnessed his flight, knowing he would be lynched if found at the scene of the killing, and I could almost hear the posses in hot but futile pursuit of the lone Mexican "with his pistol in his hand." I applauded Cortez's heroic odyssey, and winced at the frenzy whipped up by the newspapers. Most painfully, I felt the anti-Mexican sentiment coming to an ugly boil. And there was yet more intercultural drama in don Américo Paredes's little book, *With His Pistol in His Hand*. I learned about the Texas Rangers' reign of terror against the defenseless Mexicans (anywhere between 500 and 5,000 tejano casualties following Aniceto Pizaña's uprising, according to historian Walter Prescott Webb). I endured the Americans' arrogance, and, through it all, I heard the ringing ballad of Gregorio Cortez, affirming his heroic struggle and, by extension, that of his people.

Paredes's words were measured, though at times the ironic tone was a scalpel cutting through the layers of historical deception of which we were all victims, Anglos and Mexicans alike. For the first time in my life, I was being exposed to a radically new account of Anglo-Mexican relations in Texas. Don Américo related the events of those days, early in the twentieth century, in the same simple words that lent such power and vitality to Gregorio Cortez's ballad. His words were like whetstones, sharpening my perception of events about which Papa had occasionally spoken, but that until now had remained submerged in my subconscious. (Born in 1895, on the Texas-Mexico border, Papa still recalled some of the details of that legendary past, but his memory was faulty or perhaps numb, and, except for occasional flashes of anger, he had lost the sense of heroism Paredes captured with such immediacy.) But most poignantly, the book and its ballad also recounted a past filled with the great collective suffering of my people, the clarity of my future mentor's writing graphically capturing the depth of the Texas-Mexicans' oppression.

His authorial voice was sobering yet liberating. Everything I had learned in high school about Texas history Paredes refuted—the lofty ideals of the Sam Houstons and Stephen F. Austins, the tyranny of the Mexican governments, and most of all, the absence of Mexicans (except as villainous caricatures) from the state's history. With each sentence I read, the shame that had been my burden since I was in grade school was being swept away, replaced by a sense of outrage toward Anglos and pride in the courage of Cortez and the Mexicans who came to his defense. I walked out of that library brimming with confidence and a new sense of purpose. The yoke of the ox that I had worn since childhood was crumbling loose.

≡

He was there that night, César Chávez, when La Comparsa, the student chorus I led at the university, performed a medley I had arranged in his honor. The arrangement blended two ballads, "El corrido del agrarista" ("The Ballad of the Agrarianist") and another composed for the farm

Mariachi de la Tierra with César Chavez, 1976. The trumpet player
on the far left is Manuel Peña and the other trumpet player is
Steve Alcala. (From author's collection.)

labor leader himself, "The Ballad of César Chávez." Later, I was told the
performance so moved the farm worker leader that he wept. I almost
wept myself when I heard about my hero's reaction. The performance
itself, part of a concert and teach-in to raise public consciousness and
support for the United Farm Workers, was a high point in my own path
toward self-definition.

I often shared the stage with César Chávez in those days. As a
member of El Mariachi de la Tierra, a group of young Chicanos devoted
to cultivating our Mexican musical roots, I played regularly for the United
Farm Workers—at rallies, groundbreaking ceremonies, and other events
where the farm-worker leader was present. But the participation with
Chávez was only part of my involvement in Chicano political activities.
I was secretary for the local chapter of MAPA, a rejuvenated Mexican
American Political Association that was a strong advocate for Chicano
causes throughout California during the 1970s. But most significant for
my blooming Chicano identity, as a lecturer in La Raza Studies I found

myself at the center of the ideological ferment spawned by the militant and anti-assimilationist Chicano Movement. This was the tidal wave of cultural and political agitation, centered in the universities, that swept through the Southwest, its militant goal to redefine Mexican Americans and to challenge the dominant Anglo society.

It was an exciting time for me, when a different light of consciousness was dawning. A whole new and exhilarating set of strophes was being written for the ballad of this Chicano native son, this time choreographed by the power of *el movimiento xicano* and its romantic nationalism. As a newborn nationalist, I reveled in the glorious feeling of pride in my ethnic history and took every opportunity to celebrate its roots. In the company of my comrades at La Raza Studies, I was rediscovering those roots, and, for the first time in my life, the heavy yoke of racism my teachers had hung on me as a youngster, which had taught me my subordinate place in gringo society, no longer dragged me down. I inhaled deeply of the ideas of don Américo Paredes and the writings of other Chicano radicals. Rudy Acuña's *Occupied America* became my manifesto, while the poetry of Alurista and my friend Omar Salinas (the "Aztec Angel"), as well as the plays and fiery tracts of Luis Valdez, all contributed to my transformation and sense of self-discovery.

It was the gringo, I now convinced myself, in all his duplicity, greed, and savagery, who was the evil spirit let loose in America. The Chicanos and other people of color were the good and innocent victims of that evil. It was that simple: the evil Anglos against the innocent Chicanos, "them" versus "us." This discovery filled me with a sense of righteousness that must have bordered on arrogance—perhaps even racism. The feeling of empowerment could be intoxicating, even dangerously brash, as at times I engaged in behavior that placed me at some risk—both politically and domestically. (In one of many demonstrations in which I engaged, I occupied a university building with my fellow protesters.)

It had been a difficult two years since I had quit the NYC. Despite the epiphany I had experienced that fateful day of the interview with the Chicano students at City College, when my whole identity was plunged into crisis, I was drifting, without a cultural or political compass. Disillusioned with the direction my life was taking, I had quit my job as NYC youth counselor and enrolled in graduate school at Cal State to work on a master's degree in literature. I had become increasingly interested in the folklore of my youth, particularly the old corridos, and the research project seemed an appropriate way to explore the roots of my culture. It was then that I discovered the writings of Américo Paredes. Upon completion of the master's, I was approached by my bosom friend, Alex Saragoza, about starting a musical ensemble with the recently organized La Raza Studies Program at Cal State. He was the program coordinator. Since I was working only part-time at a small rural school district as music teacher, I agreed, and La Comparsa was the result.

Soon, I found myself teaching courses in Chicano literature and music history, and my ethnic consciousness began to blossom. Caught up in the movimiento, I took on with zest the task of reinventing my identity. Those were heady days, when I reached deep into my roots to redefine myself. My indigenous heritage took on a new meaning, as a gushing love for *mi Raza* blossomed. I cultivated a new interest in cultural treasures like conjunto music, which I had spurned as trash in my adolescence, and I came at last to entertain a certain pride in the hardships of my childhood. The days when I had flirted with the idea of total immersion—of losing myself—in the American mainstream were now a distant memory. I chuckled in disbelief, when I remembered how I had even sought employment with major corporations like Exxon and Transamerica. ("They'll chew you up and spit you out," my student-teacher supervisor, the wise Hiram Ching, had warned me.)

I began to understand why I had been so angry when the young militants at City College dismissed my claims to their brotherhood. Inside me—though heavily repressed—was the very cultural being they were celebrating and for whom they were staking their political lives. But I was still in denial of my Mexican patrimony, still begging for acceptance into the dominant society. I was the living and breathing "Mexican-American" that the romantic Chicano intellectuals, the leaders of the Chicano Renaissance, were trying to "save." It was my ancestral culture the nationalists sought to reclaim and protect from the onslaught of "neon gabacho culture," as Luis Valdez, a leading voice of the movimiento, put it. A former "victim" of that onslaught, I was now, in the mid-seventies, a proud member of the cultural reclamation project that was the Chicano Movement.

Postscript

*Opposed in an epic struggle for dominance, the two peoples, Anglo
and Mexican, fashion their identities and interact with each other
on the basis of difference, only to create, over time, a merging identity.
. . . step by small step, a common structuring of experience results,
with Anglo emulating Mexican and Mexican emulating Anglo in
an infinite variety of ways. Of course, since the Mexicans are the
subordinate minority, it is they who yield the most, culturally speaking.*

—Manuel Peña, *Música Tejana*

Perhaps in response to the progressive (and at times libertine) sixties and
seventies, a tide of reactionism swept through America in the 1980s and
'90s, as one by one, Lyndon Johnson's egalitarianist War on Poverty initiatives were weakened or dismantled altogether. Affirmative action, for
example, the cornerstone of the Civil Rights Act, had never been particularly successful, yet it had stood as a symbol of the good will present in the
dominant white society, and its recognition that minorities and women
were in fact denied equal access to the national bounty. Now, under the
guise of "color-blind equality" and "reverse discrimination," the whole
civil-rights project was under assault. The claims of Chicanismo (and
the black power movement) that white Americans were unreconstructed
racists seemed to be gaining confirmation, after all.

Yet despite the retrenchment in racial relations and the resurgence of
racial inequality across the American landscape, it was impossible for me
(as it was for my Chicano peers, perhaps) to resurrect the ghost of romantic nationalism, with its doctrine of ethnic pride and unmitigated hatred
toward the gabacho. After a graduate education in anthropology at the
University of Texas, I had undergone yet another transformation. The zealous ethnic romanticism had waned, and I came to a more sober view of
my relationship with the Anglo social order. The world was not painted
in the extreme colors the Chicano Movement had portrayed: the "Anglos"
were not a monolithic group, any more than the "Chicanos" were. Having
absorbed the more complex theories of social action advanced by Marxism
and, to a lesser extent, postmodernism, I abandoned the crude and essen-
tialist romantic-nationalist view for a more dynamic one. That capitalism,
with its insatiable hunger for cheap, exploitable labor, was a force in shaping

the Anglos' attitude toward Mexicans still seemed a tenable proposition. But not all Anglos were exploiters, and not all were unreconstructed racists. And Mexicans were just as capable of exploitation and prejudice as their gringo antagonists. As I had grudgingly discovered, Anglo-Mexican relations were never driven by the unmitigated hatred the Chicano Movement had depicted. They were much more labyrinthine.

But a more complex view of ethnic relations in the Southwest also implied a more subtle process of becoming "American," or even "Mexican American." My evolving and more tempered view of interethnic relations did not discount the real historical conflict I myself had lived, any more than it glorified the equally real assimilation I had witnessed between members of the two groups. The relationship was dialectical, I now realized, and the long history of Anglo-Mexican contact in the Southwest can best be seen as moving progressively (if in fits and starts) from inequality toward equality, conflict toward accommodation, exploitation toward reciprocity, hate toward love. But, as the reactionist climate at the *fin de siècle* demonstrated, the interethnic relationship was susceptible to "warping," or the onset of historical moments when the dialectical movement could be temporarily derailed. Clearly, the moment of peace between Anglos and Mexicans was not yet at hand, much less the successful bridging of the racial divide. Elusive, as well, was the historical moment when the gross class inequalities underpinning the capitalist system (and perpetuating economic disparities between races) would finally be eradicated. A good deal of rapprochement and even interethnic amalgamation had taken place, but the ugly residue of hate and exploitation was still present.

Thus, for me (and perhaps for other members of my generation) a shifting identity, grounded in two distinct cultures, seemed the only alternative possible. Balanced, still, on the boundary between two conflictive cultural worlds, my life would always be driven by a love-hate relationship with my antagonists/collaborators—the Anglo teachers, classmates, friends, lovers, patrones, and colleagues who early on invaded my consciousness and contributed inevitably to the forces shaping my sense of self. As I now realized, my social face was as much American as it was Mexican. But I was not, as my inner voice had once reminded me, a cultural schizophrenic. I was a native son of America but a unique one—a hybrid or synthesis: an American *mestizo.*

Love in the Time
of Hurricanes

20
NIGHT OF THE HURRICANE

We could hear Mama and Anita talking in the tiny kitchen adjacent to the equally tiny bedroom, where "la Minnie" and I were playing. The old toy box of a house had no electricity, and the only light in the bedroom came from a kerosene lantern perched atop the kitchen table. The evening was threatening, and in the semi-darkness, la Minnie and I could see the lightning flashes through the bed sheet we used to cover the window facing east, toward the Gulf of Mexico. Occasionally, the deep rumble of distant thunder rattled the window pane.

"They say there is an *huracán* out *en el golfo*," Mama was saying, with just a trace of worry in her voice. Weslaco was a good fifty miles from the "Gulf of Dreams," but the mighty hurricane of 1933 had crashed into the South Texas coast with rare ferocity. Its wind and rain had devastated homes and other property far inland, until it wrung itself dry on the parched slopes of Mexico's Sierra Madre to the west. The storm struck long before I was born, but as I gradually became aware, its widespread destruction was etched in Mama's memory: she, my father, and Imelda had waded through waist-high water to escape the flooding. Now, every time she heard about a hurricane "en el golfo," she fretted about the possibilities. Tonight she had asked Anita, our next-door neighbor, to spend time with us until my father returned from a trip to the port of Brownsville, where he had gone for a load of bananas. Anita had brought along her oldest daughter, Minerva, or "la Minnie," as we called her.

While Mama and Anita drifted from talk of hurricanes to more domestic matters, la Minnie and I had slipped into the bedroom to watch the lightning. After a while, the lightning died down, and we started playing "house" with some toy dishes la Minnie had brought with her, and then we moved on to "bedtime." We took a couple of blankets, spread them on the floor, and then got ready to "go to bed" for the night. Once under the blankets, la Minnie snuggled up close to me, and then she took off her panties while she began to unbutton my trousers. I was apprehensive at first, dimly aware that this was something only grownups did, but trepidation quickly turned into excitement as la Minnie began to caress my peter.

She was almost nose-to-nose against me, and although I could barely see her in the faint kerosene light flickering through the open door, I could feel her quickening breath hot on my face. Suddenly, I felt a thrilling jolt emanating from my groin and spreading throughout my whole body. My peter stood erect, hard as the piston rods from the car engine my uncle Juan Manuel had dismantled recently outside our house. La Minnie maneuvered herself under me, and with her hands she guided me toward penetration. She was trying to get me to thrust at her with my hips, but the movement was awkward, and I began to hurt. After a few moments, the wave of arousal subsided, and I pulled away—just in time, as Anita appeared at the door momentarily, calling la Minnie to go home.

The excitement of the encounter with la Minnie lingered for several days, and I kept wishing she would come over and play with me again. I spent as much time around her as I could, waiting for a repeat performance of that strangely exhilarating moment on the night of the hurricane. Perhaps sensing my eagerness, la Minnie kept her distance, ignoring my entreaties to "play house." One day, I saw her outside, running and screaming with two of her cousins, and, anxious to join in the merriment, I yelled to my mother, who was in the kitchen, "Mama, I'm going to play at la Minnie's!" La Minnie heard me, and her barking command froze me in my tracks. "No, no," she ordered, looking sternly at me. "Stay there! I don't want you over here; I already have company."

A sharp sense of rejection overcame me. The coveted Minnie had spurned me without mercy, and I felt crushed and disconsolate. With tears welling up, I went into the outhouse in the back of our lot and sat on the platform for long minutes, ignoring the stench and feeling sorry for myself as I watched through the cracks while la Minnie and her friends played jump rope.

By and by I spotted my everyday playmates, Quique and Julián Ávila (*el Güero*, as we called him—"the fairskinned one"), approaching our lot, and, distracted by their presence, I flung open the door of the outhouse and rushed toward them. They invited me to a game of marbles at el Güero's house. I agreed, naturally, and hurried inside to get the jar in which I kept my marbles.

As we walked toward el Güero's, I kept sticking my hand in the jar and sifting through the smooth, sensuous round shapes. There were several sizes and many different colors—the clear blue dwarfs we called *puritos*, regular-sized two- and three-tone marbles, and a few *pelotones*, or "big balls," as we called the jumbo ones. The slippery feel of the glass orbs had a soothing effect. As always, the older Quique's studied nonchalance and el Güero's juvenile swagger rubbed off on me, and by the time we had cleared out the loose soil from the well-worn playing holes, the memory of la Minnie's rejection had faded from my newly occupied thoughts.

It was a long time before I played with the precocious Minnie again, and it would be several years, and two or three sexual skirmishes later, before the raw thrill she had awakened would metamorphose into full-blown sexual desire. But she had lit the primal spark; she had sensitized the fuse. I would spend a lifetime stoking the firestorms of passion la Minnie had ignited.

21

JUICY-FRUIT HEARTACHE

I let go of her hand and stood up in response to my friend Miguel's nudge from behind. He was signaling for me to come out to the lobby with him. He had been sitting behind Alice and me in the darkened theater, where the students in Mmes. Guidry and O'Connor's classes were watching the feature film. It was the end of the school year, and the fifth- and sixth-graders from Mumford Elementary had made the customary trip to the Chatmas Theater in nearby Hearne. By now, Alice and I were supposed to be "going steady," and I had been waiting anxiously for the trip to the Chatmas, where I could sit close and actually touch her and be a part of her intimate history, if only for this precious moment.

"Hey, pendejo," my older friend told me as soon as we were alone. "Pinche Pascual's trying to steal Alice from you, vato, and I think he's getting away with it. While you were holding one hand, he was holding the other—I saw it myself. You better take care of business, dude. If you don't believe me, sneak behind them and see for yourself."

A wave of rage engulfed me when I stole back into to the theater and saw with my own eyes the betrayal Miguel had described. I wanted to punch Pascual Orozco right then and there, by the light of the silvery flashes coming from the screen, and to grab Alice by the hair until she asked for mercy. I did neither, but instead went to the side row and took a vacant seat next to Carmen, who was only too eager to have me so close. She whispered something to me, but I was deaf to anything but the roar

Chatmas Theatre, 1949

of anger and self-pity ringing in my ears. I completely lost track of the movie as I began immediately to rehearse possible strategies for getting back at the two-timing Alice.

≡

Every day, when I boarded the school bus, I waited eagerly for the next stop, where we picked up the freckle-faced girl with the sparkling sage-blue eyes and soft brown hair she wore in a wavy bob. I looked forward to the moment she would climb aboard and I could once again listen to the laughter in her voice and smell the fragrant scent of her supple young body as she brushed past me. When the bus dropped me off in the afternoon, I would talk to her as I walked the half-mile or so to the weathered shack we called home. In my imaginary dialogues with her, I never fumbled through the first approach; she was always already under my sway, and, dazzled by my charm, she inevitably answered, "Yes! I'll go steady with you." In real life, of course, I spent months engaging her only in my imagination. I did not have the nerve to approach her.

Worse, I was afraid she might discover my secret attraction to her, convinced that she would pulverize me with her scorn. Why would a girl like her want to mess with a poor little cottonpicker like me, who wasn't even as tall as she was? If only I had been like Joe Cassini, white, good-looking, and rich. I often imagined myself transformed into Cassini, who seemed so American and so smug in his circle of well-to-do friends. Then I would be Alice's equal, and I wouldn't feel so inadequate. Or, if she had been more like Carmen Munguía, the Mexican girl who lived on the farm down the road from us. Then, I thought, I would simply have walked up to her and taken charge: "Let's go steady, Alice. I'll take you to the movies Saturday." But Alice was not Carmen; they lived in two starkly different social spaces. Carmen was all too familiar to me, while Alice was an untouchable. The world of her white peers was as alien to me as it was intimidating.

Yet, Alice Bentley was no stranger to me. Girls like her had caught my interest at most schools I attended, particularly in east-central Texas where whites were in the majority—but they lived in a world whose daily habits I had seen only in snatches. As a child of itinerant farm workers, I often attended more than one school a year, which for me was usually no more than six months long. Despite my sporadic education, I absorbed my share of American culture in those schools, partly by watching my Anglo classmates and learning from their lifestyles, but also by reading the language texts we used in the classroom. Alice was a protagonist in all of those texts, which depicted a world of wholesome, affluent people. In the early years, she was a cherubic baby reaching for a ball ("See Baby. See the ball."), while her brother and sister played in the yard of a spacious, well-kept home ("See Dick play. See Alice run."). Surrounded by tall, easy-to-read letters was the picture of the smiling Father ("See Father walk.") dressed in a gray suit, coming home and picking up Baby, while Mother looked on in her high heels, her face beaming with contentment ("See Mother laugh."). As I grew older, the characters in the texts also changed physically, but their leisurely middle-class life remained as timeless as the green grass, blue skies, and wispy clouds that served as background for the illustrations.

The real people in the classrooms—the students who read the books and the teachers charged with their education—also seemed happy. The brisk, cheerful entrance of Mrs. Guidry and her hearty "Good-morning, children," impressed me, as did her impeccably groomed clothes. The children themselves, many from affluent families and comfortable homes, impressed me too, as they chattered about their birthday parties, little-league games, and summer vacations. I could only listen and wish I were like them, for I was never in one place long enough to participate in such juvenile pursuits. Anyway, as a Mexican farm worker I would have been out of place in their cliques. I had never attended a birthday party or belonged to a club, and the idea of "summer vacation" was as alien to me as it was to my parents and their pastoralist ancestors.

Like most of the other Mexican students, I was an outsider looking in, and I could only marvel at the wonderful things the Anglo children did with their leisure time. I spent much of my time away from school toiling in the fields, and, when leisure time was available, I used it for solitary reveries or for inventing my own pastimes (as when I discovered how to create melodies by filling drinking glasses to various levels and striking them with a spoon, much to Mama's amazement). Only rarely during the long years of campaña did I visit overnight with friends, mostly because we lived in isolated rural areas, and my parents would never have allowed me to spend the night with someone miles away. Miguel García, a special hero of mine, was an exception. He lived about a mile away from the Milano estate where my family worked in the mid-fifties, and on occasion I would walk to his place and experience the thrill of sharing his baseballs, gloves, and bats, and, best of all, his most prized material possession—a red, lacquer-smooth Schwinn bike.

And so, even as I learned in school about life in white, middle-class America, the education was second-hand, and my exposure to that life was peripheral, restricted to the small social window that opened into the classroom and the playground. As my fellow student, Alice Bentley was as near as the next row of seats on the bus, but as a member of the white majority, she was as distant from me as the divide separating Mexicans and Anglos was deep.

The first time I actually spoke to the freckle-faced girl with the laughing eyes was a lesson in ineptness. One morning she climbed onto the bus and, instead of moving to the vacant seats farther back, came directly to mine and sat next to me. She looked at me with her mischievous sage-blues and introduced herself: "Hi, I'm Alice; what's your name?" The knot stuck in my throat, but I managed to squeeze out the words: "Manuel; I guess we never met." I was terrified of her the whole time she sat next to me on that April morning in 1954. Despite all the previous encounters rehearsed in my imagination, I could not find anything to say! But Alice was just weeks away from her twelfth birthday, and she was rapidly developing the audacity of an adolescent eager to play the mating game. In contrast to my clumsiness, she talked to me with easy familiarity, and her tone was even coy at times, as she seemed to enjoy seeing me fumble for words. I was completely flustered when we finally got off the bus, but a feeling of euphoria quickly settled over me, and for the rest of the day I floated in a cloud of airy fantasies. The Alice of my imaginary dialogues had actually sought me out and spoken to me!

In the days that followed, we often sat together on the bus, and I gradually began to feel more at ease with her as her frolicsome eyes and laughing voice dissolved my instinctive fear of girls. For the first time in my life, I felt real sexual arousal stirring within me, and I began to indulge in vague romantic fancies about the two of us. For her part, Alice had decided to use her blossoming sexual power to ensnare me. I was only too willing. Without my knowing exactly when or how the "dyad of friendship" unfolded, she guided me through the appropriate steps to that fateful moment when I finally blurted out the threshold question: "Will you be my girlfriend?" She took my hand and wilted me with one of her impish looks. "What do you think?" she asked, and then she kissed me on the cheek and ran off with her friend Carmen, both of them giggling hysterically, as if no other reaction could do justice to my ludic(rous) proposition. She knew I was hopelessly in her thrall.

The next step in the courtship ritual was easy enough, thanks to Alice's presence of mind. (Once I understood her answer to be "yes," I hadn't the foggiest notion of what to do next.) Her mother, Mrs. Bentley, operated a movie theater of sorts—a large tent she had set up on the lawn next to the school, in which she showed movies on Saturday nights, with the help of Alice and her older sisters, Carla and Marilyn. Inside the tent the Bentleys had arranged about a hundred folding metal chairs in curving rows, which were usually filled to capacity. As I recall, the movie screen was merely a large canvass hanging from one of the two-by-fours that framed the tent. A divorcee, Mrs. Bentley also happened to be our bus driver, and the tent where she showed old films was just one of this enterprising woman's ventures to keep her family financially solvent. Alice invited me to come to the next Saturday-night show, where we could sit together for a "date." My dream girl's invitation sent me into paroxysms of joyful delirium. Deep down, however, doubts lingered, and I found it hard to believe that I, the little Mexican cottonpicker, had actually captured the interest of someone as privileged as this beautiful American girl.

My exalted view of Alice prevented me from appreciating differences within the dominant group to which she and her family belonged. While the Bentleys did share in the privileges of the white majority, what I didn't realize was that they were an exception to the affluence enjoyed by most of the white folk who lived in the district surrounding Mumford (a hamlet little more than a grocery store, service station, post office, and a handful of run-down homes, inhabited mostly by Mexicans). The Bentleys were what sociologists call working-class whites, as opposed to most of the other Anglos who attended Mumford Elementary. Many of these were children of the well-to-do growers who controlled the economy in this part of the Brazos Valley. A number of the students were third-generation Italians, the sons and daughters of growers like the DiNiros, the Farettas, the Scarlattis, the Bringettos, the Milanos, and the Falcones. All of them had children at Mumford Elementary.

The social differences between the affluent white students and their Mexican classmates were more or less strictly enforced through segregation, and the puppy loves that blossomed among the preadolescents were usually confined to the respective "races"—Mexicans with Mexicans; whites with whites; and blacks, who attended their own school, with blacks. But this was not the case with Alice Bentley, nor with her sister Carla, who at fourteen was now a middle-school student in nearby Hearne. The Bentley girls seemed to have harbored no prejudices against Mexicans. Indeed, Carla and Miguel García had been carrying on for most of the school year, and in the relationship between those two, Alice already had an interethnic model to emulate.

It was only when I began "going steady" with Alice that I noticed how friendly she was toward other Mexican students, and how little attention the Johnny Farettas actually paid to her. Perhaps they knew she was not, socially speaking, their equal. In any case, she and Carmen, the daughter of Mexican sharecroppers, would often be seen together on the school grounds. But working-class or not, Alice was still a member of the privileged white "caste," the daughter of a woman justifiably respected for her enterprise. Socially inexperienced as I may have been at the tender age of eleven, I knew she was far above me on the social ladder, and awed by her pedigree, I was that much more attracted to her, even as I had developed a bias against the Carmens of my world.

That world—the space occupied by my fellow "oxen at the plow"—had been peopled by too many waifs like my classmate. I had seen Carmen as a small child in the windswept cotton fields of West Texas, shivering in the cold with dirty bare feet and snot frozen under her nostrils, waiting for her parents to finish the last row before straggling home. She had stood in the steamy heat outside our shack in a labor camp near Corpus Christi, eating a soggy bean taco and sharing it with the swarms of gnats that followed us wherever we tried to escape. And everywhere we camped, the Carmens also followed in our wake. They were always grimy, wore tattered clothes, and hung around our shack like wayward kittens, waiting for my all-too-generous Mama to give them a piece of candy or sweet bread, of which they never seemed to have enough.

I had seen too much of Carmen: she was my mirror image, the "Other" that was "I," the downtrodden farm laborer from whose wretched presence I sought desperately to escape. More distressing, I knew Carmen was attracted to me. Like Alice, she was coming into puberty, and it was as plain as the brazen looks she cast in my direction that she had designs on me; and I disdained her even more for her gall. The poor girl was generically ugly—the kind of physical ugliness visited on the chronically malnourished children I had seen up close too often in my own precarious life. She had dark, coarse skin; unkempt hair; big, yellowish teeth; and she wore cheap, ill-fitting clothes. Worse, she displeased me to no end with her constant efforts to make me notice her. Every day, it seemed, she schemed some new plan to steal my attention, but she only succeeded in becoming more odious to me.

Not that all the Mexican girls were like Carmen. Even amid the poverty of the 1950s, and despite inadequate diets, Mexican beauties were not difficult to find. I can still picture Sylvia Buentello, my first crush as a second-grader, in the town of Odem (where I received my first paddling, for being caught speaking Spanish on the school grounds). She was an exquisitely beautiful Euro-mestizo girl with light olive features, luminous brown eyes, and a wholesome oval face adorned with shiny black hair. Her image impressed itself deeply in my permanent sense of the beautiful. (Interestingly, thirty years later, while I was teaching at the University of Texas, a niece of hers taking one of my classes informed me that her aunt was "still gorgeous.") Such was also the case with the delicate Emma Castellanos, from Calvert, a slender criollita with a soft, pleasing face and large iridescent eyes, who sometimes sat with me at the movies and provided material for countless daydreams. She, too, I was told years later, had grown into a vibrant and striking woman with lovely children. In their middle years, both Sylvia and Emma had eased into the comforts of life as middling-class housewives. Then there was Cora, who could pick cotton with the best, and whose chiseled curves, perfectly contoured in her skin-tight jeans, first awakened my interest in the female body.

Of Carmen I never heard again, and in later years I regretted my former disdain for her, and the passion with which I had rejected her. I convinced myself that under the unsightly mask of poverty a graceful butterfly cocooned, waiting for the proper moment to unfold its wings and show its brilliant colors. I fervently hoped that, like me, she had escaped the cycle of poverty holding her people and mine in such a protracted state of bondage, and that a free and radiant Carmen had metamorphosed out of the larva of misery that had imprisoned us both. In the early seventies, when I was "born again" into Chicanismo and its doctrine of ethnic solidarity, I wished I could reach back and embrace her, to weep at her feet, and ask for redemption. I wanted to share with her a new kind of passion—of ethnic kinship and love.

But that change of heart came much later. In 1954, all I felt for her was scorn, and the desire to escape from her brazen advances. She was not my idea of a girlfriend. The model was Alice.

≋

It was the most exciting moment of my young life. I was getting ready to go and meet the object of my romantic soliloquies for my first date ever.

This was no ordinary Saturday night, when I would normally be home, reading an Archie comic book or making music with the 'Bama-brand preservative bottles that we used for kitchen glasses. This time I was to meet Alice at her mother's tent-theater. Alice had proposed that we meet Carla and Miguel and form a foursome—a double date of sorts. Miguel was a couple of years older than me, and, at "thirteen-going-on-twenty-one," he was an athletic, good-looking kid with a tough, cool swagger that rubbed off on me every time I hung around him. I tried to act as nonchalantly as he did, but the raw thrill at the prospect of actually sitting next to Alice in the darkened tent, on a real date, had me wound as taut as the stitches on my friend's new baseball.

I had arrived at Miguel's house by five o'clock, to have dinner with him and to bathe and dress before going on our date—and to brush my teeth; I had a bought a brand new Colgate toothbrush for the occasion. The Garcías lived in one of the better Mexican homes in Mumford (the elder García worked as a laborer for the Southern Pacific Railroad), and Miguel had invited me to come and take a shower at his house, since ours had no plumbing. I had brought newly pressed khaki pants and a starched shirt, with clean underwear. The novelty of a shower was powerfully stimulating, its cool spray splashing like welcome summer rain on my body, while the thought of sharing Alice's fragrant space filled me with a sense of breathless expectation. At seven o'clock, under the warm, moist sky of a May evening in Texas, we set out for Mrs. Bentley's tent, walking the half-mile or so from the Garcías to our rendezvous with Carla and Alice.

Along the way, Miguel and I talked about baseball games we had won and lost that season, and about our teachers and other mundane things. But we studiously avoided any reference to Carla and Alice. As usual, Miguel was his fast-talking, cocky self, but as we approached the tent-theater, he became quiet, while I grew more and more apprehensive. Whether Alice shared my apprehension I never knew, for when she and Carla met us at the entrance, she was her usual carefree, buoyant self. Her easy manner had a soothing effect on my own frayed nerves, though I could not help feeling a bit dismayed at how collected she seemed, in comparison to my own sense of insecurity.

The movie was an "oater," a western with the typical shootouts between genteel "aw-shucks" cowboys and shifty-eyed villains, but the characters and plot remained hazy to me afterward (though I did seem to recall a scene with Hopalong Cassidy). My energies were completely absorbed with the precious being sitting next to me. At first we only held hands, but well into the movie, I finally succeeded in putting my arm around Alice. Miguel and Carla were sitting in front and to one side of us, and once or twice I saw their heads merge in the dark. Seeing them kissing emboldened me to do the same with Alice, but she was chewing gum, and anyway, my resolve failed each time I worked up the nerve. In the end, I gave up, cursing myself for being so gutless.

On our way home, Miguel was in high spirits. He was boasting about how sweet Carla's lips tasted when he kissed her, and he was already charting the next strategy to get her to "go down" for him.

"If Harvey can do it with Marilyn, hell, I can get Carla to go down for me."

"What do you mean?" I asked. "Harvey and Marilyn?"

"Yeah," Miguel continued. "Harvey got Marilyn to go up to the hay-loft with him. At his dad's farm. He told me himself. He said she's one hell of a lay—couldn't get her offa' him. So I think it's about time for my turn. Mamacita! I'm gonna make her see stars!"

I left Miguel at his house and walked the remaining mile to our place by myself. I had ventured across those cotton fields after dark before, and I had been a bit spooked by the pitch-black sky, draped over the rural night lit only by the stars that shimmered along the Milky Way trail. But I was not scared tonight. Tonight I felt only envy at Miguel's boldness—and an aching desire to relive my date with Alice. This time, however, I would kiss her Juicy-Fruit lips and claim her as mine once and for all. As I plunged deeper and deeper into fancy, imagination and reality merged, and I no longer felt envious of Miguel or Harvey. In my chimerical world, Alice and I kissed and dissolved into pure passion, our bodies floating upward in ecstasy, until we glowed and shimmered in tandem with the stars of the Milky Way.

Even the sight of our dilapidated shack did not dampen the euphoric aura enveloping me that evening. Weather-beaten and lacking all the amenities of modern living, the old shack was a reminder of the insur-mountable social divide I sensed between Alice and me. Although the thought probably never entered her mind, I fretted endlessly about the possibility that she might show up one day and discover the dismal sur-roundings in which I lived. Especially jarring to me was the stark contrast between Alice's clean, fragrant scent and the decrepit state of our hovel, which oozed wretchedness no matter how diligently Mama scrubbed and cleaned.

Tonight, however, nothing could burst the romantic bubble surrounding me. Even as I squeezed in between my brothers Plon and Alessio on the rusty iron bed with the sagging mattress, I did not feel the usual crunch of their heavier bodies, nor did I notice the pungent smell of working feet, or even the snores coming from my parents' nearby bed. In my romantic trance, I was still at the movies, clinging to Alice's hand. Sleep finally overcame me that night, but I never knew the precise moment when I crossed the boundary between wakeful dreams and sleeping images. Alice dominated both.

≋

It was a stunning blow when I found out about Alice's fickleness. I vaguely understood that on occasions like this, one was supposed to demand satisfaction of one's rival, but I could not work up the courage to face down the back-stabbing Pascual. To Alice I said nothing until the last day of school, when I finally confronted her: "Why did you do this to me?" Her curt, "I don't know, it just happened," and her refusal to look at me directly with her suddenly-cruel eyes spoke callously of her disregard for my feelings. I wanted desperately to ask her to come back to me, but I knew her affection was now flowing toward Pascual. There was no longer any room for me in her young heart.

That day, the walk home from the bus stop was the longest of the school year. I ached for Alice, and I kept reviewing in my mind what could have pushed her away from me. At times I convinced myself she had discovered who I really was, and she thus had no choice but to dump me. My chronic feelings of self-recrimination, always lurking below the surface, were particularly acute that day, and I was especially cross by the time I got home. Everything I saw displeased me. I wondered why we had to live in a hovel with peeling whitewash and, worse, why we had to share two of the four rooms with the newlyweds, Pablo and Esther Piña. The screen on the front door was in tatters, giving the flies and gnats free reign inside. When I walked in, I was disgusted with the yellowed layers of wallpaper—testimonials to the shack's more refined lifestyle in some distant past. Now, however, they were peeling off in blotches and revealing the termite-ravaged grayish plank walls. The gloomy bareness of the unfurnished surroundings was depressing, and I envied Miguel for having his own room, with its sumptuous bed and dresser, and walls decorated with pennants from Baylor and Rice and Texas A&M.

Late in the afternoon my thoughts drifted back to that Saturday not so long ago, when, at about the same hour, Miguel and I had readied to go meet our sweethearts. A whiff of nostalgia momentarily lifted me. But the arrival of Papa and my working brothers, and the smell of their sweaty bodies, jolted me back into reality. For the rest of that evening and the days that followed, I was in the grip of a deep sense of loss, while a dull, unpleasant emptiness gnawed at me in the pit of my gut.

I never saw Alice after that last day of school, nor did I ever learn what became of her. That summer, the patrón we worked for, Joe Milano, built a little cinder-block cottage for the Peña family nearer to Hearne, and the following school year (after our usual trip al norte to pick cotton), I enrolled in that school district. In the sixth grade, a much older version of Alice—my teacher, Mrs. Jameson—ignited the adolescent sparks crackling inside me, and not long after that, still other pretty girls came into my life to stimulate my amorous interests. I never again yearned for the mischievous sage-blue eyes.

But I had met Alice Bentley at a critical moment, when my sexual identity was in its most impressionable stage of development. Her delicate, fair image stamped itself powerfully on my psyche, and the better part of her personality became etched in my permanent model of the feminine mystique. I would meet up with that model time and again in my travels, though only once more, in the distant future, would another pair of sage-blues shake the very foundation of my shrine to Eros.

22

WHAT DO YOU WANT—A KISS?

She had walked the half-mile or so across the cotton fields to pay us a visit. Petra, or "Petrita," as everyone called her, was only months older than me, but she had already turned thirteen, and she was rapidly developing into a nubile adolescent. A bit on the plump side, she nonetheless had a pleasing roundish face, with skin the color of light *café au lait*. She was precociously sexy, and I knew she had taken a liking to me just by the way she talked and looked at me. Ostensibly, she had come to deliver a spool of thread for Mama, but she wasted no time turning her attention toward me.

I did not like Petrita; in fact, I was afraid of her, though I knew not why. Her rather brazen approach repelled me, striking me as lascivious and un-ladylike. She seemed to take every opportunity to corner me into situations that, to me, at least, seemed immodest and ultimately embarrassing. It was as if she were expecting me at any moment to pitch a romantic proposition at her. The bolder she got, the more evasive I became. In the end, I tried to avoid her as much as possible.

On this day, however, Mama had to leave the house for a spell, to go see Lencha, a neighbor who lived a few hundred feet from our cinderblock cottage on Joe Milano's estate. She took my younger sister Elia with her, leaving me alone with Petrita. The moment Mama left, I tried to escape outdoors, hoping to thwart any amorous schemes the girl might be entertaining. But as I made my move, she stood in the doorway, her arm extended and her hand resting on the doorjamb, blocking my exit.

The Peñas' cinder-block home

I walked right up, expecting her to let me pass. Instead, she stood there, looking at me with alarmingly inviting eyes.

As I awkwardly waited for her to remove her arm, she grabbed me with her free hand and drew me toward her. I was almost face-to-face with her when she asked the dreaded question: "*¿Qué quieres—un beso?*" "What do you want—a kiss?" Her audacious words bounced provocatively in my head, and I hesitated for a moment, my resistance threatening to collapse under her dark, beguiling eyes. I almost answered "yes," but my instinctive fear of her prevailed. "No!" I cried, as I backtracked and ran out of the room, scurrying out the door at the other end of the house. My heart was pounding, but I never knew whether it was out of loathing, panic, or sexual excitement.

Eventually, as the months wore on, Petrita gave up on me, and her shameless advances ceased. By Mexican cultural standards, she had matured into an adult, and her changed status may have contributed to a new aloofness toward me. Whatever her motives, a year later, now drowning in a tidal wave of adolescent hormones, I looked desperately into the indifferent eyes of a suddenly-irresistible Petrita, aching for a lascivious look from her. On occasion the previous summer, I had spotted her in the cotton field adjacent to her house, chopping weeds with a hoe. Now I kept going by that field, hoping to see her and hoping I would have the courage to walk up and tell her how badly I wanted a kiss.

But I was never alone with Petrita again.

23
LAS BODAS DE PANCHO PEÑA

My father got married yesterday. I took him to Crestview in a dense tule fog to pick up his betrothed, and the three of us then drove to the county courthouse in Fresno for a marriage license. He introduced me to his new sweetheart: "This is my son Manuel. He's going to take us to the city. We need to obtain a license before we can be married." "Happy to meet you," she said in Spanish, her hand extended and a shy smile peeking out of her large innocent eyes. "María Carrizales at your service." She was a short Indian woman with a very fat body, and she smelled faintly of garlic. "Must've been cooking before we arrived," I thought as I grasped her soft, chubby palm.

We squeezed her into the back seat of my two-door coupe, a '64 Pontiac LeMans, while Papa sat in front with me, in the passenger-side bucket seat. They were both quiet for the first few minutes of the trip, but by and by she broke the silence. "They kept him from me for a while," she said, "but I knew *el hermano* Pancho was meant for me." She called Papa by his nickname, "Pancho." "The Lord had promised him to me." *El hermano Pancho.* That's what his fellows call him—the "brothers," or members of Papa's church, *La Iglesia Apostólica de Cristo* (The Apostolic Church of Christ).

I could still remember the day my father had been "saved." He was sprawled on the floor, vomiting blood from what would be the last binge of his life, this one to celebrate his sixty-fifth birthday. The doctor had already warned him: "Frank, one more hangover could kill you. Your liver has taken a lot of abuse from all the alcohol you've consumed." Ever since he was in his teens, he had been a binge drinker—going sober for weeks, only to slip into alcoholic bouts that could drag on for days. He could never enjoy just one drink or two; it was always a parranda or, at the very least, a parrandita—a big binge or a little one, depending on the occasion.

But he had to do it once more, even after the doctor's warning—steal right up to the black veil of death—before he could be convinced. And so, bedridden from the poisonous effects of the whiskey, and feeling utterly guilty for his reckless behavior, he had welcomed los hermanos when they arrived to pray for him. Mama, who had converted to the fundamentalist Apostolic Church a couple of years earlier, had invited the brothers to come and pray for her fallen husband. He wept that day as los hermanos pleaded fervently for him, asking the Lord to have mercy on this wayward sinner, and by the time the visitors left, he seemed to be dramatically better. He never touched liquor after that—until his ninetieth birthday, when he downed two quick glasses of chenin blanc at a dinner party his children celebrated with him.

Papa met María somewhere in Texas, perhaps at a regional conference of the Apostolic Church. She is from Ciudad Juárez, across the river from El Paso. She has relatives in Crestview, and she moved in with them to be a little closer to Papa, who lives in Camarillo—which is why he has been coming up to Fresno so often these days. When María and Papa met, he was on the rebound from a failed marriage he leapt into shortly after Mama's death, and he immediately proposed to her. María declined at the time, but she did move to California in the hope of getting to know him better.

Family rumor has it that Papa and the previous wife, a woman named Liliana, or "Lili," had been carrying on even before Mama's death. According to my sister Imelda, the pair had engaged in a long-distance romance for months, but it was only after Mama passed on that he finally had the chance to visit her in Texas and make intimate contact. Whatever the nature of the relationship, he waited a mere nine months after his wife of forty-three years died before he tied the knot with "la Lili," as Imelda called our new stepmother (the adjective "*la*" signifying disdain). Papa left California rather suddenly, and it was only after the fact that I learned of his marriage to la Lili. Nor did I ever learn how Papa made his new wife's acquaintance, since Camarillo, California, is a good 1,700 miles from Harlingen, in the "Magic Valley," where la Lili lived. But apparently my tía Virginia, his trusted younger sister, had acted as go-between at some point.

Unfortunately for Papa, his marriage to la Lili was a stormy one from the start. According to Imelda, the new wife was the exact opposite of Agustina Jasso. While Mama was a meek, subservient woman who catered to his every whim, the new wife was a "bossy bitch" who tried to change Papa in radical ways, such as insisting he observe the manners and etiquette of the gente decente—the norteño gentry—of which she was a member. That is to say, la Lili, who at age fifty-eight was considerably younger than Papa, was a woman of modest means, with a comfortable, fashionably furnished home (by barrio standards, at least) and a middling-class lifestyle that was in sharp contrast to Papa's rustic, working-class habits. In trying to remake him in her class's image, la Lili created inevitable friction, especially since Pancho Peña was so thoroughly steeped in the ways of Mexican working-class machismo. No woman was going to tell him how to behave.

Or so one might have thought. But Papa was enthralled with la Lili, and, to hear Imelda tell it, he "bent over backward" to accommodate her desires, even learning to bathe daily and to use a knife and fork at the dinner table, in contrast to his lifelong habit of using the tortilla as a spoon. He seems to have failed in his attempts to please his new bride, and in the end, he suffered a macho's most humiliating ordeal—la Lili betrayed him with another man, who, to Papa's utter devastation, turned out to be a gringo. He showed up at my sister's one day, looking ashen and agitated. "I must leave for California immediately," he told her. "Will you and Noé take me to the McAllen airport, please?"

Taken completely by surprise, Imelda and Noé nonetheless did as he asked them, and, despite the torrential squalls of a dying Hurricane Fern (which lingered as a tropical storm over South Texas for several days), they drove him to the airport, unaware of his reasons for leaving so abruptly.

"He was all worked up," my sister was telling me. "And then he pulled out a bottle of Pepto Bismol and drank half of it. 'What's wrong, Papa,' I asked him, 'was it something you ate?' 'No, hombre,' he said, 'it's just that my stomach gets nervous when I'm planning a trip.' But I knew something more serious was happening to him; he just didn't wanna let us in on it."

My tía Virginia knew exactly what had happened. As he had done so many times in his life, when misfortune struck, he immediately went to his clairvoyant sister for advice. "*Vete inmediatamente de aquí*," she had commanded him—"leave this place immediately." As I learned later from Tía Virginia herself, he had confided to her that one day, as he was returning home early from a trip across the border, he noticed the front door was ajar. He came in, expecting to find his wife busy as usual, knitting, doing housework, or attending to her rose garden, when he heard a man's voice drifting from the rear. His suspicion aroused, he tiptoed to the back porch, where he found the gringo and his wife in an amorous embrace. He left abruptly, without making his presence known to la Lili, and, after consulting with his sister, he went to Imelda's house in Weslaco to ask for a ride to the airport.

La Lili never heard from him again, but she knew where to find him in California, and a few weeks after he had returned to Camarillo, he received the annulment papers from her lawyer. Included in the lawyer's correspondence was a statement for him to sign, disclaiming any right to her worldly possessions, of which she boasted a few (including her house), while he had nothing in this life but the clothes in his suitcase. He and the new Mrs. Peña had been married less than a year, and at seventy-six, he was once more a *soltero*—a bachelor.

After a twenty-minute drive, Papa, María, and I arrived at the courthouse in Fresno, where I swung into the underground parking garage. We then took an elevator to the ground level and walked up the long, sloping ramp that led to the courthouse grounds. María was breathing heavily by the time we ascended the ramp, her plump brown face turning a maroonish color with the exertion. We finally reached the ground level of the County Courthouse, where we took an elevator to the fourth floor and the Office of Vital Statistics.

As we stepped out into the hallway, we were immediately greeted by a sign that read, "MARRIAGE LICENSES." Underneath the sign, someone had scribbled the message, "Turn back! It's not too late," which the office managers had either not noticed or neglected to erase.

"*Vente, vamos,*" Papa said with a sense of urgency, while nudging her gently out of the elevator.

"*Sí, vamos,*" María answered, and, suppressing a giggle, she added, "before we change our minds."

The woman behind the desk smiled halfheartedly when I addressed her: "These two young people want to get married." She handed Papa an application, which he turned over to me to fill out. The first section required information from the groom:

NAME: Francisco T. Peña
AGE: 77
BIRTHPLACE: Salineño, Texas
FATHER'S NAME: Manuel S. Peña
MOTHER'S NAME: Anastacia Garza
MARRIAGE NUMBER: 3rd

The second section elicited information from the bride:

NAME: María Carrizales
AGE: 63
BIRTHPLACE: Cd. Juárez, Mex.
FATHER'S NAME: Ernesto Carrizales
MOTHER'S NAME: Socorro Martínez
MARRIAGE NUMBER: 1st

I handed the clerk the completed application, and she scanned it rapidly, as if this were something she had done innumerable times. Without comment, she sat at her typewriter and entered the information we had provided. Papa and María sat down on two chairs in front of the secretary's desk and whispered to each other, while the typewriter clicked furiously under the dexterous fingers of its user. In less than two minutes, the woman handed me the completed form and asked me to check for the accuracy of the information. Papa and María then signed the document, while the secretary informed me the fee was six dollars. Our business completed, the clerk gave Papa a marriage license and instructed him to take it to a judge for notarization.

"That was very easy, hermano Pancho," María said as we walked out.

"Yes," Papa replied, "we're practically married now. I think this was the hardest part. We'll go to Crestview now and see about finding a judge to marry us."

On the way to Crestview, Papa suddenly remembered the suit he had planned to wear for the ceremony. "*¡Ay, hombre!*" he exclaimed, "I left my suit at your house, Manuel. I had it ready, but I wasn't sure I would need it today, and in the end I forgot about it and left it on top of the bed."

"Do you want me to turn back to Fresno and get it, Papa?"

He weighed the decision for a moment. "*O, qué le hace*—what does it matter. I'll get married in the clothes I've got on." Always attentive to his dress (Mama had never let him leave the house in wrinkled clothes), he was wearing a handsome brown suede coat, well-pressed khaki pants, and, of course, the indispensable Stetson hat he always wore on his bald head. Reluctant to turn back, I assured him the clothes he was wearing were more than adequate for the simple ceremony he and María were planning.

"Do I look presentable in these clothes, María?" he asked.

"O, sí, hermano," she replied, giggling in the back seat. "We don't have to dress in the latest fashions. *No es boda grande*—it's not a big wedding. And, anyway, we aren't young and *ilusionados* [starry-eyed] anymore."

"Don't call me 'hermano,'" he said, with a hint of irritation. "It sounds too formal, and, anyway, you're practically my wife already."

María had been staying with her cousin in Crestview, Mrs. Soria, where we picked her up yesterday to go to Fresno, and we returned there after obtaining the marriage license. Mrs. Soria's husband, a retired man on social security, volunteered to be an official witness to the marriage (I was the other), and he was to join us when Papa and María were ready to take the vow. Papa had wanted to get married as quickly as possible, but no one had made any of the necessary arrangements, so it fell on me to find a judge. After calling the justice court in Crestview, I finally located a Judge Kruger, who, I was told, could marry the couple later in the afternoon, after His Honor had returned from lunch. Since it was only eleven in the morning, María and Papa agreed it was best to wait at the Sorias, and, feeling uncomfortably out of place, I decided to pay my old classmate from Weslaco High, tejano expatriate Art Ballí, a visit. Art runs his own insurance agency in Crestview, and, since I had not seen him in over a year, it seemed like an opportune moment to reconnect and have lunch with him.

"Don't be too long," Papa warned. "I don't want us to be late to our appointment with the judge." I could tell that he was anxious.

After lunching with Art, I was driving the five or six blocks from his office to the Sorias when—surprise!—I espied Papa scurrying down Crestview's main street. I pulled up beside him and asked what he was doing out on the town. His normally reddish-bronze face had an ashen look to it, which accentuated his prominent nose. He seemed distraught, or ill, perhaps.

"Is something the matter, Papa?" I asked.

"No, hombre," he brushed off my question, trying to reassure himself as much as me. "*No es nada*. I'm just getting a bit of diarrhea, and I came down to the drugstore to get some Pepto Bismol." He climbed in the car and hastily opened the extra-large bottle he had bought, gulping down about a third of the liquid. Papa is not one to settle for half measures. As he would say, if a little is good for you, a lot is even better. "There," he said, "that should settle things down."

"Just take it easy, Papa. You shouldn't get too terribly excited. It'll soon be over and you'll be married."

"Sí, sí, hombre—I'll be all right. It's just a case of nerves in my stomach. Let's hurry; we've only got another forty-five minutes." And with that, he stuffed the bottle of Pepto into his coat pocket.

"JOHN W. KRUGER and ROBERT J. HARDIG, Attorneys-at-Law," the sign outside the judge's office read. We entered the long, narrow reception room, where a slender woman with a distinctively Armenian nose greeted us.

"These two young people want to get married." The receptionist, who was not particularly friendly, did not respond, and I immediately wished I had not repeated the cliché.

"It will be a moment," she informed us. "Please be seated."

Judge John W. Kruger, a giant, heavyset man, showed us into his office, with its equally ponderous desk, which filled most of the small space. "So, you want to get married?" He looked at both Papa and Mr. Soria, unsure who the bridegroom was.

"Ah'm the one," Papa said, in his thick Mexican accent, laced with more than a thread of Texas twang.

"Well, it's never too late, and you've come to the right place."

"Yessir," Papa added. "Ah'm seventy-seven years old, but I b'lieve I cayn go one more round."

Judge Kruger picked up a black book that looked like a miniature when he placed it in his massive hands. "I want you to stand here and you here," he instructed, as he flipped through the pages. María, who had been standing timidly close to and slightly behind Papa, moved in halting steps toward two chairs in front of the judge's desk, her hands clutching her large black purse against her prominent round stomach.

"No, no, ma'am," said the judge, "not there. *Aquí.*"

"*¿Donde?*" María turned to Papa with a confused look.

"*Aquí, mujer.*" Papa pulled at her old charcoal tweed coat impatiently.

"Is there a ring for the ceremony?" Judge Kruger asked.

"*¿Qué dice?*" Papa, who was hard of hearing, looked questioningly at me.

"No," I intervened, "there is no ring."

"Oh, a ring. No, no, we don't need no ring," Papa added.

I stood next to María, while Mr. Soria stood on the other side, next to Papa, as Judge Kruger began to read from the diminutive book nestled in his hands:

"Marriage is a divinely sanctioned institution which you must enter into only after the deepest consideration and conviction. The law has authorized me to legalize on earth what God sanctions in Heaven. 'Francisco T. Peena,'" he mispronounced the last name, pausing to glance at Papa, "I will read the following, and I want you to repeat it after me—"

"I, Francisco T. Peena—"

"I, Francisco T. Peña—"

"do solemnly swear—"

"do solemnly swear. . . ."

As Judge Kruger read from his book, I could feel next to me María's expansive diaphragm rising and falling rhythmically with each breath she took, as she stared intently at the man's imposing hands. The faint smell of garlic was still with her. Papa, meanwhile, kept moving his jaws up and down in a nervous chewing motion, and this produced a clicking sound from his dental plates. I felt María's body stiffen when it came to her turn, as she cleared her throat and adjusted her glasses.

"María doesn't speak English. Do you want me to translate?"

"Yes, please." He repeated the words out of the ceremonial book:

"I, María Carrizales—"

"Yo, María Carrizales—"

"Yo, María Carrizales. . . ."

"I now pronounce you man and wife," Judge Kruger finally concluded. "You may kiss the bride," he added, with a smile in his voice.

Papa and María looked at each other and embraced gingerly. He kissed her on the cheek and chuckled. "Thank you very much, sir," he addressed Judge Kruger while extending his hand.

"Yessir," replied the judge. "Good luck to the two of you. Are you going on a honeymoon?"

"No, sir. We just go back to Camarillo. I been livin' with muh daughter, but now we have to look for a place for the two of us."

≋

I could still remember that scene, when I was about five—Mama suppressing a sob and rushing into the kitchen to busy herself. Weeping did not come easily to my mother. In fact, in all the years I spent at home, I only saw her shed tears on one or two occasions. But this time she had seen "*la Borrada*"—the "hazel-eyed one"—riding side-by-side with Papa and lavishing attention on him, her body rubbing against his in the old candongo. Papa was a foreman for Pfluger Farms, and he had a whole crew of men and women under his supervision. As everyone in the family seemed to know, *andaba chiflado con la Borrada del diente de oro*—he was beside himself over one of the women working for him, the "hazel-eyed one with the gold tooth." And, as Imelda would recall years later, he had made no attempt to conceal his adulterous affair with "la Borrada." Mama was consumed with jealousy—"lost so much weight she got sick," according to my oldest sister—but Papa seemed insensitive to her suffering.

The fact is that my father was an *enamorado*, a man with an enduring zest for feminine charm. The affair with "la Borrada" was the only one to gain notoriety within the family, but according to Imelda, "Hazel Eyes" was but one in a long line of women dating back to the time she was a little girl. "You never saw him in his prime," my oldest sister recalled years later, when Papa was in the twilight of his life. "He could spend his last penny on any woman who wiggled her fanny at him, especially one with a big butt. He went ape over big butts." "Liquor and women," she concluded, "were his undoing." For Imelda, that was why "mi madrecita" had languished in chronic illness all her life. "She loved him so much," Imelda recalled, "she depended on him so much, and he—all he could think of was liquor and viejas [broads]."

Imelda may have been close to the mark in her assessment; yet it would be unfair to characterize my father as an inveterate womanizer, at least not while I was growing up. During the ten or so years we spent on campaña, so much of Papa's life was spent in toil and on the struggle to keep hunger at bay that he could not have had the energy to pursue his amorous interests. Of course, during periods of unemployment, especially during the fallow months after the pizcas, when time and a little money were available, he did spend his share of nights in the cantinas, where, family rumor had it, he slipped into his old habits.

In any case, once he passed into the autumn of his life and retirement—now with considerable leisure time at his disposal—Papa resumed his old ways: he began to cultivate his penchant for sensuous women. As a young man of eighteen at the time, and even well into adulthood, I could not help notice how ingratiating—even fawning—he could be with women who attracted his attention. Listening to my sister's recollections reinforced my memory of Papa as a "lady's man," and I thought I understood why, even when he moved to California later in life, he kept his own separate mail box at the Post Office. I ran into him one day, opening his box at the very moment when I had gone in to mail a package. He offered no explanation, and I asked for none. It was as if we both knew why he was there. He was seventy at the time.

Francisco "Pancho" Peña was a man of two faces (as perhaps all of us are)—one public the other private. The private man could be fearsome in his domestic wrath, which on occasion wrought violence upon his wife and children. Especially when drunk, he could become another Farrington, the Dubliner who bullied his wife and children to compensate for the failures in his sordid life. I can still remember one Joycean scene in particular, when Papa came home after midnight, drunk, and demanded that Mama get up and prepare his dinner. She had not been feeling well, and when she protested he threatened to pull her out of bed himself. *"¡Levántate, cabrona!"* he ordered, *"si no quieres que te agarre a patadas*—Get up, bitch, if you don't want me to kick the hell out of you." Alessio and Plon heard the commotion and got up to confront Papa. Both were in their teens by then, and it was the first time they had ever summoned the courage to challenge him.

"You are not going to make Mama get up," Plon told him, with shoulders squared, as if ready to fight. "You've been out on the town, drinking and living it up with your friends, while Mama's at home sick. No one can stop you from going on your binges, but you have no right to come home and abuse our mother. If you're hungry, prepare your own dinner. She is not going to get up."

Papa blustered and threatened to beat Plon and Alessio, but in the end he backed down. "I was scared as hell," recalled José years later. "But we weren't going to put up with his abuse any longer. Luckily, he was getting a bit old by then. I don't think we could have stood up to him ten years earlier."

But Papa could, in turn, be quite effusive when inebriated; his emotional barometer was that volatile while under the influence of alcohol. Then again, his violence was as much cultural as it was personal. The custom of Mexicans on the Border had long favored tough, disciplinarian husband-fathers and submissive, doting mothers—even if in practice strong women (my tía Virginia among them) did contest the patriarchal norm. Steeped in the male culture of the Border, Papa was quite naturally a stern, if sporadic, disciplinarian, and his domineering character (and Mama's acquiescence) impelled him toward a controlling, occasionally violent, parenting style. He thus left no doubt as to his authority in the family.

I learned early on to respect and fear that authority, a lesson made tolerable, however, by my early identification with his male dominance and by his undeniable charm and effusiveness, the latter often breaking down into sentimentality. Despite his macho exterior, he cried easily. In short, Papa's demonstrative nature softened his sometimes-tyrannical behavior. His wrath could bring terror to my heart, but his gentler, charismatic side was soothing by contrast. In fact, as an "ox at the plow," Pancho Peña was often too tired from toiling in the fields to exercise his authority, and he left the day-to-day disciplining to the gentle lamb that was his wife. His abusive side thus emerged only in sporadic fits of wrath, tempered, as it was, by the harsh labor that sapped even his domineering will.

And, of course, there was the other Pancho Peña—the public man whose colorful character was most often on display before outsiders, but who on occasion, during tranquil domestic moments, would regale his family with humor and hearty entertainment. As a child, I remember being enthralled by his storytelling skills and his knack for verbal antics. Having been brought up in a world steeped in folklore, where the mass media was nonexistent and traditional verbal arts were the principal source of entertainment, Pancho Peña possessed a wealth of folktales, legends, proverbs, and other forms of lore (some of which he invented himself). Narratives were transformed into artistry through his consummate rhetorical skills, and characters came alive in his performances.

One of my favorites was the story he told about "El arroyo de los morteros," a type of personal narrative known to folklorists as a "memorate." According to Papa, *El arroyo de los morteros*—The Creek of the Cannons—was notorious for the strange and supernatural events believed to take place in the vicinity of the small bridge that spanned its width. Papa's own story combined local interethnic history with an experience he had while riding alone at dusk on the trail that crossed the arroyo.

One day, he related, while approaching the creek from the north, he spotted another horseman on the opposite bank, and he judged the two would meet somewhere near the bridge. *"En aquel entonces,"* he continued, in that clear, resonant voice that immediately commanded one's attention—"In those days, people in Salineño were quite superstitious, and I remember that several spots were considered haunted. Such was the case with El arroyo de los morteros, which connected to the Rio Grande. It was thick with chaparral, so thick you could easily lose your bearings, especially on a dark moonless night. There was a road—more like a trail, actually—which descended steeply from the high banks that flanked the arroyo on both sides. According to local legend, gringo soldiers who invaded the border during the Mier Expedition of 1843 had been ambushed and killed at the creek crossing by local Mexican irregulars. Texas was independent by then, but the Border was still ours, and the gringos were trying to extend their control. That was the reason for the Mier invasion. In any event, several gringos were killed—*según se decía*, or so it was said—and many people believed their spirits still roamed the area, in search of heaven-knows-what."

By this time we were all in the thrall of Papa's riveting account, which, as always, was marked by an impeccable grammar and all the inflections and pauses that a skilled storyteller commands. We listened intently, as he proceeded to tell us how he rode down into the bottom of the arroyo and approached the bridge, expecting to meet up with the ghostly rider and wondering whether he was one of the local rancheros. "I finally crossed the bridge," he reminisced, "all the while looking around, to see if I could spot the rider. Nothing. I rode on along the trail, still looking and expecting to meet my counterpart at any moment. I ascended the other bank, and still no sign of the *jinete* [horseman]. For a moment— remembering the stories I had heard—I felt a chill run up and down my spine, but then I said to myself, 'Perhaps he turned back, and that's why I never met up with him.' In any case, I never again witnessed any kind of unnatural movement at the arroyo, and, since I was not much given to superstition, I convinced myself it was either an optical illusion or the rider had in fact done an about-face."

Long after his death, Pancho Peña was fondly remembered by those who knew him for his "Pancheñas," as Tía Virginia's husband, Tío Federico, called his whimsical antics, especially the idiosyncratic names he invented for people. His nicknaming powers were legendary; original and humorous, they stuck like tar on anyone unlucky enough (or lucky, depending on the nickname) to earn a Peña alias. For example, he nick-named my music teacher, Eugenio Gutiérrez, "*El Escamoso*"—"The Scaly One"—because of the latter's habitual scratching due to a chronic rash. A neighbor whose front teeth were set apart became "*El dientes de colar atole*"—"the man with the gruel-straining teeth," while another, a fellow known for his womanizing, became "*El Garañon*"—the "Stud-horse." A cousin who was dark as night became "*El Comaladas*," suggestive of the jet-black color of a comal, or griddle. And then there was "*El sartén sin cola*"—"the skillet without a handle"—an alias he pinned on a friend with a fat, round middle. Some of our patrones also succumbed to Papa's bap-tismal powers. One, a man with a taciturn attitude and a peculiar gait, got pinned with the alias "*El Burro*," while another earned the title of "*El Saíno Viejo*," or "the Old Boar," due to his snout-like nose and bristly hair. Such was Papa's notoriety for nicknaming that Tío Federico bestowed on him the ultimate moniker, "Alias," in recognition of his verbal flair.

It was in public, then, among friends and neighbors, that Papa's communicative skills and charm were on full display. Here, in public performance, he gave ample play to his theatrical bent and great oratorical skills. But Pancho Peña was more than a nicknamer or storyteller. True, he was as gifted a narrator and orator as I have ever heard, but he was also a man of remarkable inner strength with a natural aptitude for leadership. His commanding presence earned the instinctive respect of all who knew him, as did his capacity for empathy. The latter was evident in acts like his quick adoption of the wayward young man he nicknamed "Pénjamo," and his volunteer work late in his years for Nancy Reagan's Foster Grandparent program at Camarillo State Hospital.

Yet Papa had grown up in the abject poverty of the Texas borderlands, in Salineño, a third-world village where publicly funded schools were nonexistent. And so, while I could explain his sympathy for the less fortunate, I never completely understood where and how he had cultivated the silver tongue that dazzled everyone who came under its sway. He was born on September 16, 1895—Mexican Independence Day—and as a child, he had attended a little makeshift school run by a matron from the local rural gentry. The three or four years he spent in the village school marked the extent of his more-or-less formal education. Beyond that, his sheer intelligence and motivation had driven him to read every Spanish-language book he could find. And that self-education, coupled with his native skills, ultimately served him well, transforming him into a communicator of rare persuasive power.

In later years, I came to the realization that Papa's efforts to improve his speaking, reading, and writing skills were driven by a deep-seated desire to escape his poverty and to emulate the culture of the norteño landed gentry. He was *"un hombre pobre pero de orgullo,"* as people would say of certain individuals raised in his circumstances—a man who, despite his humble origins, harbored a fierce pride that drove him to escape the shame of poverty that had been his inheritance. In this effort to erase his past, however, Papa never succeeded—not because he lacked the intelligence or the motivation, but because there was a force in his life—a hubris, perhaps—that drove him toward both heroic acts and profane ones simultaneously. He seemed condemned to wrest defeat from the jaws of victory, as when he squandered generous sums earned as a fruit buyer for a packing company during World War II—all, seemingly, for his love of women and liquor.

Papa's charismatic persona and formidable language skills earned

Pancho Peña, 1912

him the admiration and respect of both his peers and superiors; yet despite his abilities, he seemed convinced that he was predestined to life as a lowly "ox at the plow." As he admitted to me in one of those riveting conversations we held toward the end of his long life, when I was an anthropologist and he a willing "informant," fear of success stalked him always. "Instead of taking advantage of my successes," he recalled, "I succumbed to my vices"—the parrandas that brought him to his knees and remained his most enduring legacy to his offspring.

And, as he often reminded his children, Pancho Peña was raised in a social climate driven by the intense conflict that marked Anglo-Mexican

Pancho Peña with Nancy Reagan, 1980

relations in the Southwest in the days of his youth, prior to World War II. Unlike my generation, his had experienced the aftermath of the American conquest of the Southwest in all its unmediated brutality. Thus, despite his intelligence and his gregariousness, which could ingratiate even the most racist of gringos, he was the object of discriminatory acts on more occasions than he cared to remember. He recalled, as an example, the time he and his compadre Esteban Ramos were pistol-whipped and hauled to jail by a Texas Ranger, simply because they did not produce their World War I draft cards. *"Era puro alemán el desgraciado,"* he said—a "German

SOB through and through," in reference to his conviction that Germans were the most prejudiced of all gringos, especially those in Central Texas, notorious for their mistreatment of Mexicans. Ironically, Papa remembered his German patrones as unusually generous toward him, perhaps because he had a faint Teutonic look about him (he even spoke a little German), and perhaps because he worked hard and was such a master at disarming his antagonists.

Thus, despite the stigma he suffered as a Mexican, on repeated occasions his natural leadership and his silver tongue impressed the patrones, who singled him out and charged him with command over others. One example, in particular, stands as apposite in my mind—the time Joe Milano started importing braceros to help harvest his cotton fields in the Brazos Valley. Papa was a logical choice for the role of majordomo, and Milano put him in charge of the largest crew. All went well, until the inevitable happened: the majordomo went on one of his periodic weekend drinking sprees, and when Monday arrived, he was in such a pathetic state he could hardly get up. But he did the usual—he drank a beer to "cure" his hangover and went off to round up the braceros. But his *cruda* (hangover) was unusually harsh, and he was desperate for another drink, so he stopped at Trudy's, a country tavern, to pick up another cold one while the men waited on the loaded truck. Unfortunately, Lofton, the general foreman, was on to Papa, and he arrived just as my old man was coming out of Trudy's. Lofton threatened to have him hanged by his balls, and an argument ensued. Papa lost his handle, and he stalked off on foot, walking the mile or so from the tavern to the cinder-block cottage we called home. He left Lofton seething and his shocked crew stranded on the parking lot at Trudy's.

I saw him when he arrived, looking haggard and red-eyed, as if he hadn't slept in a week. "¿Qué pasó, Francisco?" my mother asked, with a look of dread in her face. "*Este hijo'e su chingada madre*—that son-of-a-fucked-bitch," he answered, his face drawn and turning even more ashen. "He's been waiting for an opportunity to nail me. I knew he had it in for me the moment Milano appointed him general foreman. Well, he's not going to fuck with me anymore. I told him to go *chingar su madre* and that's it. Things have gotten pretty rotten around here, no thanks to Lofton, but he'll have to find some other Mexican to beat on, because we're getting out of here."

Pancho Peña family, 1912

We left Milano's farm immediately after the incident. Papa informed us on the very next day that we were leaving the estate on which we had sharecropped for the last three years. The harvest was not finished yet, and the thirty acres we sharecropped were still unpicked, but Papa had gone over to Milano's place, and he had told our patrón he could not work with Lofton any more. Milano told him he was willing to forget the incident, but Papa had made up his mind. "Vámonos," he announced, and with that, we loaded the tiliches on cousin Reynaldo's truck. Reynaldo had a crew picking cotton up the road in Waco, and we joined him and his pickers the very next day. (We found out later, much to Papa's satisfaction, that Milano had fired Lofton within six months after we left. The general foreman was replaced by an old work mate of ours—Charlie, Slogam's son.)

That summer of '56 was the last time Papa would hold a job with leadership responsibilities. For the next four years, until he turned sixty-five and applied for Social Security, he and his family drifted in and out of harvests, as we ranged far beyond our usual haunts, visiting places like the Midwest and California. Papa and the older boys even spent three months in Florida. In time, I came to understand that the Lofton incident was not only the most shameful Pancho Peña ever experienced, but a summing up of the paradox surrounding this extraordinary man—the personal magnetism that marked him as a leader running up and colliding with the urge to self-destruct through his compulsion to risk everything for the sake of his addictions.

≡

Even if, as some of his children accused him, Papa had committed an "indecency" by marrying la Lili so soon after Mama's death, I had excused his amorous fling as an eccentric act attributable to advancing age and a quixotic attempt to recapture his lost male vigor. Frank and José, especially, were highly indignant about our father's actions. Both had converted in recent years to the fundamentalist Apostolic Church, and Frank was by then an ordained minister, so they were particularly sensitive to any action by a member of the family that might reflect negatively on their own Christian morality. To them, he was a sinful old fool, making a futile and immoral attempt to prove his macho virility. I, on the other hand, was undergoing a moral radicalization at the time, thanks to my experiences at the Welfare office, where my rebellious friends were eroding many of the values I had absorbed at home and at school. I thus looked upon my father's actions with a bit of levity, even applauding him for breaking the rules of his puritanical church. When he married la Lili at the age of seventy-five, Papa was boldly going where most people his age were too old and feeble to even consider. In my view, his leap into marriage was thus an extraordinary display of male prowess, and I was pleased with the mettle he showed at such an advanced age. So what if my prudish brothers are scandalized by his daring act, I reasoned. Now that they have renounced carnal pleasures, what do these Christian ascetics know about sexual passion and forbidden desire?

Perhaps, I thought, he had married because he needed companionship. In the months following Mama's death, he stayed for a spell at Elia's house in Camarillo, and I would sometimes see him, gazing vacantly into space for long minutes at a time, oblivious to the bustle of people all around him. Having seen him in such a despondent state, I could sympathize with his wish to remarry. La Lili would no doubt be a comfort to him, providing him not only companionship but food at the table, pressed clothes, a clean home, and a sense of stability. These were all domestic services he had come to consider a married right during his long years with Mama. And, I thought, if he wants to satisfy some sexual fantasy, why not? All because, as my brothers claimed, he should devote the rest of his life to God? Or, as my own mother-in-law hinted, because it was indecent for an over-the-hill fool to crave sex? Nonsense, I argued. He owes nothing to his children in his old age, least of all his morality.

And so, while my brothers were scandalized by what they saw as Papa's reckless and unchristian act, I secretly cheered him on. (Fortunately, sisters Imelda and Elia seemed more tolerant than my brothers, perhaps because they had now been relieved of their motherly duties to him, and someone else could take care of his needs.) But Frank and José saw Papa's as the sinful actions of an immoral man, and they were indignant. The family had never forgotten (or forgiven) his days as a womanizer, and, as far as his converted sons were concerned, he had never really "accepted Christ." In their view, his lack of the proper respect for his wife's death betrayed his worldly ways. He was, once again, a "fallen" sinner.

After Judge Kruger concluded the boda by pronouncing Papa and María man and wife, I embraced my new stepmother. As I put my arms around the squat Indian woman, I was overcome by a sense of disquiet. Suddenly, the pungent smell of garlic, which I had long associated with Mama's delicious guisados and her special healing salves, seemed repulsive to me. I had never seen María until today, and now she was to take the place of another woman, one who had nurtured both Papa and me almost until the day she died. A shudder swept through my body as the reality of the marriage sank in, and at that moment María became the embodiment of my father's longstanding infidelity to my mother. A wave of disgust engulfed me, and, suddenly, I almost sympathized with the sense of outrage my brothers expressed when they found out he had married la Lili. But outwardly I maintained a smile and welcomed María into the Peña family, wishing Papa and his third wife success in the future.

"Bueno, vámonos," Papa said as he picked up his Stetson hat and put it on his bald head. We went out into the early February fog, which was now beginning to lift, Papa and María walking arm-in-arm. It was almost two o'clock in the afternoon.

She wanted to spend the rest of the day with the Sorias, and have Papa come and pick her up later, perhaps after dinner when Mrs. Soria, a nurse's aid, had returned home from her job. "Oh, no," Mr. Soria intervened. "You go with your husband. From now on you are his wife, and you are no longer free to do as you please."

She looked at Papa from behind her thick glasses, her magnified dark eyes blinking innocently, as if she were some timorous, naive girl getting married for the first time. "*¿Me voy contigo*—shall I go with you?" she asked haltingly.

"Let's go to Fresno and stay with Manuel for a while," he said; then, with a soothing, gentle tone he added, "We can come back to Crestview tonight, after you have finished crocheting that shawl you've been making for Mrs. Soria's daughter. *¿Cómo la ves?*—what do you think?"

"Ah, bueno," she agreed, happy that she could come back at least once more to the security of her cousin's home.

We then drove back to Fresno, Papa and María in the back seat, sitting close together in silence. They were holding hands.

"*Cuñao.*" Noé was at the other end of the telephone line. He always called Frank, José, and me "*cuñado*" (or the clipped version, "*cuñao*")—"brother-in-law." "Yes?" "*Cuñao, ya murió Papa Pancho*—Papa Pancho has died." I looked at the clock: it was 1:35 in the morning.

"We'll go down tomorrow, as soon as we get ourselves together," I told Nóe. "He's dead," I said softly to my wife María. "Papa has finally met his maker." Groggy from the deep sleep I was in when the telephone had awakened me, I felt no particular emotion at that moment, only a void deep in my stomach, which bordered on nausea.

He had been ill for some time, and over the last six months his strength had gradually deserted him. He had suffered one respiratory infection after another, and they had taken their toll. When he couldn't walk anymore, he was taken by Elia and Consuelo to the hospital, where he was diagnosed with pneumonia and admitted. María, our three children, and I had spent the past weekend with him in Camarillo, but since the doctor had informed us his condition was stabilizing, we had returned to Fresno to take care of our business at home. "He's a real fighter," the attending doctor told us. "At his age many people succumb to pneumonia, but he seems to have a strong will to live." Just three months shy of his ninety-first birthday, Papa was stubbornly holding on to life, talking to his children and still showing traces of his once-hearty appetite by eating most of the supper the orderly had brought him.

When the end finally came for the old ox-at-the-plow, Consuelo, his wife of ten years, was at the head of the mourners' cortège, seated in front of the newly dug grave. Papa's flower-laden casket rested on the scaffold, ready to be lowered. He had wed his fourth wife to a chorus, once again, of indignant protests from his Christian children. Papa had arranged to annul his marriage to María Carrizales when he discovered, to his consternation, that she was legally married in Mexico. She had evidently hooked up with Papa with the intention of obtaining her legal residency in the United States and, maybe eventually, that of her husband. Somehow, Papa found out about her marital status, and her intentions, and he wasted no time dumping her.

But Pancho Peña was not finished in his conquest of women yet. He had one more boda left in him—one more knot to be tied. Furthermore, not being a man to be swayed by pious detractors, once he had established contact with his wife-to-be after reading her *pesquisa*—a personal "introduction" she had placed in a Spanish-language newspaper—he moved swiftly to bring her to California and to legalize the relationship. Considerably younger than he, Consuelo, a stout mestiza from the port of Tampico, Tamaulipas, had seen to his needs during their ten-year marriage (although, according to Imelda, during his last years she had become abusive and tyrannical with him). Consuelo was an alert woman, and she took immediate steps to become a legal resident, even as she started bringing her children into the United States from Mexico, until one by one, all five of them had also gained legal residence.

When Papa died, Consuelo lost a spouse, but in return she assured herself of a government check for the rest of her life. His Social Security was the only inheritance Papa "owned" that he could pass along, and his last wife was the only heir who was eligible for survivors' benefits. Combining the government check with her own industriousness and hustle (she was an excellent seamstress), Consuelo lived frugally but comfortably for many years after Pancho Peña left this world. She was surrounded by her sons and daughters, all of whom had Papa to thank for their opportunity to share, however modestly, in America's bounty.

As for his own children, his legacy to them was the paradox that was his life—the charm and the wrath, the inner strength and the moral weakness, the pride and the shame. And, for me in particular, the will to go where the ox does not plow.

24
FEAR OF "BIG BALLS"

We were picking cotton on the twenty acres we sharecropped with E. B. Gruene. The sky was dotted with building cumulus clouds, and some of them had already spiraled upward into the familiar thunderheads. Intermittently, we could hear the distant thunder from a towering cumulo-nimbus hovering not far to the east. "*Hay que apurarle*—we need to hurry it up," Papa was saying, "and see if we can get one more weigh-in before the rain arrives."

I had long been fascinated by thunderstorms, having acquired an interest from Mama, who was terrified of them. To her, thunderstorms were nerve-wracking experiences to be endured—especially the violent ones, accompanied by wind, lightning, and hail. To me, they were exciting adventures into the heart of nature. Whenever a thunderstorm struck, Mama would cower in a corner, praying that it would soon end and that we would be spared its fury. When we lived in our little shoebox in Weslaco, which was a bit better furnished than the spartan shacks we occupied on our campañas, she would scurry to the tiny bedroom and throw a blanket over the dresser with the big round mirror. Someone had told her the reflection of lightning in the mirror had a magnetic effect, which could draw the electricity into the house and cause everyone inside to be incinerated. The thought horrified her, and, when we lived in the unfurnished shacks up north, she often expressed her relief that at least we didn't have to worry about dangerous mirrors.

As Papa, my brothers Frank and Plon, and I were getting ready to abandon the field in the face of the rainstorm bearing hard upon us, I remembered Mama's instinctive fear of thunderstorms, and all the names the people of South Texas had for them. These included *aguacero* (rainstorm), *tempestad* (tempest), *tormenta* (storm), and one peculiar to the tejanos, *pelotón de agua*, or simply *pelotón*. The last is difficult to translate. *Pelotón* literally means "big ball," but in the context of the South Texas vernacular, the phrase signified a powerful thunderstorm with heavy rain—in short, a "big ball" of rain, a deluge.

The threatening weather had brought to mind all of these terms that Mama and tejanos used, and, curious about their comparative degree of severity, I asked my father, in Spanish, "Papa, which is worst—an aguacero, a tempestad, tormenta, or a pelotón?"

My father, who at the moment was concerned with covering the trailer to protect the cotton from water damage, listened to my question with only one ear, but did respond. "Oh, I don't know, son," he said. "In the end I suppose they're all pretty much the same thing."

"Well," I said to him, "the reason I ask is because I often hear Mama say that she is afraid of *pelotones*—of 'big balls.'"

On hearing this, Papa burst into a hearty and prolonged fit of laughter, while leaving me totally perplexed. That evening, as we were waiting for supper to be served, he told Mama about my question, and when she heard about it, she too burst into laughter.

The little vignette was repeated endlessly to relatives and friends, and it never failed to elicit at least a chuckle. But it was only after I had tasted of the tree of knowledge that I understood why my parents and others found my childish question so humorous.

25
THE DEATH OF AGUSTINA JASSO

My dearest Children,

I received your letter and was filled with jubilation and happiness.

As for me, I can't get rid of the pain in my leg—a sort of rheumatism. . . .

I'm glad my Nanito is a bit spoiled. He is alone and doesn't have anything else to spend his time on, except entertain himself with something that scrapes and makes noise. So give him many kisses and tell him his grandparents will let him get away with anything. . . .

I bid good-bye with kisses for the three of you from your loony Mama. Answer my letter by hare or by turtle, whether it's soon or whenever you can.

Letter from Agustina Jasso, May 13, 1969

"Manuel," I heard Papa calling me. His tone did not sound particularly urgent, but there was nonetheless an ominous edge to it. María, my sister Elia, and I were sitting at the kitchen table in the cramped apartment, playing Scrabble and drinking coffee, when Papa called me. I got up and stepped into the tiny bedroom next to the kitchen, and I immediately became aware of the reason for Papa's summons. He was standing over Mama, who was prostrate in the bed where she had spent more and more time over the past few weeks. Motionless, she was foaming at the mouth.

"Call the ambulance, m'hijo," he said, trying to remain calm. "I think your mother is dying." He placed a towel over her face.

I was walking to and fro outside, waiting impatiently for the ambulance to arrive. We knew Mama was dying of cancer, and so the onset of death was not particularly surprising. But the suffering she had endured rankled inside of me, and I was crying out of anger with God for inflicting such pain on one of the saintliest human beings I had ever known.

≣

"That's it, over there, Alonso," I pointed out the house to my future brother-in-law as we approached the address at 500 East Torritos Street. The car pulled off the dusty unpaved street and stopped in front of the darkened house, the one we had renovated three years earlier. Its angular, single-gable roof was clearly outlined against the cloudy sky illumined by the city lights below. It was hot and smelly inside the crowded car, in which Alonso, his wife Chelo, their two small children, María, and I had driven the 1800 miles from Wrangler City, California, to the Rio Grande Valley of Texas. I stepped out and breathed the warm, humid Gulf air, which offered little relief against the sweat drenching my body. The atmosphere felt suffocating, in comparison to the arid climate of California's San Joaquin Valley. Alonso opened the trunk, and I pulled out the blue metal suitcase, a well-worn witness to the many campañas the Peña family had endured in years gone by. I took leave of my fellow travelers and stood for a moment contemplating the scene before me.

It was past ten in the evening, and the house was in darkness, except for a dim shaft of light issuing from the window in my parents' bedroom. I looked forward to seeing Mama and Papa. I had been gone for only three months, but it seemed as if I had been absent for a much longer spell than that. "God bless you, m'hijo," Mama had said when I left. "Don't forget to send your mamacita a few pennies." "How you are, woman," Papa intervened, with a tone of irritation. "You know he needs money for his college, and you know we can't help him, so don't bother him with silly demands." But I did send Mama "a few pennies" from California that summer of '62, and I did manage to save a few more for my first year at Pan American College.

And now I was back, glad to be near Mama and Papa, for whom my appreciation had deepened in the three short months I had been away. I had missed them sorely, in the way, I imagined, that absence heightens our yearning for loved kinfolk. Papa was on Social Security by then, and when I left, my parents seemed to be enjoying a period of relative tranquility in what at times had been a troubled marriage. Mama's frequent ailments had contributed to the marital strain, but Papa's impatience with her, his marital infidelities, and periodic bouts of alcoholism had also been a source of friction. Older now and permanently on the wagon, he seemed a bit more mellow and content in his retirement.

As I paused momentarily under the large mesquite tree in front of the house, thinking about my parents, a gust of wind suddenly set the leaves in motion. The melodic wooden sound of the ripe, sugary pods striking against each other brought a flood of memories—playing marbles with Quique and Güero; watching Manuel Ábrego scream in pain when he fell off the mesquite tree in Güero's yard and broke his hand; hunting rabbits in the mesquite thicket with Quique and Chalo Tamez. I could still see Chalo, looking incongruously out of place in the dress slacks and Arrow shirt he had worn to a party the night before, a cigarette in one hand and the 38 Smith and Wesson in the other. So many memories associated with this ancient emblem of my homeland, the mesquite. I took one of the pods, snapped it open, and, sucking on its tart seeds, walked toward the house.

I knocked on the door, and Papa answered shortly. His robust, erect frame and his ruddy face let me know he was in excellent health. That was the picture of the old man I had always carried in my head—brimming with health, energetic, virile. On the eve of his sixty-seventh birthday, he had definitely regained a good deal of the sprightliness he had lost during his last days as a binge drinker, when the ravages of alcohol abuse sapped much of his usual vitality. As was his habit when reuniting with his children after a period of absence, he immediately burst into tears when he saw me.

"M'hijo! How good it is to have you home safely, thanks be to God." he stuttered between sobs as he embraced me. Then, regaining his emotional control, he asked about José: "¿Cómo están él y Lula, y las muchachas?"

"They're all doing well, and they send you their love, Papa. Where's Mama?"

As Papa and I exchanged greetings, the state of the surroundings registered half-consciously in my mind. Was the kitchen always painted this gaudy yellow? I noticed a new—or at least different—dinette set. The blue ceiling in the living area looked awfully faded. "We need to paint it," I thought. My eyes rested momentarily on the old sofa we had bought from a neighbor when we renovated the house, the one I slept in when I was at home. It looked even seedier now, and the brocaded bed cover carelessly draped over it only partially concealed the tears on the worn fabric. But my conscious mind was quickly drawn toward the irritation in Papa's voice.

"Where do you think? She's in her bed, sick, as usual."

"She's still sick?"

Papa had mentioned in one of his letters that she had not been feeling well. But, as he added, this was not at all unusual for Mama. "*Ya ves como es tu Mamá,*" he had written, "*no le falta un achaque para quejarse*—You know how your mother is: she's never lacking an excuse to complain." He had made no further mention of Mama's condition, and I assumed she had gotten better.

"Why didn't you let me know she was still sick?"

"Because there's nothing seriously wrong with her. Don't worry, the doctor has assured me of it. Nerves, he tells her, it's her nerves, but she keeps right on complaining. Every day it's the same story—el mismo *¡ay, ay, ay!* She is driving me crazy; I don't know what to do with her. But you know how it is with your mother. When it's not one thing, it's another. Agustina! Your son is home."

Papa was right about Mama's perennial complaints. Chronic illness seemed to be the rule with her. Indeed, that is the picture of her I shall always carry in my mind's eye—a sickly, sad, vulnerable woman curled up in a bed surrounded by medicine bottles and a pained look on her dark, exquisitely shaped Indian face. It was a gentle, loving face on Mama's good days. *La cara de bondad,* as people used to say of our mother—the face of kindness, which lit our lives when it was free of pain. "How are you feeling today, Mamacita?" we children would ask. The question was redundant, since her condition was already written on her expression. On good days she radiated warmth and comfort, the mischievous smile in her dark eyes communicating good cheer. But too often her inner turmoil invaded the soft contours and chiseled its punishment on her furrowed brow and drooping mouth. "*Ay, m'hijo,*" she would respond. "*Este dolor en el estómago que no se me quita*—this pain in the stomach that won't go away." On such days she was withdrawn and self-absorbed.

I entered Mama's bedroom and was immediately taken aback. I had not expected to see her in such a declining state. She sat hunched in bed, propped up by pillows, shoulders sagging, her scoliotic spine pronouncing the frailty of her body. Her thick, gray hair looked dirty and disheveled, and her high cheekbones stood out like knobs on her grimacing face. The wrinkles on her forehead were deeply etched, accentuating her distressed appearance. She looked much older than her fifty-four years. When I caught sight of her, the feeling of joyful anticipation I had experienced upon arrival drained out of my body like siphoned blood.

"I'm sick, Memito," she moaned as soon as she saw me.

"Nonsense, mujer," my father interjected. "It's all in your head. *No tienes nada.* The doctors have examined you, and they have assured me it's all in your head. It's a habit with you, woman, something you do to get attention. I'm sick and tired of your complaining."

"That's not true. You talk like that because you don't—you have no. . . ." Her voice trailed off weakly, melting into the humid air that drenched the room.

"As God is my witness, you've been like this all your life, mujer. I've lived with you for over thirty-five years, and it's always been the same '*ay, ay, ay.*' *¡Caramba!* How much more of this can a man take?"

"You see, m'hijto? This is the way he treats me. He has no sympathy for my suffering; he has no compassion."

"Why don't you go ahead and die? Then maybe I could find some rest." In exasperation, Papa waved his hands in the air and walked into the kitchen, where he poured himself a cup of coffee.

I approached Mama and put my arm around her, a heavy pall of sorrow blanketing my whole being. "Tell me, Mamacita, what is it you feel?"

"Something inside me, Memito, in my stomach. I can't even eat anymore. I have these horrible images, of hideous sores festering in my intestines. Every minute of my waking life is filled with misery. What could it be, m'hijo? What is wrong with me?"

"I don't know, Mamita. If the doctors can't find anything wrong, then maybe it is your nerves. You must try to calm yourself, to relax. And make sure to take your medicines. They should make you feel better soon."

"But I do take them; they just don't have any effect."

Papa had returned from the kitchen. "Of course they don't have an effect. She doesn't take the medicine as she should. Look, look at all those bottles she has on that night stand. There are enough to fill a blasted drugstore. I've spent hundreds of dollars on her. And for what?"

"Get out of here!" Mama wailed. "Manuel, tell him to leave me in peace; tell him to go away, please!"

"Let her be, Papa. It does neither you nor her any good for you to get so upset."

"I'm trying to keep my sanity, son, trying to see to her needs, but my patience is at an end. All my life with her has been like this, one illness after another. You have no idea how bad it has been, you cannot understand—." His energy sapped, Papa stepped into the kitchen and slumped into a chair. He remained silent for a long time, sitting there, grinding his teeth in frustration.

I was standing in the doorway, looking now at Papa in the kitchen and at Mama prostrate in her bed. At that moment I wondered how such an incongruous couple could have survived nearly thirty-six years of intimacy. Papa was the energetic, domineering father, a man driven by his strong will and lust for life. Mama was the self-effacing and downtrodden woman, heavily dependent on Papa for everything, even for her identity. But then again, I thought, perhaps their extreme difference results in a mutual dependence—she for her very existence, he for his sense of superiority. Both, I would come to realize later, were very much the offspring of Border culture. Papa played the role of the indomitable patriarch, Mama the suffering and submissive wife. And, in keeping with the ideals of that culture, both were bound to each other for life, the concept of divorce as alien to them as the practice of birth control.

Suddenly, I became aware of the quiet that had descended over the house. Papa was still sitting in the kitchen. Motionless, he was apparently deep in thought, with his eyes shut, arms crossed, and chin on his chest, while Mama seemed to have dosed off. The sounds of the night began to register in my ears. A cricket's steady chirp rang with metronomic precision outside Mama's open window. The hissing sound of boiling liquids coming from a nearby cannery reminded me that the world beyond Mama's window hummed along, as people went about their business. The rumble of a passing truck rang in my ears, and I heard voices coming from the street, late as it was at night. But it was a Friday, and even at this hour, Weslaco and its barrios were still alive with people.

Mama sighed, and my attention was drawn to her once more. The look of pain never left her face, even in sleep. In the hushed light from the little table lamp, I could see her wrinkles, deeply etched on her forehead. "Her chest looks so sunken," I thought, "and her back seems more hunched than I can remember." Had she always been so deformed? No, not this badly. She had been like that, hunchbacked, ever since I first became aware of her presence. As everyone knew, her long life of suffering, from her stomach and other assorted ailments, had caused her to age before her time. And, my sister Imelda would add, from childhood malnutrition, abandonment, loneliness, and God knows what other hardships that had all been visited on this orphaned child.

As I stood there, contemplating the scene before me, I suddenly became aware of an unpleasant odor in the room. What was it? Thoughts and sensations raced through my mind, and then the sense of smell made the connection, sending a shudder through my body: it was the odor that hovered over the one-room shack where the Cerdas had held a wake for their dead baby. They lived on Joe Milano's farm in Hearne, where we were sharecropping at the time. The Cerdas were illegal immigrants, and, when the baby died of dysentery, they hastily buried it in a makeshift grave, rather than report the death to the authorities. The image of the wake scene and Mama's present state converged in my mind's eye, and a wave of anxiety swept through me. I felt a strong urge to flee from the room and its smell of death.

I walked out to the dirt patio in the back, where the gentle breeze, the night sounds, and familiar surroundings began to ease the fear in my gut. Gradually, the sense of impending doom gave way to a feeling of profound sorrow. Papa came out shortly, and he approached and gently laid his hand on my shoulder.

"Don't cry, m'hijo." His voice had the soothing quality I remembered from the time in Edroy, long ago, when he had personally nursed me through a serious bout with pneumonia because Mama was deep into one of her depressive spells. "God is just; he will set things right. Sometimes he works in ways we cannot fathom." Listening to him, I immediately felt better.

"She seemed so healthy when I left, Papa—more alive than I had seen her in a long time. What happened?"

"I don't know. For two months she's been like that. I try to be strong and patient, to give her hope. But at times my own strength is put to the test, and sometimes I fear that I, too, could be dragged down with her. But we must trust in God; He is great in His mercy. Oh, I had forgotten to tell you—Henry Rodríguez called today, about some papers for your college. He wanted you to call him as soon as you got in."

Late as it was, I went back in and called Henry on the telephone Papa had installed while I was away—the first we'd ever had. Henry was a high-school buddy who was already attending Pan American, and he had obtained the necessary forms for my application while I was in California. He arrived shortly and asked me to join him for a late snack at the Keno Restaurant, where he was sure we would to find Gene Pérez, Henry's brother Roland, Bobby de la Rosa, and the rest of the clique. These and several other old friends were at the Keno, and after hearty greetings all around, someone suggested we get some beer and have a party out in the country, at Sunrise Hill.

"You wanna go with us?" Gene asked.

The picture of Mama lying in her bed flashed through my mind, and I felt a twinge of remorse.

"Yeah," I answered. "What the hell, we may as well have a little fun. It's been a while."

≣

"Ahi viene la jorobada—here comes the hunchback," I heard Quique say as Mama approached. That was the insult my playmates whispered conspiratorially, in reference to Mama's scoliotic spine. I imagine she must have been self-conscious about her condition, and even coming from a nine-year-old, the insult no doubt stung her pride. She had overheard Quique, and she looked at him with a frowning half-smile, then responded with a typical Agustina witticism: *"Oye, ojos de gato, no seas mal hablado; vete a descular hormigas, huerco feo*—hey, cat-eyes, don't be a foul-mouth. Go busy yourself dissecting ant butt-holes, you ugly whelp."

That little scene with my playmates captured much of Agustina Jasso's predicament. She was a sad, reclusive, disfigured woman who could still spray witticisms with machine-gun frequency when the occasion presented itself. Her disfigurement no doubt contributed to Mama's reclusive habits. As my sister Elia would recall years later, "On top of all the other problems she suffered as an abandoned orphan, Mama considered herself an unsightly woman, and this kept her from expressing her sense of—you know—femininity." Thus, during my childhood and adolescence, especially, she never primped herself or applied a trace of makeup, and she never wore but the simplest of house dresses. (The only "makeup" she ever wore on the occasional visit to friends' was baby powder; to this day, the smell of talcum evokes Agustina Jasso, not babies.) And she never went any place, except for the infrequent trip to the market with Papa. The usual forms of entertainment were beyond her reach: she never attended a dance or saw a movie—for that matter, she never participated in any sort of celebration. She wasn't at my high-school graduation or even at my wedding, but it was as if we all understood why: like Quasimodo, she was the freak cut off forever from society by the double jeopardy of her infirmities and her misshapen body.

To make matters worse, throughout the fifties and early sixties Mama suffered recurrent spells of panic disorder. The panic was part of the "curse of the Jassos," as my father labeled the condition that wound through Mama's lineage. Much to her distress, Mama was afflicted with this syndrome all of her life, though there were times, especially in her later years, when she was spared its worst effects. But some situations were certain to provoke the fulminating fear and desperation of a panic attack: being confined in a train, for example, where escape seemed impossible or, worse, in an airplane. Particularly agonizing to Mama were winding mountain roads. Traveling on them could be excruciating for her, and later, when she and Papa moved to their final destination in Camarillo, California, she dreaded having to visit her children in nearby Fillmore, because it was necessary to negotiate "*el caracol*," as she called the spiraling mountain road that connected the two communities.

And of course there was Mama's intense fear of hurricanes and thunderstorms. Finally, as if the demons of panic did not generate enough terror, during her middle years Mama suffered from agoraphobia. Crowds frightened her; the hustle and bustle of the market place set her adrenaline flowing, even as it paralyzed her brain. She became a virtual recluse, confined to the security of her home and the immediate barrio neighborhood.

Mama felt particularly clumsy and out of place among the americanos. She always held affluent Anglo women in special awe, and there was no question in my mind that she felt horribly insecure in the presence of "*gringas orgullosas*," as she called them—haughty Anglo women like my sixth-grade teacher, Mrs. Jameson who, to Mama, were nothing short of superwomen. I can still remember the time another teacher, Mrs. Emerson, visited our shack unannounced, to express her concern to my parents about my chronic tonsillitis, which she felt could only be remedied by removal of the tonsils. Mama panicked when she saw my immaculately dressed teacher step out of her car, and she rushed to the box of miscellanea where she kept her baby powder, hastily dabbing some on her face and neck. It was an awkward and embarrassing scene, the smugly confident Mrs. Emerson trying to communicate with Mama, who did not speak English and who was obviously petrified despite her game attempts to keep a smiling face. She remained jumpy and in a state of alert for the rest of the day.

In Mama's mind, Anglo women had everything she lacked—poise, charm, beauty, power, intelligence, and wealth. Compared to the paragons of grace and confidence that were the americanas, she was a lowly misfit, a timid, hunchbacked brown woman who had nothing to offer but pride in her domestic labor and unflinching devotion to her husband and children. I could understand why Mama felt inferior to the gringas; I too was overwhelmed by their presence, especially teachers like Mrs. Jameson and Mrs. Guidry. Indeed, I was ashamed to be seen in the gringo sections of town with Mama—she seemed so small and puny and, well, so Indian, in comparison to the imperious and beautiful americanas. Like her, I would long stand in awe of them.

But not all people frightened Mama—only the anonymous faces "out there," in the bald glare of the public places. In the intimacy of her home and the surrounding barrio, with its circles of friendship and reciprocity, Agustina Jasso could be an ingratiating and charming woman, known for her utmost generosity and a wry, pixiesh wit that delighted the Peña family in her sprightlier moments. Among her vecinas as well, the poor brown women of the barrio, she allowed her native intelligence and abundant talent to display themselves, though always with a disarming sense of humility and understatement. She was consequently admired and much loved by her compañeras, whose devotion provided whatever social pleasure and fulfillment she could eke out of her stormy and tortured life.

Her relationship with Eva García, my mother-in-law, was typical. Although the two comadres did not often see each other, on the few occasions they did visit, doña Eva was one of Mama's most avid listeners. She absolutely feasted on Mama's narrative bounty. On at least a couple of occasions, I overheard Mama regaling her comadre with some of the folkloric stories and jokes she had learned during her otherwise sordid youth. In the company of women like Eva García, Mama plunged into the role of performer with a passion, sharing an impressive range of narratives, from riddles and folktales to a type of bawdy joke common to Mexican men but often shared by mature Mexican women with intimates. María always remembered the laughter and merriment one of Mama's bawdy jokes elicited during one of their visits.

It was about the two women who, like Mama and Eva, had been brought up in a repressive patriarchal culture and a technologically primitive environment typical of the rural areas along the Texas-Mexican border. In a moment of curiosity, one of the women asks the other, "*Oiga comadre, nunca ha cogido usted con condón*—say, comadre, have you ever fucked with a condom?" Confused, or perhaps piqued, the other comadre replies with her own question: "*¿Con don quién?*—with don who?" The humor in this joke, as Eva García fully appreciated, is in the confusion created by the two words, "*con condón*—with a condom," which, when run rapidly together can be taken for the words "*con don*—with don (Mr.)," leaving the sentence hanging: "with don [someone]. . . ." Of course, it is the underlying theme of forbidden pleasures among presumably chaste, simple women that doña Eva (and Mama) found so humorous, perhaps because it resonated deeply in their repressed sense of sexuality. But that was the glaring paradox surrounding Agustina Jasso—a strongly repressed and self-effacing woman possessed with a liberating sense of the carnivalesque and its subversive wit. Eva García and other barrio women could well appreciate that wit.

In the safety of her barrio surroundings, then, Mama was not averse to the play of her folkloric imagination. In ludic moments with friends and family, when her buried desires lifted up on the wings of laughter, the jester in her peeked out and let loose in mirth. Momentarily freed from the demons of her afflictions, social and physical, she became a master of humor.

Like my father, Mama was supremely adept at nicknaming. I remember one moniker in particular, which she pinned on a vecino, a rather wimpy neighbor whom Mama considered henpecked. His wife was a strong, voluptuous woman who exuded the self-confidence of someone

Agustina Jasso, 1949

fully conscious of her dominant sex appeal, and who my parents suspected of carrying on an affair with a compadrito of theirs. At times I was convinced that Mama was envious of the woman's sexual magnetism and her flirtatious nature, but such behavior also violated the chaste-wife archetype deeply ingrained in the psyches of women like Agustina Jasso. Thus, the vecina's brazen display of feminine sexuality, coupled with a certain disdain toward her husband's weak masculinity, was something Agustina Jasso could not consciously condone. To verbalize her disapproval—not of the woman, ironically, but of the man—Mama soon hung an apt nickname on the acquiescent husband—*Calzoncez*, which may be translated as "his Panty-ness," or, even more devastating, "his Pussiness."

Thus, despite her disabilities, Mama boasted a truckload of talents that matched those of my father. Like her husband, Agustina Jasso was the carrier of a vast fund of folkloric knowledge gained while growing up in Ciudad Mier, across the river from the city of Roma, Texas. Born in

1908, she had grown up amid her people's rural customs, which strongly valorized traditional skills associated with oral competence, in particular verbal arts like narrative, nicknaming, double entendre, and other folkloric genres. Naturally blessed with such verbal skills, Mama rivaled Francisco Peña as a master narrator, even if their rhetorical styles differed radically—his histrionic and direct, hers ironic and understated. Unlike her husband, however, Mama's talents were global: she was a gifted artist as well, though she confined her ability to pencil drawings of animals, flowers, and an occasional human face. A special gift was her musical ability, which unfortunately was the one she most neglected. She had a clear alto voice with a natural richness and a pleasing vibrato. Hers was a folk style, devoid of the artifice of trained singers, but her melodies, sung for our moral uplifting in the form of church hymns, had a sweet, plaintive quality.

And, as her neighbors often observed, Agustina Jasso was the most unselfish of housewives. Between her bouts with assorted illnesses, she was as industrious a homemaker as anyone I ever knew. I always picture her hunched over the tallador, scrubbing her family's clothes, then carefully starching and ironing every wrinkle out of the clothes her husband and children wore. As a youngster, I in particular was known as *"el catrín"* by the neighbors—the "dandy," in recognition of the creaselessly ironed clothes I wore to school every day. And, of course, Mama's attention to the kitchen was unassailable. *"Ay, Tinita,"* the women neighbors would invariably say, *"tú siempre en la cocina."* Perhaps nothing personified her dedication to domestic responsibilities more than the tenderly delicious dishes that were part of the Peñas' everyday diet, even in lean times when our meals consisted of the bare essentials, beans and potatoes.

But all of her kindness, wit and industriousness deserted Tinita every time she plunged into illness. Adding to Mama's chronic woes was perhaps her most crippling "disability"—what I later understood to be a powerfully repressed sense of her individuality. Over the years, she had almost become an appendage to Papa's personality, a weaker alter ego that he constantly used as a foil for his own sense of superiority. Unable to challenge his authority, she would characteristically defer to Papa. *"Pues ahi lo que tú pienses, Francisco*—Well, whatever you wish, Francisco,"* was her usual response when she judged him to be against something she desired, such as a new washing machine, a stove, or even a dress for herself. "Go to town and buy yourself a washing machine," one of our neighbors once told her. "Don't be a pushover; don't let Pancho talk you out of it. You're the only one in the barrio still slaving away on that tallador." "Heaven forbid," replied Mama, "I'm sure he would put me through the wringer." Fearful of incurring his wrath, she let him make all the decisions. But more than that, she depended on him almost entirely for her sense of social identity—or rather, his identity was so overbearing that hers remained recessive, and in a chronic state of self-denial.

And yet, as we all knew, deep within the timid, acquiescent persona that she projected, a magma of artistic talent swirled, bubbling to the surface often enough—a poignant reminder to us of the vibrant being residing at the core of her meek exterior.

≋

It was cousin Chabela's fourteenth birthday, and Mama's tía Chana had a special dress made for her daughter's birthday fiesta, complete with bright laces, a wide skirt with ruffles, and matching ribbons for her hair. Mama, who then lived with Chana, could only look at her cousin with envy, dressed as she was in her hand-me-down rags. Perhaps feeling a twinge of guilt, Tía Chana took some of Chabela's old ribbons and tied them on Mama's hair. "Why are you wearing my ribbons?" her cousin screamed at her. "They look awful on you. Take them off, and stay away from me and my friends." "I was so humiliated I hid in the chicken coop until the fiesta was over." This Mama told my sister Imelda many years later.

Agustina Jasso's youthful experiences with Chabela and other kin are the morbid stuff of fairy tales and their grim outcomes, before these were sanitized by Disney for the edification of American children. Hers was a Cinderella-like youth (sans Prince Charming), during which she lived through extreme hardship, beginning with the death of her mother soon after her delivery. The baby Agustina was left to the care of her grandmother and two aunts, Tías Chana and Toña. Her father, Aurelio Jasso, and his brother Anselmo were involved at the time in a revolt inspired by the Flores Magón brothers against the dictator Porfirio Díaz. When the revolt was squelched by the Díaz forces, the Jasso brothers fled to nearby Texas, where they remained for the rest of their lives. Abandoned by her father, Mama knew no other family than that of her aunts and grandmother.

Jasso grandmother and aunts, 1915

Tía Chana, a woman of some wealth, assumed primary responsibility for the orphan. She was married and had several children, of whom one, Chabela, was about the same age as Mama. Chabela despised her live-in cousin and, according to Imelda, she made Tinita's life as difficult as she could. But Mama was a docile and obedient child, and she did her best to please her tía Chana, taking on extra chores around the house, from looking after the goat herds to watching after Baldo, Chana's youngest child. Her aunt was not necessarily unkind to her, but she did nothing to prevent her children from tormenting Mama. However, Chana did make sure little Agustina finished the *primaria*, the Mexican equivalent to an eighth-grade education in the United States.

But Tinita needed the loving care of a real mother, and from what I heard from relatives, she was a lonely child, given to intestinal problems even during her youth. Besides her time in school, she spent her days mostly alone, tending goats, knitting, singing, reciting poetry to herself, and memorizing the vast store of folkloric knowledge that would be her artistic strength in her adult years. Papa recalled the first time he saw her, when she was about ten and he already in his twenties. "She was a scrawny little thing," he said, "and what struck me was how badly dressed she was. I remember thinking, 'poor little orphan. How sad that she was left motherless so young.'"

"I think that is why Mama was so unselfish, so giving of herself," Imelda was saying. "As an *arrimada* [unwanted live-in] herself, she knew what rejection and loneliness are really about. People sometimes took advantage of her generosity and her eagerness to please others. Do you remember Antonia, the lazy fat woman who lived behind the alley in Weslaco? She used to come around two or three times a week, just when Mama was making tortillas for lunch, and she would say, '*Ay, Tinita, qué lindo huelen tus tortillas.*' Mama would instantly offer her one, and then Antonia's kids clamored for tortillas themselves, and before you knew it, Mama had fed the whole brood, and she would have to start preparing new dough. 'Oh, Mama,' I would tell her, 'why do you let that lazy wench talk you into feeding her whole family?' 'Ay, m'hijita,' she would say, 'God tells us to love our neighbor, and we must always give of ourselves to others. God will repay us many times over.' But that was Mama—always giving, never asking."

When Mama turned eighteen, her father Aurelio finally decided to reclaim her, and he brought her up to Yorktown, Texas, where he had lived for years. He had remarried and had a family with his second wife, and Mama became part of the reconstituted Jasso household.

But she did not remain with her new family for long. Papa, who also lived in Yorktown, had long been friendly with Aurelio and often visited with him, and he saw Tinita in a new light, now that she was, according to him, a handsome young woman. He romanced her and won her heart, and at the age of eighteen, Mama became Señora Agustina Jasso de Peña. He was thirty-one.

"The patient is a timorous fifty-four-year-old Mexican woman who appears older than her age, due, partly, to the effects of scoliosis. She presented with rectal bleeding, and upon digital examination a mass was discovered, which, after microscopic analysis, proved to be malignant." I was reading the report of the surgeon who had performed the colostomy on Mama two years earlier, in 1963. After my return from California, when I found her sick in bed, her condition had deteriorated even further, and eventually she was diagnosed with rectal cancer. In 1965, when Mama had recovered fully from the operation, she, Papa, and little sister Elia moved to Crestview, California, and her physician in Weslaco had sent me the surgeon's report so that we could deliver it to her new doctor. Despite the removal of the malignant tumor, Mama continued to suffer from her "nervous stomach," and to better assess her condition, the doctor in Crestview had asked us to obtain the records from her physician in Texas.

Always at the core of her sense of self, "el estómago" was the storm that buffeted Mama's life, a destructive force that eased its grip only in her later years when she had seemingly recovered from cancer surgery, before a hidden metastasis regenerated to deliver the fatal blow. Eventually, I came to suspect Mama's mental anguish was driven by chronic depression linked to what is now known as "irritable bowel" (or "migraine of the gut," as it has recently been dubbed). "She was especially depressed after you were born," Imelda often reminded me. "I became your substitute mother, since she couldn't breast-feed you or even look after you. At times she was so sick and withdrawn that I had to prepare your bottle, bathe you, and basically take care of you. Some people thought you were my baby. I used to carry you around all the time."

And as if her intestinal problems were not enough, during her years of menopause, Mama was often laid up for days, the victim of a double punishment—irritable bowel and what is now known as PMS, or premenstrual syndrome. ("Irritable bowel seems to fluctuate with the ebb and flow of hormones during the menstrual cycle," reports the *Harvard Health*

Letter of June 2000). Although she struggled to keep up with her domestic chores, daily routines sometimes collapsed, and Papa was forced to do the cooking for the family. He may have been a strong and charismatic man, but Pancho Peña's cuisine was not one of his virtues, and we children grimaced, if silently, when we learned that he had been the cook for the day.

I would always wonder: was Mama Tinita's timid and withdrawn nature a part of her biological makeup? Clearly, her notorious bouts with panic disorder, which afflicted other relatives and which she passed along to her offspring, were tied to the "curse of the Jassos," as may well have been her depression (considered by some medical authorities to share the same "neuronal pathway" as panic disorder). Of course, in the forties and fifties no one in the barrio ever spoke of depression, but in retrospect, we were convinced many of Mama's symptoms were associated with that dreaded condition.

But yet another sad fact surfaced whenever we children talked about Mama's ordeals—the turmoil in her early years and its possible lifelong effects. I would always wonder about that, too: Were her childhood experiences somehow implicated in her suffering as an adult? Imelda and Elia were convinced that her abandonment and isolation resulted in a stunted personality that left Mama with a constant fear of being rejected. Whatever the connection between adult fears and childhood hardship, Mama was never her own advocate. Not once did I see her argue with anyone or defend a personal opinion. On the contrary, she would go to great lengths to avoid conflict.

Imelda and Frank recalled an incident that summed up Mama's reaction to individuals who challenged her. The ever-quarrelsome Plon had gotten into a fight with a new neighbor's kid and bloodied his nose. His mother, a tough-talking woman named Germana, was so incensed that she stormed out of her house and charged into our yard. "Tinita!" she yelled. "Come out here, you bitch. Your bullying son beat up on my child, and I'm gonna see that you pay for it. Come out here, now, before I go in there and pull you out by the hair." Germana was livid and ready to take out her wrath on Tinita. Mama, who had been baking empanadas, was terrified when she saw the fuming Germana. But she quickly sized up the situation and approached the screen door, calling out to her neighbor in her gentlest voice:

"Germana, my friend, please, don't be upset. You know how kids are;

they fight today and make up tomorrow. It's not worth getting so angry. Besides, you're pregnant, and getting all worked up is not good for you. Look, I have just baked these empanadas, and I have some freshly brewed coffee. Won't you come in and have some with me? They are fresh and delicious. Please don't be upset; come in, come in. Try my empanadas"

Gradually, Mama was able to placate the enraged Germana, and in the end, the neighbor did come in and help herself to Mama's pastry. She became one of Tinita's most devoted friends.

But that was Agustina Jasso—always eager to appease her antagonists. Yet her acquiescent nature could work to her disadvantage, especially with Papa. She yielded to his wishes on every occasion and only rarely pleaded her case with him. She seemed so desperate for his approval, for his love, while he took her devotion for granted and always seemed to look elsewhere for the satisfaction of his amorous pleasures. Was he a father figure? I would always wonder about that as well. And one final, troubling question: were her chronic complaints desperate messages from an inner voice caught in the emotional hurricane churning in the ocean of her interior? Were they alibis for a deeply repressed passion drowning under the weight of Pancho Peña's domination and surfacing only in the spume of her artistic creativity?

Mama implicitly accepted the supremacy of her husband, and although she occasionally confessed to Imelda her offense at Papa's abusive behavior (the night he came home drunk and threatened to beat her comes to mind), she never questioned her subordinate role in the home. Unlike women such as Tía Virginia and Eva García, who rebelled against husbandly authority and willed their way to power, Mama was too docile to claim any right to womanly sovereignty. As my articulate sister Imelda insisted, the patriarchal order Papa represented ground her down, stifling her creative powers and channeling them into acceptable pursuits like homemaking and religious fervor. In the end, she was left with nothing but her artistic talents, and her saintliness, to compensate for a life that was never her own—that and the ailments which swarmed over her like Furies eager to suck dry any fountain of personal freedom that might bubble up from the depths of her rich creative core.

"Dios es amor," read the small plaque over Mama's grave, and underneath, "Agustina Jasso Peña, 1908–1970." We had just buried her, and my anger at God's injustice was still smoldering inside me. Here was a woman—*un alma justa,* as everyone referred to her, an innocent soul—who had not only suffered every imaginable affliction during her wretched life, but upon whom God had imposed the ultimate agony: death by cancer. "Where is Your justice?" I had been asking since her death. "What crime did this gentle, defenseless lamb of Yours commit to deserve such harsh punishment?"

I felt Papa's hand on my shoulder. I was so engrossed in venting my wrath at God that I did not hear him approach. "Your mother is dead, hijo," he said, in his most serious and eloquent tone. *"Pero no murió en vano*—but she did not die in vain. Yes, she was a suffering woman, but all her life she toiled for you—for all of us—to make sure we did not want for anything. And remember this, my son: it is from her that you children inherited all your talents. It was through her, m'hijo, that you became who you are—a singer, a musician, and now a man of letters. She lives through you in particular, for she was especially proud of your accomplishments, so honor her through your deeds and through your work."

I put my arms around Papa and wept uncontrollably.

26

LOVE IN THE TIME OF HURRICANES

Swirling spiral, heat-driven torrent
rarest storm of all:
a category-five hurricane
churns in my Gulf of Dreams
veering relentlessly toward my vulnerable shore.

And still it gathers strength.

Born in the tropics of my heart's desire
you were but a gale last spring;
now in the waning summer of my life
you rage unchecked
and thrive upon the warm currents of my ocean.

To steal into the calm eye of your vortex
and cradle in the bosom of your throbbing mass
Watch sixty-thousand feet of wind-whipped clouds
spin round and round past your elusive heart
While I dream awake, enchanted,
Caught in the magic circle of your unpredicted path.

Where will you strike next?

But my continent is vast, you know—
it will contain your fury
Your sheets of slashing rain
will turn to showers on my parched brown slopes
A few moist remnants—a lingering autumn squall, perhaps—
before your sultry breath gives way
to winter's frost.

"I know this is not logical, Ruth, but I have fallen for you, despite my better judgment."

"No, it isn't logical. There was no reason for this to happen."

"I think I've been attracted to you—or your image—ever since the light of consciousness first dawned on me. But I just don't know anymore. I guess I felt at some point there was something happening between us."

"There was nothing. There was no reason for you to take this so seriously. We've been friends, nothing more. You seem to have misunderstood. Perhaps something about your culture led you to believe otherwise. . . . But I really must be getting back to the office. I've been very busy these days."

She stood up and walked toward the concrete steps leading out of the "pit" onto the adjacent plaza, but then turned back abruptly to the table where we had just shared lunch. She had forgotten the paper bag in which she'd packed the chicken drumsticks. It lay neatly folded on the table.

"I thought maybe you had left your heart behind."

"Not in a brown paper bag."

"Well, I left mine in a silver Camry."

She smiled faintly and gave me one last look with those mischievous sage-blues of hers—eyes that could be both frolicsome and cruel. I watched her graceful figure climb the steps and then disappear behind the shrubs above the sunbathed pit. It was a bright first day of June, and it was the last time I would share her company.

After two years of sporadic rendezvous, of hoping and waiting, of romantic hints on my part and subtle deflections on hers, especially after my frank declaration and her blunt rejection, this final encounter was anticlimactic. But I laid open my bruised heart anyway, more to unburden my disenchantment than try and convince her of anything. She grew impatient with me, and she reproached me for letting myself end up like this.

Perhaps she was right; I had misread her actions and confused friendship with romance. Was this confusion the result of my machismo, as she intimated—this primordial Mexican sense of overweening male prowess? Yet I still felt a sense of betrayal, of somehow having been led down a romantic dead end. Worse, I knew the quest was over, even as her last glance lingered in my mind's eye while I sat at the table under the awning, looking out at the June glare. I pictured her opening the glass doors leading to her office, the memory of my confession already fading from her busy thoughts.

≣

I was spellbound from the first moment I caught sight of her. After the wrenching affair with Vicki Haverty, which nearly wrecked my marriage, I had vowed never to yield again to the allure of sensuous white women. Yet there she was, brushing past me in the dining hall with all the majesty of a Rosenkavalier waltz. Her sudden appearance was like an epiphany—a resurrection of memories and feelings buried since my childhood, when Alice Bentley stirred within me the first pangs of sexual desire. Standing before me was the embodiment of American woman in all her imperious presence, as I had encountered her at age twelve in the person of my sixth-grade teacher, Mrs. Jameson. Dressed in perfectly modest fashions, that middle-aged woman had ignited my sexual fires—her smooth, freshly rouged face, full moist lips, soft perfumes, and ample, curving hips driving me into my first orgasmic fantasies.

Mrs. Jameson was the absolute contrast to the weathered black and brown women who lived on the East Texas cotton plantation where my family worked. I was dimly aware even then that her sexual magnetism was somehow tied to her pearly skin and, especially, her affluent breeding, which in its smug gentility was at once awe-inspiring and seductive. Her fashionable suits might subdue a voluptuous body, but they evoked authority and sexual power in their own right. She was, as I tacitly understood, a beautiful white woman who exercised the same dominance over me that the bosses did over my father and the two older brothers who worked alongside him.

In my transgressive yearnings, I breached the code of power inscribed in Mrs. Jameson's role as teacher, adult, and white superior, in this way bringing her into an intimacy born of my own surging male potency. My reveries about Mrs. Jameson provided a vent for the sexual flames exploding inside my adolescent body. More than that, as I understood much later, my imaginary relationship with my teacher also encoded—and inverted—the social relations based on race and class authority that controlled my life and those of the black and brown people around me.

And now, thirty years later, long after I had renounced all desire for

Mrs. Jameson and her kind, the buried embers of those youthful fantasies burned anew, rekindled by the sparks radiating from this enchanting but inaccessible woman. I knew after my first sighting that any personal contact with her, however improbable, would be risky.

That first encounter must have taken place in 1983 or '84. But I didn't see her often in those days, and besides, I thought, a stunning American beauty like her would never notice a plain Mexican like me—let alone become romantically involved. As James Baldwin might say, not even the intercession of the Virgin could have delivered her to me. And anyway, I had enough personal troubles to discourage me from romantic adventures. It was enough to long for her from afar.

Then one day, near the end of the spring semester of 1991, I saw her in the dining hall. I was having lunch with colleagues when she came in with a group and sat a few tables away from ours. Again, I found myself magnetized by her presence. But this time I gazed at her with reckless intensity, almost daring her to notice me. She must have sensed that I was watching her, for she turned toward me and we exchanged glances for a brief but, for me, riveting instant. She looked away, but I was convinced our glances had intertwined, even if momentarily.

I saw her again in the cafeteria a few days later, and again I thought our eyes connected in fleeting acknowledgment. Though still wary, I began to entertain the possibility of somehow approaching her. The opportunity arrived sooner than I had expected. A week or so afterward, I was coming out of the campus post office when my heart bounced against my rib cage: she was walking along the sidewalk leading to the East Mall Building. This has to be my break, I thought. Since I was headed in the same direction, it was only a matter of timing my pace so that our paths would converge. My head felt giddy and the knees unsteady as we met, eyed each other, and voiced almost simultaneous hellos. The knot stuck in my vocal cords, as again the feeling of *déjà vu* swept over me (Alice and the school bus in Mumford!), but I spoke to her: "We've never met; my name is Manuel." She said hers was Ruth, and we immediately struck up a conversation. Filled with dread and elation, I had entered the risk zone.

She sat down on a bench outside the building and we spoke for perhaps five minutes. We made small talk and found out where each of us worked, and as I said good-bye and started to leave, I turned around on an impulse and asked if we could meet sometime for coffee. Taken aback by my own audacity, I froze momentarily, but she readily agreed, and regaining my composure, I promised to call soon.

As I walked toward my office, I felt a mixture of anticipation and fear. After all these years, I had finally met the woman who personified the ultimate temptation—a dazzling gringa orgullosa in all her seductive glory, and I wondered whether I could be a match, or even a foil, for her overwhelming presence. In the late summer of life, however, Ruth's was a mature attraction—not the nubile sultriness of a young Mariah Carey, but the lush scent of a fully ripened flower that sent waves of hot chills rippling through my body. I wanted to memorize her every feature, lest I never get this close to her again, and I tried to note every line in her slightly aging face, every wave in her rich brown hair, and every sparkle in her playful sage-blue eyes. The eyes, especially, transported me to a time before Mrs. Jameson, when Alice Bentley had wilted me with her own pair of sage-blues. Unlike the cherubic Alice, Ruth was not actually beautiful when I studied her irregular individual features, but as an ensemble—or a "gestalt," we might say— her face electrified my whole being. Her husky voice, with its Midwestern melody, echoed in my head long after I left her. And just as I had imagined, she seemed witty, intelligent, poised—and still possessed of the spellbinding aura that had ensnared me at first sight.

The raw thrill at the prospect of sharing her space, if only for a cup of coffee, had fired up since early that morning. I had called as promised, and Ruth agreed to a get-together that afternoon. I went directly to her office, and we walked out the bronze-and-glass doors of the building, engaging immediately in serious talk about a colleague's op-ed polemic in the local newspaper on the evils of multiculturalism in the university. Knowing intuitively that I would voice a strong reaction against his position, she asked if I planned to respond. I had not given the matter any thought, although I was disturbed by his intemperate attack against "diversity." "If I do," I told her, suddenly motivated to respond, "it will be on equal terms—a guest editorial like his, and not in the form of a letter, which would get lost in the shuffle."

We sat across from each other and savored our coffees, and I asked if her last name was related to that of an administrator on campus. "Divorced," she said, matter-of-factly. Since I was wearing my wedding band, I assumed she saw no need to question me about my marital commitments. For fifteen years she had worked at the university, the last five as an associate editor, reading, evaluating, and occasionally writing articles for the university newsletter. I told her of my own career at Cal State—my early years with Chicano Studies and my move to the Humanities Program. Our conversation was otherwise casual, lacking any overt emotion—a friendly exchange of bits of information between two strangers, with neither displaying any outward sign of romantic interest on our second contact.

But already stirring within me was a groundswell of passion and desire, and I left with a smoldering urge to see her again and somehow penetrate the urbane image she projected. I had a gut intuition Ruth was a woman of strong sexual impulses held in check by a lifelong cultivation of the niceties of middle-class culture. Of genteel social origins—her father had been a member of the diplomatic corps, her mother an artist—she was perfectly fluent in the nuances of refined cultural communication. She relished intellectual stimulation, and as I learned later, was especially partial to men she considered exceptional writers. But her inner fire was only muted, not entirely suppressed, by her genteel manner, and I eventually understood that her attraction to strong male writers was as much sexual as it was intellectual.

I learned Ruth was also intrigued by difference and novelty. She confessed to being curious, perhaps even "nosy," when it came to meeting the culturally different "Other" and exploring the possibility of new contacts and fresh experiences. Indeed, she spoke several languages fluently (as I found out later), and when I visited her office, I noticed it was decorated with artifacts from the African subcontinent. Somehow, her curiosity and penchant for the unfamiliar seemed a complement to what I sensed were Ruth's vigorous sexual passion and an adventurous nature held in check by her adherence to "moderation." (She would later joke about her impulse to buy a fiery red sports car, only to settle for a staid gray Camry.) Perhaps I might represent a new and exotic adventure.

Over the next few days, I contemplated our differences and what an encounter with a stranger like me might mean to Ruth. I could not forget, of course, my ambivalent feelings toward her people in general, but her sex appeal and symbolic attraction were so strong that I was willing to gloss over all the disparities between our two worlds. In time I came to see us as racial-cultural counterparts, two people raised in radically different cultural economies who nonetheless shared a similar orientation toward life—what we might call a liberal or progressive outlook. Both of us took seriously such truisms of liberal-democracy as equality, opportunity, cultural diversity, and, especially, the notion of an equitable distribution of the public wealth.

And, I was convinced, deep down we shared the conviction that sexual and intellectual expression are but two sides of the same life-force, or libido, as Freud called it—the one a procreative, the other a creative impulse, but both vital to our individual quest for power and self-fulfillment. Though we never discussed it openly, I felt that our mutual attraction was based on this conviction. She considered me a capable writer and was drawn to me, but I was drawn to her for the same reason, for it soon became apparent her sexual magnetism was a physical counterpoint to an exceptional gift for the literary turn. At one point, I even suggested she help me with a research project as an avenue for expanding her expressive capabilities beyond the occasional campus article she contributed. Her presence was a potent stimulant to my own creativity, and inspired and brimming with intellectual energy, I wanted to share this productive bounty with her. Indeed, her praise of my writing motivated me immensely. I redoubled my literary efforts, and under the spell of her influence, I not only contributed my own column on multiculturalism to the local paper, but eventually brought to life a long-delayed book.

But at this early stage in our relationship I was certain I must present a sharp contrast to previous men in her life. Ruth was the well-bred white woman, the daughter of elite-class socialites. I was the exotic "Other," the son of lowly Mexican American farm workers, a child of poverty who had made the improbable leap from the cotton fields to the halls of academia. And always confronting me was the conflict her people and mine had waged for 150 years in the American Southwest—for the subordinate and stigmatized Mexicans a "war of position," as the revolutionary Antonio Gramsci might see it, one that made for strained relations even in the waning years of the twentieth century. Had not 70,000 brown bodies marched recently in Los Angeles against the anti-Mexican Proposition 187? Didn't the Anglos of Fresno squelch an effort to rename a street in honor of César Chávez, the beloved hero of the Mexican Americans? And had I not felt the sting of racial hatred when, as a youngster, I was thrown out of a hamburger joint simply for being Mexican? An incongruous match, I thought, even in my fantasies. Yet as in the days of Alice and

Mrs. Jameson, the racial and social divide made the forbidden Ruth even more seductive.

Summer set in, and I did not see her again until the fall. We ran into each other on campus, and I asked if we might get together again. "Well, give me a call," she replied. Heedful of the cultural mismatch, my contradictory feelings toward Anglos generally, and the painful consequences an involvement with her would bring to everyone close to me, I did not want to become ensnared by my own chimeras. But seeing her after three months was an electrifying experience. I yearned for her company—her sultry voice and coquettish eyes, the warm glow of her presence, and the still-supple figure that had inflamed my passion when my eyes first saw and desired her. I called her within a day or so.

Once again, I was enthralled by her measured elegance, her inner warmth, the wry humor and melodious voice, and the easy manner in which our intellects seemed to blend. Were it not for the basic dread she elicited in me (and the fact that I was a married man), I would have surrendered totally to the spell she cast over me. We made friendly conversation—so casual I began to wonder whether I could ever penetrate the wall of civility she had erected. It was so easy to approach, yet so seemingly impossible to dissolve into intimacy. I was thoroughly disheartened. "No possibilities here for any romantic involvement," I thought, unable to fully grasp the disastrous results such an involvement would set in motion. I did not seek her company again for several months.

Spring was in the February air when I met Ruth outside the cafeteria. She seemed genuinely glad to see me, and I immediately asked her to join me for coffee. "Yes, of course," she said. "Call me." I did and was again confronted with her spellbinding charm—and the wall of civility that set limits on how near I could approach. But I was determined to move closer. "Lunch—can we have lunch sometime soon?" "Well, not soon, but give me a call and let's see if we can arrange it."

We went to a fish restaurant. It was early March, and the air was clear and brisk after the passage of a cold storm front. Great weather for Fresno, we agreed, and indeed, I felt as if I were riding atop the glistening clouds piling up on the mountains to the east. She looked as resplendent as the March sky. As we walked together after a leisurely meal, my whole being throbbed while the light conversation lifted up over the mountain of my desire, much like the clouds over the sierra range, obscuring the rugged peaks and canyons of the emotional terrain over which I was stumbling. But try as I did to articulate the poetry welling up inside me, the most I could get myself to blurt out was an admission that, at the risk of sounding maudlin, being in her company was as exhilarating as the fresh air after the storm. She did not respond. The wall of civility kept the rush of intimacy at bay.

There was no turning back for me now. I was willing to risk great chunks of personal discretion to breach the fortress surrounding her and become part of her privileged history, to be illumined by the inner fire that animated her and generated the magnetic force trapping me in her gravitational pull. Ruth's fragrance, her libidinal charm, and especially her worldly elegance had become for me the supreme embodiment of the feminine. If I could only touch her! Consumed with desire, I was ready to sacrifice almost anything to stand in her grace and worship at her temple.

I asked her out for a break; we went out. I asked to have lunch; we had lunch. We took another break together, and then I asked for lunch again. But I was afraid to overplay my strategy, to appear indiscreet. The plan to possess her, clumsy as it was, must go forth at her pace, not mine. In fact, there were strong hints that she would have it no other way. She spaced these encounters well, and there was nothing I could do, especially since I could not ask her out for an actual date, such as dinner or a philharmonic concert. At times her manner seemed abrupt and indifferent, even distant and cold. "Not soon," her response more than once when I asked to meet her for a break or lunch, became a code-phrase for her reluctance, just as "How about next week?" became a shorthand for my persistence. In sum, there was real hesitation on her part, and I sensed it. And that was a formidable brake on my impulses, which otherwise would have swerved beyond my control.

But the fateful encounter was inevitable. I could not postpone my assault on her fortress of civility forever. Summer was almost upon us; I was impatient. My male pride was at stake. Do it! She knows by now how you feel about her—else why does she prolong this "dyad of friendship"? We were having a brown-bag lunch, sitting on a wooden swing suspended from the plum trees behind the Engineering building. Under different circumstances, this shady, out-of-the way corner could have been an ideal setting for a romantic proposition. But I was uncomfortable, and the conversation had turned superficial (that small talk again!). I was feeling increasingly fidgety, knowing the moment of revelation had come—though I tried not to show it.

As we walked back to her office, I braced myself and asked the threshold question: "Will you go with me to Berkeley next week? I have some research and other things to do there, and I would be delighted to have you along as company."

"I can't," she answered, her eyes flashing and her voice uncharacteristically brittle as she reached for the finger on which my wedding band was tightly encircled. "I can't go with you because of this!" Her words went off like little hissing explosions, as when heavy raindrops strike red-hot embers. The wall of civility had been breached, but not by romantic passion. The spell had been unceremoniously broken; the absurdity of my quest starkly exposed. I fought for my rhetorical life, but no explanation that would turn the tide, repair the damage, seemed possible. But wait! Perhaps the time had come for an honest, come-clean accounting of my actions. "Please," I said, "let me explain; let's talk about this; I need to talk. May we, soon?"

My professional life took a drastic turn in the next few days. On June 8, 1992, I was laid off, as twelve years of seniority and a full professorship evaporated in the heat of a budgetary crisis that gripped the university. Shocked and angered by the administration's cavalier attitude toward my scholarly contributions, I began looking for other possibilities, late as it was in the season. I was fortunate. By coincidence, my friend Tatcho Mindiola had an unspent visiting research fellowship for the 1992–93 academic year with the Center for Mexican American Studies at the University of Houston. He offered it to me, and I accepted. Stung by my university's callous action, I wanted to demonstrate that I was marketable enough to find other employment, even at such a late date. Besides, the visiting scholarship in Houston included the possibility of permanent employment. Disillusioned with Cal State, I wanted to explore new possibilities.

But equally unsettling to me was the way Ruth's presence intruded upon my current misfortune, and I yearned to resolve the recent episode. To my great relief—and to my surprise, given her brief but explosive outburst—I found myself in her company a week later. As we walked toward the spot she had selected, I sought to convey just how great an impact she was exerting on my life. "Like Jupiter does to Uranus, you have put a major wobble in my orbit," I said, but my words seemed to dissolve into the black hole of her enigmatic silence. We did talk, finally, for about forty-five minutes. I tried to explain my situation to her, but it was not explainable, and she must have known that. I was, after all, a married man, though feeling restless (as in the 1970s). And so, as desperately as I might wish to extricate myself and surrender to her, I could not seriously entertain such an action, much less convince her of it.

≡

My feelings toward María were ambivalent during this period. An old contradiction was haunting me again: As in the days of Vicki Haverty, I was intoxicated with desire for another woman, but I was inextricably bound to my wife. Yet I sensed our marriage had slid down the rut of ennui; the waves of desire Ruth set in motion were missing with María. In fact, my marriage to María had always been driven by the ebb and flow of love and its perpetual compromise. We both loathed open conflict, but each had a distinct personality not immune from selfish action. Our relationship was thus one of waning and waxing passion, of battles and truces, and of the constant accommodation of two strong wills jockeying for power.

We had met as adolescents, and María had been one of the few girlfriends I had. We married young—she was nineteen, I twenty-two—and the first years had been a period of friction and reconciliation, particularly since I felt she was too controlling, while she complained that I was not attentive enough to her needs. Eventually, the wear-and-tear of daily clash led to more serious breaches, especially in the seventies, when my moral compass shifted and I plunged into the hustle and bustle of movimiento activities. I drifted further and further from her and, disenchanted and seeking to redefine myself, finally separated from her. But we seemed irrevocably bound to each other, and eventually we reconciled and patched over our differences. In time, we convinced ourselves that the turmoil we had been through had actually strengthened the relationship. For several years the marriage was strong and relatively free of acrimony.

But the decade of the '80s presented a difficult challenge to us. I succumbed to "the curse of the Jassos," with bouts of panic-disorder that incapacitated me and increased my dependence on María. She bore with my illness, but I knew it weighed heavily on her. More than that,

I felt my self-dignity slipping away inexorably, and on several occasions I broke down completely. On a trip to an ethnomusicology conference in Phoenix, for instance, I was unable to drive beyond the desert city of Blythe. (Flying was out of the question: the claustrophobia was crippling.) María urged me on, but it was in vain—we turned back to Fresno. Over these years my self-esteem was shaken, and I sensed a loss of respect in her eyes. But María remained stoic throughout, and she seldom betrayed any impatience. She hid her disappointment well.

When I met Ruth, I had recently emerged from the long tunnel of despair, and her impact on me was like a bolt of energy revitalizing the very core of my being. The last vestiges of panic vanished before the powerful tonic of her presence, and as my feelings for her quickened, I realized that for María and me, the long years of mutual suffering had left a trail of emotional litter and a compromised relationship. I could now see more clearly the weariness in our marriage; the insidious progress of the panic disorder had transformed love into obligation. The periodic struggle to cope with my condition had sapped the vitality out of the union, and our few joyous moments were overwhelmed by the drudgery of daily living, particularly in the late eighties, when clinical depression worsened the panic. The relationship survived on obligation and moral commitment—especially on María's part.

María was fully aware that I had emerged from the grip of the disorder, and as time passed, it became clear my newfound independence was threatening to her, particularly when I told her of my plan to go to Houston alone. I spoke to her frankly of the unhealthy dependence I had developed during the difficult years. I knew I had been a burden on her, but more than that, a real wedge had opened between us in the form of a certain weariness on her part, perhaps even a desire to escape. Now, I told her, I needed to be alone, to be free to experience my autonomous self. I never told her about Ruth.

≡

"She's quite attractive," Ruth was saying, in reference to María. Although they did not know each other, both had attended a recent staff reception to honor university employees with many years of service. Ruth had received her fifteen-year certificate, María her tenth. Ironically, both had master's degrees in letters, and they shared the same occupational classification: Technical Specialist. "You know," I said, "it's funny, but there is something about the two of you—not a real resemblance, of course, but certainly an affinity of features, shall we say." And that indeed seemed to be the case, with the brown hair, fair complexion, soft facial lines, and similar stature combining to present a common physical type. And in a perverse way, perhaps, the perceived affinity increased my appreciation for both—my Mexican María becoming less familiar and the Anglo Ruth less alien.

But they were different in many ways as well, these two remarkable women. Despite her European features, María was the offspring of my culture and, like me, the child of lowly workers. She too had struggled against formidable odds to overcome poverty and ethnic discrimination. (She never forgot one experience in particular—the day a gringa student, the daughter of a rich farmer, had beaten her out for a spot on the high-school cheerleading squad, this despite the fact the girl had fumbled her routine badly, in contrast to María's flawless performance.) Ancestrally, then, we were entirely compatible, María and me, although I felt we were not as well matched intellectually. María was less bookish than I—or, perhaps, more politically cautious—and at times I felt she did not fully appreciate my forays into radical positions like Marxism, Freudianism, and the more extreme forms of Chicanismo. Still, we had been through several life-changes together, ranging from our shared experiences as agricultural workers to participation in the Chicano Movement of the sixties and seventies, and, of course, to entry into the middle class, as we moved together up the educational ladder. Our shared life experiences thus helped cement the marital bond, creating a mutual feeling of identity.

Despite our racial-cultural differences and the long-running conflict between Anglos and Mexicans, Ruth and I seemed intellectually and politically compatible. And that, I thought, canceled all disparities related to our racial and class origins. Beyond that, of course, was the explosive effect she had on my own sexuality. I wondered incessantly whether I might have the same effect on her, and indeed, I could not rid myself of the suspicion that no matter how distant she sometimes seemed, deep within her a small flame burned whose glow shone in my direction and drew me inescapably toward her.

In fact, however, there was another man in her life. By a remarkable coincidence, he was, like me, an ethnomusicologist, a student of the music-cultures of West Africa (hence the reason for the artifacts in Ruth's office). "You are like him in many ways," she said, "your ideas are quite similar." And he too descended from a minority group—one, however, not nearly as marginalized in American life as the Mexicans. Of Jewish descent, he taught at a large university in Southern California. How had she met him, I wondered, but never asked. I learned he had been in her life for a long time; indeed, he may have played a part in the breakup of her marriage. But I did not ask about that, either. I thought I should feel jealousy toward my rival, but I did not. What I thought I could almost feel was the profound sense of loss and despair her former husband must have endured upon losing this extraordinary woman who had, for all I knew, betrayed him for the love of another—the Jewish ethnomusicologist, perhaps?

"I might get married," she at length offered, in what seemed to me an offhand manner. Her tone was flat and lacking in faith or commitment. Her announcement was not very convincing. I looked deep in her eyes and asked, "Ruth, had I been unattached, would it have made a differ-ence, for you and me?" "If that were the case," she replied, "I would have to reassess my whole situation." At that moment I understood perfectly her hesitation and the wisdom of her decision not to become entangled in what she labeled a "triangle." Still, I wanted to say, "Take me, and I'll run away with you," but I knew that would be an empty promise, one I could never fulfill. I said nothing.

She expressed sympathy for my predicament with the university. She also seemed truly impressed when she learned of the lucrative fellowship I had been offered by the University of Houston. More than that, she talked fondly of that city, where she had spent some time in her youth. A cousin of hers lived there, and Ruth had promised she would visit soon. She espe-cially looked forward to attending a performance of the famed Houston Grand Opera. I jumped at the possibility of convincing her to visit during my stay. Far from this place, I thought, I might convince her, and myself, to explore a sublime new relationship. She seemed intrigued by the idea, and I pleaded with her: Give a relationship between us a chance to blossom; meet with me in that faraway city, where we can explore new and intimate pos-sibilities. When we finally parted, I thought I had almost enticed her to visit Houston in the next few months. I left with a renewed sense of hope.

We met once more that summer of '92, for coffee on a sultry August morning. I had been working on a poem for her, "Season of the Hurricane," finished coincidentally just before the category-five Hurricane Andrew wrecked much of southern Florida. The only poem I ever wrote ("too many adjectives," my poet-friend Leonard Adame said of it), "Season of the Hurricane" likened the passion she generated in the late summer of her life to the force of a hurricane feeding on the energy stored in the waning summer of the tropical sea. I presented her with the finished work, and she glanced over it without comment. Disappointed, I imagined she was determined not to let anything I said affect her, as if my entreaties represented a challenge to—what? I could not decipher her motives.

I repeated my invitation to meet in Houston and urged her not to let what I felt was a potentially grand relationship wither on the vine. I could tell her position had hardened since the last time had we met, and I pleaded with her: "Don't let things end this way, Ruth." "You've never been more than a distant possibility," was her response. As I left her that day, I felt for the first time a real sense of defeat in my mad quest.

I was on my way to Houston a few days later, having left a little gift and a love note on her desk. She had flown out of Fresno earlier that week on a "business trip" to Florida (to visit her ailing father, I learned later). I had called before her departure to arrange one final meeting with her, and she had agreed to a "farewell cup." But when I called later to confirm, the iciness in her voice froze the earphone. "I cannot see you anymore," she said. "There is nothing to discuss, and anyway, I'm leaving on business, so I won't be here tomorrow. You have taken all of this too seriously." Her tone was disengaged—as if all our previous discussions had absolutely no significance for her. If I thought there was anything other than friendship between us, that was my mistake. Perhaps something in my culture had led me to believe, incorrectly, that there was anything more than friendship between us.

My first few days in Houston were a sobering experience. I had not been away from María for more than a day or two since 1977, when I had left her in Fresno and moved to Texas to begin my doctoral studies in anthropology. Vicki Haverty was the cloud hanging over us then. That had been a time of reckless indulgence, when I shared my love with two women, even if only one was legitimate.

Vicki swept into my life at a moment of discontent and moral flux. Immersed in the process of reinventing myself, I had plunged into the thick of movimiento-inspired political activity with passion, and a sense of adventure had fired up old libidinal impulses. Feeling hemmed in by marriage, I had actually moved out a couple of months earlier, leaving María in a daze—the pain in her face seared into my memory forever, even as I shut out her sobs of distress. But I was intoxicated by the attentions of a pert and voluptuous young woman—Mercedes—a former singer in an ensemble I directed at the university. In my thirties and ready to unleash long-frustrated urges, I gave in to the unfulfilled fantasies of my adolescence. Mercedes yielded to my advances, and our sexual excesses engulfed and disrupted my life. I wanted to suffocate in the young singer's wet, slippery loins, to smother the fire raging inside me—only to be disappointed by her immaturity and her own free spirit.

At this moment, enter the irresistible Vicki—a chance encounter on a cold February evening at a dance at the Rainbow Ballroom. I had gone to this popular Mexican nightspot after dropping off Mercedes for her graveyard shift at the county hospital. Vicki's fluent Spanish, dancing blue eyes, maddeningly nubile body, and, especially, her mixed Anglo-Mexican ancestry captivated me on the spot. Here was the woman who not only matched the blueprint for womanly charm inscribed in my memory—she also bridged the yawning gap between my Mexican roots and the dominant culture with which I had carried on a love-hate affair for so long. I was in love with Vicki by the end of the evening. My relationship with this schoolteacher-*folklórico* dancer, though lasting only a year, was deeply cemented if at times wrenching, principally because I could not forget María's pain and my own strong attachment to her. I was convinced Vicki and I loved each other with passion and commitment, and I was certain she was the ideal woman for me. There were times when she could absolutely overwhelm my senses—to this day the image of her dressed in a white Vera Cruz costume rivals the most resplendent vision I have of Ruth. But I tore away from her at the end of the year, and María joined me in Texas permanently in the winter of 1978.

The reconciliation was torturous. María's trust had been badly shaken, and I had to work hard to convince her of my loyalty, even as Vicki's memory burned inside me. But we were determined to make our marriage work, and I refused to indulge my desire, maintaining my silence and never contacting Vicki. Paradoxically, the stronger the yearning for my absent lover, the closer I moved toward María, and eventually the marriage reached a new level of trust and solidarity. Only the chronic memory of the irresistible Vicki remained. I resolved never again to succumb to my chimeras and put María and myself through such bitterness and pain.

I spoke to her today. I knew she was hurt at how easily—even eagerly, it seemed to her—I had left Fresno. But I had to get away, I now realize. This Houston fellowship has given me a chance to think. I yearn for Ruth, but I realized today how deeply María's roots extend into my being, and how painfully profound and unshakable my love is for her. Her voice at the other end of the line was like a beacon in my dark night of loneliness. "I don't know why," she said, "but I've been having flashbacks to the time of Vicki. Something seemed so wrong when you left." I choked inwardly as she spoke, and I remembered the day she had left me in Austin in 1977, and taken my two sons with her. At the time, I was still torn between her and Vicki. The sight of the worn-out tricycle our little toddler Isaac had left behind sent me into convulsions of sorrowful weeping, and a crushing wave of loneliness for María and my children descended over me. I relived those Austin days after we hung up today, and I hated myself for my perversity and for being another Pancho Peña. I swore I would never contact Ruth again, let alone betray María for her.

I finally called her today. I waited six weeks but could wait no longer. I was anxious to talk to her, but I was frightened by the prospect of rejection, and the danger in reopening still-fresh wounds. I dreaded the icy, heartless voice that had rebuffed me before, and it took several starts before I finally yielded to the insistent inner voice. I picked up the phone and dialed her work number. Using the most humorous, self-effacing greeting I could think of—"Hello, Ruth, this is the voice that's been banished to Houston, Texas"—I waited breathlessly for a response. She appreciated the humor and broke out in laughter; she seemed pleased to hear from me. I was

relieved to hear again the lifting music in her voice, the good cheer I had
come to appreciate, and, especially, the willingness to communicate. I kept
the conversation light and steered away from amorous suggestions, hoping
to impress her nonetheless with my own good cheer and happiness at being
able to share some of my new experiences in the big city. She asked about
Houston, and I described the extremes of the city: its opulent skyscrapers
overshadowing neighborhoods ravaged by third-world squalor. We parted
with friendly exchanges; I wanted to ask, "may I call again?" but did not,
hoping to do so just the same.

≣

Upon my return from Houston, I immediately called Ruth. I had kept in
occasional contact with her, hoping until the very end that she would make
good on her wish to visit the city. I had actually spent time with her on a
trip to Fresno during the winter academic recess. We went to her favorite
Chinese restaurant, where I heard her speak to the waitress in what seemed
fluent Mandarin. (She had learned the language as a child, when her family
spent several years in Beijing.) Her voice had a richly melodic, almost cloy-
ing quality when she spoke Chinese. We drove to lunch in her silver 1992
Camry—a car whose classic lines and subtle elegance had always impressed
me. Now strongly associated with Ruth, Camrys became talismans evoking her image. I looked for them everywhere in Houston, and when I occasionally saw one that matched hers, I thought I could sense her presence
hovering over it. More than once I caught myself smiling at the irony of my
predicament: here I was, a Marxist, violating Marx's critique of capitalism
by transforming a market commodity into a personal fetish.

Many a time I imagined picking Ruth up at the airport, taking her to
a premier restaurant in Houston, going to the opera or a symphony concert perhaps, and then, finally, merging in a delirious bond of passion. But
she never came, and she never called. I shall always remember that city
and that year as a place and a time when I waited in loneliness and with
wavering hope for a destiny that could never materialize—a confabula-
tion dug up from the depths of adolescent dreams and unfulfilled desires.
Like Mrs. Jameson, Ruth was the fair lady who would erase forever the
blight of racial and class shame that had been my patrimony. The wait
was endless.

The sultry voice was on the other end of the line: "You're back?" "Yes, I am. The Music Department has offered me a position, so I'll be staying at Cal State, at least for now." I wanted to tell her once and for all how much I ached for her. And so I asked her to meet with me again, and she agreed to lunch in the sunken patio called "the pit." I went into the dining hall across the plaza, bought a sandwich, and waited for her. Moments later she appeared, wearing a white skirt and a blouse of soft summer pastels. Her face was radiant, and she looked more beautiful than ever. She had brought her own brown-bag lunch.

"I'm engaged," she said. The words sent a shock wave through my body—an 8.2 on the Richter scale I told myself, in a bizarre moment of metaphoric self-assessment. But outwardly, I tried to appear nonchalant, and I asked her to show me the ring. "That's the ring he gave you?" I asked in mock surprise. "Did—did he bother to give you the Crackerjacks, too?" She smiled at my awkward attempt at humor, as she proudly held up her finger for my inspection. *Pinche judío*, I thought, he finally gave in. But the delusion had been shattered; as in the cyber-world of the computer, my virtual game had vanished at the stroke of her casual announcement. She heard me out just the same, and in the end she gently, almost apologetically, excused herself—the wall of civility intact, the divide between us unbridged.

When Ruth left, I remained in the pit for what seemed a long time, sitting at the table and looking out at the June glare. The conversation had drained me of all energy. The depth of my self-deception finally dawning on me, I felt defeated and disconsolate and foolish. I had not only betrayed María's trust—again—but trashed my long-held resistance to Anglo women. I wondered why I had let myself slide into such destructive and self-indulgent behavior. Was this woman worth such personal debasement? For that matter, was she nothing more than another of my chimeras—an image dredged up from the depths of my adolescent fantasies, when I yearned to be part of white America? And yet the two years of pursuit, of anticipation and disappointment, of ups and downs, of incredible longing, of the endless wait in Houston—all seemed appropriate to a perverse but bittersweet object: privation endured for the sake of the ultimate but forbidden prize. But the whole scheme collapsed the moment she announced her engagement. I felt a need to scream and unload my heartache, but I had compromised too much of my dignity already, and now my body seemed empty of emotion.

At length, I got up and slowly climbed the concrete steps onto the plaza. I heard her voice call out, "Honey—Manuel!" The familiar tone triggered another shock wave. It was María. All the while Ruth and I had been talking of misguided romance and cultural misunderstandings, my wife had been sitting no more than forty feet above us, beyond the bushes and out of sight, eating lunch alone. Blinded by obsession, I had overlooked the possibility of running into her while in Ruth's company.

I composed myself and walked over to her. The turmoil within me resolved, or at least squelched, by Ruth's final announcement, I suddenly felt a sense of liberation—or was it emotional exhaustion? For the moment incapable of shame or remorse, I only knew that María, with whom I had shared the "immense complexity of love"—ecstasy and pain, excitement and boredom, solidarity and conflict—would be my companion forever. More than that, at this moment I grasped, finally, the real value of this woman, with whom I had been through so many life changes. As her laughing, comfortably familiar eyes confirmed, she was an extension of my own being, just as the two of us were breathing, feeling, inseparable links in a shared ancestral culture. To forsake either María or that culture was to risk my own self-destruction.

Suppressing a choke and putting on my "leather face," as we would say in Spanish, I approached, took her hand in mine, and accompanied María into eternity.

ACKNOWLEDGMENTS

Even a personal book like this "auto-ethnography" owes something of its existence to other individuals who contributed in some way to its creation. In the spirit of appreciation, I want to acknowledge those individuals. First, I want to give recognition to professors and friends Gene Zumwalt and Bob O'Neill, who first awakened in me a serious desire to write. I took nonfiction writing classes with both in the 1960s and early '70s, and both encouraged me to keep writing. In fact, "Day of the Storm," "Juicy-Fruit Heartache," and "Ballad of a Chicano" morphed out of essays I originally wrote for Zumwalt and O'Neill.

To Doug Foley and Lillian Faderman, two gifted scholars whom I greatly admire, I wish to express my heartfelt thanks for reading and critiquing the entire manuscript. To Lillian I owe a special gracias for nurturing the project from its inception, giving much of her time to both encourage and criticize. To my dear friend and colleague Helene Joseph-Weil, I express my deepest gratitude for the time she spent poring over some of the chapters and offering many valuable suggestions. To all three of these very special friends I shall always be deeply indebted.